T0314744

Bello
hidden talent rediscovered

Bello is a digital-only imprint of Pan Macmillan,
established to breathe new life into previously published,
classic books.

At Bello we believe in the timeless power of the imagination,
of a good story, narrative and entertainment, and we want to
use digital technology to ensure that many more readers
can enjoy these books into the future.

We publish in ebook and print-on-demand formats
to bring these wonderful books to new audiences.

www.panmacmillan.co.uk/bello

TRACK OF AIRCRAFT TAKING OFF BETWEEN CORAL REEFS

Emily Bay at high water. The darker patches in the water are coral reefs, and the width of the passage between them can be gauged by the size of the houses and sheds ashore. The walls of the old convict prison show up clearly.

Francis Chichester

ALONE OVER
THE TASMAN SEA

Introduction by
Group Captain Frank D. Tredrey

First published in 1933 under the title of "Seaplane Solo" by Faber & Faber Ltd.

This edition published 2016 by Bello
an imprint of Pan Macmillan
20 New Wharf Road, London N1 9RR
Associated companies throughout the world

www.panmacmillan.co.uk/bello

ISBN 978-1-5098-2581-3 EPUB
ISBN 978-1-5098-2579-0 HB
ISBN 978-1-5098-2580-6 PB

This book remains true to the original in every way. Some aspects may appear
out-of-date to modern-day readers. Bello makes no apology for this, as to retrospectively
change any content would be anachronistic and undermine the authenticity of the original.

Pan Macmillan does not have any control over, or any responsibility for,
any author or third party websites referred to in or on this book.

A CIP catalogue record for this book is available from the British Library.

Typeset by Ellipsis Digital Limited, Glasgow

Visit **www.panmacmillan.com** to read more about all our books
and to buy them. You will also find features, author interviews and
news of any author events, and you can sign up for e-newsletters
so that you're always first to hear about our new releases.

Contents

Introduction

Those who know *Alone over the Tasman Sea* put it on their shelf somewhere near Childer's *Riddle of the Sands*, Masefield's *Bird of Dawning* and Lawrence's translation of the *Odyssey*, all books that come down every now and then to be read again. For the things of which Francis Chichester writes are the things of man's old quest and spirit; danger and adventure and achievement, the sun and the wind, the "many-laughing waves" and the steady thunder of the seas on island beaches.

It is England's habit to produce men like Chichester in every generation, especially when she needs them most and sometimes even when she appears least to deserve them. Little is known, his biographer may say, about his early days except that he played football for Marlborough (second fifteen); but in 1919, at the age of eighteen, he sailed for New Zealand and, in preference to lazing in deck chairs, worked in the stokehold as a trimmer for most of the voyage. In New Zealand he farmed, felled trees and sawed timber, learned to ski in the Southern Alps, worked for a year in coal mines and gold diggings, and travelled in an old Ford selling a farmer's magazine. Then later, having saved some money, he started with Geoffrey Goodwin the first joy-riding company in New Zealand, engaging ex-Royal Flying Corps pilots to fly two Avro Avjans and take up six thousand passengers in little more than a year. In 1929 he sailed for England again, giving himself nine months in which to qualify as a civilian pilot, buy an aeroplane, and learn enough about airmanship, night-flying, meteorology, navigation and the other things he would need to know to fly that aeroplane back across the fourteen and a half thousand miles to

New Zealand. In the England of those days, when a trip in a, sports car to Brighton was the finest flowering of many adventurous spirits, and when adulation was lavished on the smart weekend set lounging in the cocktail bars of flying clubs, he was already beginning to show as a man of a different temper.

By the time he got to Brooklands to start flying lessons it was already June, and three of the nine months had gone in travelling and in a hospital at Los Angeles; and while he was having great difficulty in learning to land—since youth he has had to view the world through strong spectacles—his business in New Zealand slumped so badly that paying for his lessons and buying an aeroplane and oil and petrol became a serious problem. However, he went solo and bought a De Havilland Moth. In October he set out to fly round Europe, and the names of the great traveller-cities of the world began to appear in his logbook—Paris, Lyons, Milan, Venice, Zagreb, Lemberg, Warsaw, Berlin, Leipzig, Dessau, Brunswick, Rotterdam, Antwerp. Then, back in England with this self-imposed apprenticeship in route-flying finished, he laid plans to challenge Hinkler's record to Australia; and in December he set off, at two-thirty in the morning from a frost-bound aerodrome, six months after he had first gone solo. Again the string of names— Pisa, Tripoli, Benghazi, Alexandria, Gaza, Baghdad, Basrah, Bushire, Jask, Karachi, Nasirabad, Calcutta, Rangoon, Singapore, Batavia, Darwin; and in January 1930, Sydney.

A few months later, in New Zealand, the idea of the flight described in this book began to take shape, and with it many new problems of which the air pilotage textbooks did not at that time treat. He was therefore driven back on the old seaman's manuals of navigation to unravel the mysteries of the chronometer and the sextant and spherical trigonometry. *Norie*, which "was conned to destruction by sea-apprentices when the frigate-built Indiamen entered Blackwall with yards and gunports squared, bunt-jiggers bowsed up for a harbour furl, and stun'sails rigged out to the mark." *Lecky*, with such interesting contents-page titles as "The Dutchman's Log; the Mariner's Creed; How Wrecks Occur; Big Ben and his two Chums; Sun the World's Timekeeper; Fog and

Floating Ice; Sextant the Seaman's Sure Friend." *Raper*, who says somewhere that "in navigating among the coral reefs of the Feejees . . . the lookout, when placed half-way up the rigging on these occasions, sees better than from the masthead, where the eye is dazzled by the glare." From these and similar books, borrowed from a cargo-steamer mate or bought in an old bookshop in Wellington, Chichester learned his first astronomical-navigation. He finally pinned his faith in Raper, "because he was a great man on position lines;" then he devised a method of running down a position line that is still used in the Royal Air Force. He borrowed a small brass sextant made for artillery work that had been taken off a captured German officer, and practised with this by taking shots of stars reflected in a bowl of wafer, and by taking sun shots while running up and down the beach. Then, with his 1839, thousand-page Raper stowed under the seat in case he should need to use its tables, and with the pocket sextant to take sun shots while he held the aircraft control-column between his knees, he set off on this flight in which one error in the estimations or calculations would have meant the end. The aircraft was the same wooden Moth in which he had flown from England, but this time with floats fitted, and with extra tanks to permit him to carry enough petrol to bridge the one and a half thousand miles in three stages, each of five hundred miles, mainland—Norfolk Island—Lord Howe Island—Sydney. Norfolk Island is "a squat rock dumped in the Pacific . . . no larger than a New Zealand sheep farm;" Lord Howe is only five square miles in extent. He reached each island in turn, but while he was preparing for the last stage of the flight the seaplane was wrecked in a night gale. The refusal to be beaten that runs through every chapter of this book drove him to strip the wreck down to the last nut and bolt and, with the help of a few islanders, rebuild it again. Weeks later he flew on through a great tropical storm of blinding rain, waterspouts and high winds, using navigation instruments, chart-plotting, log-keeping, all in the open cockpit of a plane vibrating so harshly that he could not write if his elbow touched any part of the fuselage. It was a flight that the best R.A.F. pilots would think hard about to-day before they would essay it; in 1931 it was unique.

The Tasman flight accomplished, the autumn of 1931 found him off by air again. Chinese and Japanese customs' stamps now follow the blue and red and violet stamps of Arabia and Persia and a dozen other countries in his log. Then, because he crashed in Japan and was severely injured, there is a gap until 1936, when the city-names begin to appear again. Sydney, Bangkok, Hongkong, Foochow, Pekin, Nankin, Rangoon, Calcutta, Cawnpore, Ambala, Jodphur, Baghdad, Benghazi, Tripoli, Tunis, London. This time, to get married and to return to New Zealand by sea.

Then, just before Munich, he saw the red light and came home, thinking that it would not be hard to get into the Royal Air Force as a fighter pilot. Three times he volunteered, but he was not young enough and his eyesight was too bad for flying duties. His next move was to recruit the keenness of six other civil pilots like himself and to propose to the Air Ministry that they should be allowed to become the nucleus of a "commando" squadron which would go in low to bomb small enemy targets, such as particular buildings, in bad weather. It was a serious attempt to get into the war, but this too failed; so he went to work with an aircraft instrument firm on the development of navigation aids and, in his spare time, wrote article after article on his special subject. How he had now come, through years of study and of flying at his own expense, to be a leading writer in England, and in the English-speaking world, on air navigation may be sensed from the titles of some of these articles. 1938: *Bombing by star navigation, What can the air sextant do?* 1939: *Bombing by super-navigation, A square deal for the navigator, Long-distance and night navigation, Raiding by celestial navigation (four long articles).* 1940: *The echo altimeter, Transatlantic flight navigation, Star curves, Factory versus bomber, The need for research, The Mark IX sextant, Bombing unseen targets.* During these years he also produced a number of textbooks on astronomical navigation, and many navigators now working with our Pathfinder and heavy bomber squadrons, and in the aircraft keeping watch and ward on the long sea routes, read them with profit during the first years of the war.

In 1941 Chichester was commissioned as a Flight Lieutenant and went into the Air Ministry. There he worked for two years, helping to revise the air-navigation training syllabuses and writing lecture notes for R.A.F. navigation instructors and for cadets training for operations. These notes are the work of a first-class navigator, navigational thinker and teacher, and they are used in R.A.F. and Dominion air schools all over the world.

There is much of the Elizabethan in Francis Chichester. He was one of the first to navigate by air the seas that Drake was the first marine navigator to enter. He also belongs to the Elizabethans by descent, for a John Chichester married Thomasine Raleigh in 1365 and, as you may read in *Westward Ho!*, the Chichester daughters in the Armada times lined the road to greet the seamen returning from the West Indies. Now he is flying again, this time with senior R.A.F. officers when they do their advanced day and night navigation exercises at the Empire Central Flying School. I think the early navigators and captains would be well satisfied to know that one of their breed has added to the lustre of their trade.

August 1944   F. D. Tredrey

Chapter I

IMPULSE

I wanted to fly the Tasman; and a dirty stretch of water I knew it to be, breeding a vicious type of young storm that rampages up and down for days before the meteorologists get wind of it. None dirtier for the long-distance pilot unless he include a turn round Cape Horn in his flight. And though it may be less wide across than most oceans, it has the considerable disadvantage for any aeroplane which falls into it of not being traversed by great steamer routes.

"Then why fly it?" demanded a friend to whom I confided the project.

"Because I want to continue from Australia the flight round the world which I left off there a few months ago. And what is the sport in flying round the world if one's plane is unable to fly on to the track to be followed, but has to be carried there?"

Though really I had a strange feeling that I must attempt the ocean flight whether I wanted to or not. This seemed as if I considered it my destiny. That could not be, for I definitely did not believe in destiny. Man was "master of his fate"—that was the great thing about him; he could do whatever he wished, or refuse as he liked. So the reason for feeling myself bound to make the attempt must be simply that if I jibbed, I should have no rest or peace of mind. And yet, was that sufficient cause? No, the incentive must be that no man had yet flown this ocean solo. And that solo ocean flying was undoubtedly something new under the face of the sun—since only one solo ocean flight at all had been completed.

There was something strange and wonderful in the thought of man spanning an ocean in that way by himself. It held the lure of the unknown.

Or was I driven by the challenge held out, "Could I do it?" like an itch that irritates the more, every time it is scratched. Or by the reward dangling in my imagination—the great moment of romping into Sydney from the east, having already flown to it from the west.

But, often, I thought the reason was fear. I suppose everyone is afraid of something: and that all fears, whether of incurable disease, of death, or merely of spiders, are equally terrible to their owners. Mine was the thought of heading across an ocean in a plane, and it was fast becoming a habit for that thought to give me the cold shudders. And every time this fear came to me, the thought bit deeper into me that I could not allow it to make me feel a coward and that I must exorcize it by experiencing it myself.

This was all very well, but to obtain an aeroplane capable of spanning the 1,450 (land) miles separating Wellington from Sydney was quite another question.

I was not able to buy one; I could not borrow, because for one reason there was not a plane in New Zealand with the range. And to beg would have affected me as it did the man in the Bible.

I must think of some other scheme—and quickly, if I wanted to fly that ocean solo before anyone else. Then one night, I awoke with an idea. I would raise the money by taking up passengers in my Moth, the same which had carried me from London to Sydney; and I think this scheme would have been a great success had not the passengers refused to be taken up. They liked flying in any other plane well enough, but not in mine. This puzzled me greatly until I came to hear their opinion of my *Madame Elijah*, of how she was held together partly by pieces of string and partly by odd pieces of wire—that she must inevitably fall to bits—and at any moment. I will not mention their opinion of the pilot, such as that he was blind in one eye and unable to see much out of the other, and that the phenomenal good luck which had enabled him to keep alive so far must inevitably break up, and at any moment.

The day I heard all this, by a strange coincidence, I temporarily forgot the power lines bordering the field where I was landing the plane. The propeller chewed its way through all three—11,000 volts—with a grand flash like lightning. This cut off the town's supply of electricity, and my own supply of passengers, except for the priest, the local undertaker, and the usual brave souls ready to risk death with me provided there was no charge. Furthermore, the electrical authorities demanded payment for repairs to their power line although I explained that it should be charged to general expenses as what the insurance companies call an "Act of God". "Who did I think I was?" they demanded.

I was extremely angry at the remarks passed on my aeroplane. I considered it thoroughly sound, though both motor and plane had flown over 33,000 miles in England, Europe, New Zealand, and from London to Sydney. "Confound it," I thought, "I'll prove her sound; she shall be the plane to carry me over the Tasman."

But the question was how to make a plane with a 950-mile range cross a 1,450-mile ocean. Though three petrol-tanks were already fitted, I wrestled with the possibility of adding a fourth till I could see a way of increasing the range to 1,270 miles. I thought there might even be a slight chance of piling on tankage for as much as 1,430 miles. But certainly not for an inch further. And that range, it seemed to me, fell just short of my requirements.

But one day, a friend lent me a globe, and it was placed beside the looking-glass where my eye strayed to it while shaving. Three hours later, a search party arrived to find me, razor in one hand, globe in the other, having "discovered" two small islands in the North Tasman.[1] I was almost ready to believe they had been especially dumped there for my plane. Norfolk Island was 481 miles from the north end of New Zealand; Lord Howe Island 561 miles from Norfolk Island; and Sydney 480 miles from Lord Howe Island. A line drawn through all four places resembled a rainbow curve in shape. I was excited. For how could a blundering flight straight across be compared with a delicate picking of one's way from island to island as stepping-stones? There was something

_____
1   See map of North Tasman Sea, at end.

strangely stirring in the mere thought of flitting to an island from out of the blue.

One or two difficulties arose. I could not find out if Lord Howe Island was inhabited. Nobody seemed to have heard of it. At last I dug information out of an old encyclopaedia that it was of 3,200 acres and had 120 inhabitants. But as neither it nor Norfolk Island had ever seen a plane before, there could be no landing-places, and from charts I secured, they both appeared too hilly to provide even a level field. Nor could I find out if this were so or not. It took four days by steamer to reach Sydney from Wellington, and another week doubling back to Norfolk Island. Even then, the obscure steamer which made the island trip, only did so once a month. I could obtain no information of any use to me. A good thing too, as the fox said when unable to reach the grapes . . . the information was sure to have been sour. I thought of my feelings had I arrived at the island to find a layman's idea of an aerodrome to be a plantation of tall trees, encircling a field too small for a boy's kite-flying.

I was stumped—till the idea occurred to me of exchanging the wheels of *Elijah* for a pair of floats and alighting in the sea.

"Good heavens!" exclaimed the experts, "whoever heard of flying a long distance by oneself in a seaplane? What about mooring? And as for a Moth seaplane to cross the Tasman—why! rigged as a seaplane, it is only a toy. For another thing, it will never be able to rise from the water with half enough petrol."

I had heard it said that seaplanes occasionally could not rise at all from a glassy surface, even when empty of load. But never having been near one, I only half believed these tales. And the idea of blowing in and settling on the lagoon of an untamed island caught my fancy. I must learn seaplane flying at once. And over this, I had an undoubted stroke of good luck. For, when I approached the Director of Aviation,[1] he said: "As you are now in the Territorial Air Force, you can do a course of seaplane, instead of landplane, training."

I proceeded to the Air Base at Auckland in my brand-new uniform

---

1   Wing-Commander S. Grant-Dalton, d.s.o., a.f.c.

and when not scheming to dodge the regulars for fear of awkward saluting problems, I spent the time hoping to be sent up for fifteen-minute periods of seaplane instruction. Once allowed out solo, I found that where landplane flying had thrilled, seaplane flying thrilled five times as much. There was something wild and free about it. Instead of artificial aerodromes to deal with, the seaplane must twist and turn in a tight-sided valley to settle on the floor of water like a dog turning itself a flat bed. There was the joy of skimming the steep tree-covered slopes, the cliffs, the promontories of harbour-arm; of the plane settling on to its water cushion, the give of the water and its drag on the floats taking to it; of choosing for oneself the best water on which to alight and the joy of depending on oneself alone for accurate estimate of wind, tide, and surface obstructions. But I was surprised to find that to fly a seaplane required more skill. It could not climb or manoeuvre as quickly; therefore the height of the cliff ahead must be taken into consideration; and water was usually land-locked, whereas an aerodrome was chosen for its flat approaches. With big floats, the seaplane lost flying-speed and stalled more easily, changing the lightness of an air-borne plane for the weight of a dropping stone; with the least excess of bank in turning, the floats caught the air, were forced outwards and tripped the plane on to one wing. Then, not only was it an aeroplane to fly, but a fast motor boat to handle and a delicate yacht as well. Once the motor was on, it could not travel through the water slower than a motor boat, and immediately the motor was off, it drifted back as fast as a yacht sailing—with wings to grip the air as much as possible, and floats to grip the water as little as possible.

As for forced alightings on the sea, it would weather as big waves as a canoe could weather, no more, no less.

I quickly found it necessary to keep alert the whole time, especially near the Air Base, where a group of power lines had been stretched across the harbour-arm as a sort of booby trap. But these were 110,000 volts, and I felt that 11,000 had been quite enough to manage. As I had to fly over or under them at each alighting and as they were not particularly noticeable from a plane, they dealt many a jolt to my ease of mind when, nearly into them, I suddenly remembered their presence. Who would be the first pilot, momentarily forgetful, whom they would catch and kill?

On the surface, there was the chance of running aground while turning, or fouling a launch or jetty, of being capsized through a gust catching under the weather-side wing-tips; and a-small accident which could be repaired at the cost of a few pounds with a landplane, might mean total loss with a seaplane: fouling a lee jetty—crunch! both lee wings crumpled: a wave lifts—crush! tail crammed between jetty-floor and water: wave drops away—zip! an iron bolt rips open the thin float-shell. The plane has sunk to the bottom of the harbour before a rescue party has had time to crank up the motor of its boat.

I began to wonder if I had bitten off more than I could chew. I should have no specially trained wading party to bring the seaplane ashore after every flight, to haul it up a specially constructed slipway. I should have to deal with men used to handling heavy boats, unaware of a seaplane's fragility. I must moor out every night, must effect the mooring by myself, must carry ropes, anchor, drogue; must take off with enough petrol to reach my objective, must, must, must . . . They were right, a Moth *was* a toy for a long-distance seaplane flight. There were so many other difficulties, too. Hadn't I better chuck it up?

I pulled out the chart of Norfolk Island. It appeared to be a squat rock dumped in the Pacific, walled up from the ocean by 300-foot cliffs; bare and grim and bleak, it had no sheltered anchorage; the deep-sea rollers must be forever lurching against it, snatching at it, pounding on it. And the whole was no larger than a New Zealand sheep farm. Ugh! what a place for a small seaplane. The project was impossible, I must give it up.

I turned to the chart of Lord Howe Island. This was shaped like a Cupid's bow with a coral reef for a bowstring. The lower arm of the bow went beyond the bowstring and there were two knots on the end of it. These were the mountains, Lidgbird, 2,500 feet, and Gower, 2,800. Yet the whole island was Only 3,200 acres, or five square miles in extent. I forgot everything and sat absorbed by the hour. Finger Peak, Sugar Loaf Passage, Look-out Mound, North Hummock, Intermediate Hill, Boat Haven, Smooth-water Lagoon, Fresh-water Creek—the sight of those names alongside the feathery drawings of hillocks and reefs and creeks set me afire with a slow, fierce combustion of excitement and desire to plop my *Elijah*, on to that lagoon, with its "coral reef awash here", "heavy surf here" and "boat passage at high water"; and in the evening to stroll, rifle in hand, from the farmhouse with its clustered outbuildings, across the close-cropped pastures and up the slopes of Mount Lidgbird to stalk a young rabbit or two. I must fly there at all costs. I lay awake half the night conjuring up pictures of it and tingling all over at the thought of coming upon it suddenly from out of the blue. The island grew to have for me the lure of a maid for a man.

And if that were not enough to fire me, there was the thought of Ball's Pyramid, a solitary rock twelve miles south-east of Lord Howe Island. Only four hundred yards wide and eight hundred long, it shot straight up from the sea to a height of no less than 1,810 feet. Always I was picturing in my mind that pinnacle of rock standing alone in the ocean; thrust through the surface like a jagged finger of fate. And then I knew I could never rest till I had flown up to it, gazed at it framed by the wings of my plane in a setting of azure blue, had flicked past it, wheeled about it, and spiralled down it a thousand feet, wing-tip and rock flirting with each other a few inches apart.

But meanwhile a difficulty had arisen. How should I find these islands? Norfolk Island was only four and a half miles across at its widest, and as a target seen from New Zealand (on the map) only filled an angle of half a degree. And since there was not so much land as a gull could perch on within 500 miles, it was a compulsory landfall. I must make a bull's-eye of it, or . . . And the smallest compulsory landfall yet made by an aeroplane, had provided a target of seven degrees—fourteen times as wide. That was the Hawaii group made from San Francisco and picked up by direction-finding wireless. But it would be impossible for my small plane to carry the weight of direction-finding wireless—on second thoughts, that fact was of no moment, because neither island had a direction-finding wireless station. As for depending on a light aeroplane compass for the job, I had known a compass deviation to change nine degrees within three weeks, so how should it be relied on to find a half-degree target? The only possible chance of my finding an island was by the sun. "Hasn't been done", said the experts, "—man flying solo, piloting the plane and finding the way by sextant, all together. Can't be done." "Well," I argued, "the mate of a tramp steamer can find his way by sextant observation of the sun. In that case, so can I in an aeroplane."

I must learn astronomical navigation.

By the time I had learnt as much as necessary to navigate a ship, I began to realize the difference between navigating an aeroplane with a speed of 80 m.p.h. which cannot stop, and a tramp steamer of 8 m.p.h. which can. The steamer was quite content to obtain its position by two observations, one early in the morning and one at noon. The sun travelled halfway across the sky in that time. But the faster-moving aeroplane required the same information inside an hour, and the sun did not change its position sufficiently in an hour to provide it. And besides moving faster, the aeroplane was more erratic. Whereas a ship was seldom more than a mile or two out of its dead reckoning in a day's steam, many a pilot would attest how easy it was in rough weather for an aeroplane to be forty miles out at the end of an hour's flying. I must concoct a scheme of navigation to surmount both difficulties. And not only must it be simple, it must be foolproof as well. Solving mathematical problems in a ship's chartroom and solving them while flying an open plane, were as much akin as reading a book in a study to writing a letter in a typhoon. Gradually I evolved a scheme of flying along hourly position-lines. It was a perfect little system (I decided); all that was necessary for success was for the plane to leave at the exact moment calculated for that particular day. Ah! little did I know of seaplanes.

As the ordinary sextant was not good enough for air work, I ordered a special one with an artificial horizon, and until I could test it in a plane, practised by the hour while motoring along the road, walking round the house, or running round the garden. My only worry about it at that time was my inability to prevent childish errors from creeping into every third or fourth observation. Stupid mistakes such as jotting down a figure wrongly. However, I supposed that my brain knew this was only practice and that it would exert an extraordinary effort necessary for accurate work when the time came.

At this juncture, Menzies of Australia flew the Tasman solo west to east from Sydney. (This was in an Avro landplane which had been built for Kingsford-Smith to make his record flight from England to Australia. Menzies crashed it in a flax swamp on the west coast of South Island, New Zealand, on arrival. It was repaired and shipped back to Sydney where, its wings collapsing when in flight, the owner, named James, and a passenger were killed.) However, the point was, the flight had now been done. West to east, it was true; but still, it had been done. Well, the idea of flying to my islands, in mid-ocean and the problem of finding them by my own scheme of navigation had such a hold on me by now, that forty ocean flights would not have quenched my desire for this one.

But a fresh difficulty now cropped up. I was astonished to find that a new pair of floats with the necessary undercarriage alterations would cost £500. I lost much sleep trying to devise a scheme for evading this little obstruction, until I noticed an old discarded pair at the Air Base. They had belonged to the Moth sent up to bomb the Mau rebels at Samoa (with pamphlets); and were the relics of that machine after it had been dropped accidentally twenty feet on to the deck of H.M.S. *Dunedin*; however, I thought they would serve me all right if patched up. Unfortunately, the Government refused to let me have them.

I went the round of all the oil companies in the hope that one would back me in return for (possible) advertisement. One said Menzies had already made the flight, another said the financial depression prevented, a third said it could not associate with such a risky enterprise for fear the public might blame it if I failed.

At this time I had my first chance to try my hand with an

ordinary sextant when flying solo. The observation was 180 miles in error. Altogether, affairs did not seem to be at their best for me.

I found I was beginning to charge obstacles like a bull, goaded by any check as by a pricking dart. That was no way to accomplish things. "Softlee, softlee, catchee monkey"—one could catch any monkey provided one kept on going "softlee" after it long enough—that is, so long as it did not die of old age first. I must completely throw off the burden of the whole business for a while.

So I retired to a tent in the hills for an arduous fortnight, felling bush and scrub in the heat of the year. Even so, I could not at first altogether shake off thought of the flight. Coming to a young tree, the fancy leaped into my mind—unwanted, as it were—that if I could fell the tree with one stroke of the axe I should get across the Tasman, and if I could not, then I should fail. It was a pretty stout young sapling as thick as the width of my palm. I swung the axe and brought it down with all my force—with more force, it seemed, than I knew I possessed. The tree reeled—but it stood. Heavens! I had failed. I gave it a shove. It tottered. Slowly, it fell with a crash of breaking foliage. Yet even on the ground a few strands still bound it to the stump. The axe-haft was split in two. I stood for a moment pondering the omen of it. Had I felled it with one stroke or had I not? It would not have fallen without my shove. And still a few strands remained uncut. The axe broken, too. But the tree, certainly, was felled . . .

It was no good to work among the hill-tops if I continued to think about flying. I must grow a beard—one could not possibly remain over-serious about anything else with a beard breeding.

Up there the poison of worry sweated out of one's pores; until blood felt ready to burst through its vein-walls; until vitality and power were burnt in by the sun, and fired by swinging the axe to the mark. How grand life could be! with this consciousness of ability to achieve anything, to tackle anyone. My God! this was the life I loved. The true life—that made one feel the joyousness of existence, strength, health. To return to camp after toil with the mist of fatigue creeping over the brain and veiling worthless cares from it, soothing. To emerge from the mountain stream aglow and tingling. To hear the dull "pop" of a red-hot stone in the camp fire. To feel the bite in nostrils of the acrid manuka leaves smouldering. To swear carelessly at the smoke curling into the tent and following one's eyes about to make them smart.

My God! why was I returning to a life I did not love? A life without even the glamour of an unknown experience. The terrible fatigue at dawn. Nerves wearing thin through sixteen hours of strain a day, through ceaseless beating from sound-waves of the motor's roar, through eternal oscillation. Wondering each morning how much longer one's luck could hold. My God! what did I stand to gain? Health? I was leaving it behind in these hills. Happiness? What happiness was to be derived from long-distance flying? Months of worrying work preparing for a flight which any one of a thousand things could prevent. And even if it should start, what enjoyment could be obtained when in a constant state of exhaustion? Money? I stood to gain none, only to lose it—both ways, by business neglected, by spending every shilling I could lay hands on. Fame? I was attempting a flight that had already been accomplished, and in any case, who would choose to fly the Tasman in search of fame? Few people had even heard of it, let alone knew it. Let me stay where I was and derive happiness from life! It would not be a case of "quitting". I had no money, could get no floats, my navigation was uncertain, plane inadequate. Let me accept the inevitable, cease the futile struggle and live the life I loved.

But it was no use reasoning like that. I felt I could not escape the flight. I was bound to go on whether I wanted to or not. But surely that was an admission of fate? And as man was master of his fate, it could not be correct. No, the reason why I was bound to go on must be that once I had begun, I must finish. I must drag myself back to the city and have at it again. I was just as much compelled to as Sisyphus was compelled to heave his boulder everlastingly up the mountain side.

I approached the Government once more, and sought the loan of the old floats. But I found that, not only was it holding on tight to them, but a new official had been appointed to the Ministry of Defence whose sole job was to effect economies.

The autumn was drawing to a close. Soon the stormy westerlies would set in across the Tasman. Contrary winds. And with a contrary wind Norfolk Island was out of range. The utmost fuel that even I could hope for *Elijah* to lift as a seaplane was only ten hours' supply.

It appeared that I was completely blocked. I could see no way through the difficulty. Well, I must make a change in tactics—desert reason and obey a premonition connected with a strange feeling that the flight was to go forward. On the surface, to obey a premonition seemed to savour of fatalism, but of course there must be some other explanation for doing such a thing. The premonition said, "Return to the Air Base as if all were going well." So I immediately climbed aboard the night train for Auckland, and did go.

I had left on Friday the thirteenth (of February) I found—a discovery which caused me an uneasy feeling. Pouf! nothing in superstition—it was only an illegitimate offspring of fatalism.

In the air, I tried my special Booth bubble sextant with the artificial horizon and was 740 miles in error. On hearing this, the Wing-Commander wrote an official letter saying that I now ought to abandon the flight. "Lost Airman" publicity would set back aviation with the public. They still had in memory Hood and Moncrieff, who set out to fly the Tasman and were never seen again. I replied that I was confident I could make an ordinary sextant do by flying lower and using the sea, instead of an artificial horizon.

I wrote again to the Government through the Wing-Commander, urging it to lend me the floats, or failing that, allow me to pay for them when I could.

Wing-Commander Grant-Dalton, who had been building up a surprisingly efficient Territorial Air Force in New Zealand from the collection of pilots available, thought I was doing good experimental work in navigation, and said that he, personally, recommended that the floats be lent to me.

I became ill and was sent into Auckland Hospital. I found the day I returned to the Air Base to be Friday the thirteenth (of

March). I was distinctly uneasy at another Friday the thirteenth turning up.

Reason: "But we could easily have remained in hospital till the fourteenth."

Instinct: "Then why didn't we?"

Reason: "For one thing, we didn't know the date; though, in any case, to be quite frank I would rather risk superstition than another day of that bread-and-milk diet."

Yet it was good luck that seemed to follow, because on return to the Air Base, I found the Government had relented, and loaned me the floats.

A week later I had an absolute presentiment that the flight would be started the following Saturday. In fact, so strong was it, that I immediately prepared navigation for that day, working out the position of the sun for the various times it would be needed. I soon suppressed the presentiment, telling myself that I was only doing the work for practice. And, indeed, how could I possibly start the following Saturday with the floats still unrepaired, with *Elijah* still on wheels? She had never yet been flown as a seaplane and I should not have the faintest idea till she was launched, whether she could carry enough petrol to bring Norfolk Island within range or not—and the experts declared she had not a hope of doing so.

By next day I had forgotten all about the presentiment and was astounded when on Thursday a wireless arrived from Dr. Kidson, the meteorologist, to say that a favourable wind was likely for the next weekend, and was I going to make the attempt? I showed the message to the C.O.[1] I felt guilty of putting him into an unenviable position—I was nothing but a liability, for if I succeeded he would get no praise, whereas if I failed he might be blamed—but I promptly asked him if he would try to get me away to the extreme north of New Zealand on Friday, preparatory for an early start on Saturday.

"You know," he said, "I dislike this flight of yours. I doubt

---

1   Squadron-Leader L. M. Isitt, now (1945) Air Vice-Marshal, O.B.E., Chief of Air Staff, R.N.Z.A.F.

whether, alone, you can find your way by sextant. Even if that is possible, suppose there is no sun for the sextant. And even if you succeed in reaching Norfolk Island, there is nowhere to put down a seaplane. While, if you succeed in getting down, you won't be able to take off on account of the swell. If there should happen to be no swell, that would mean no wind and it will be quite impossible to take off a Moth loaded up like yours without a stiff wind to help."

He knew his business, and I knew he knew his business but I advanced some specious argument against each of his.

Once he had stated his opinion about it, I think he felt his duty done, and that he could give full rein to his unofficial bent which was a sporting inclination to help me as much as possible. But by midnight on Thursday, the plane was still not a seaplane, though he himself had helped work at it with the aircraftsmen.

Elijah was not ready for the water till the Friday afternoon. The wading party wheeled her down the slipway on a trolley; she made her début on the water like a duckling and took off into the air like a wild swan. Was I proud of her? After 34,000 miles as a landplane, she had a heart! But would she take the load? With all my gear, boat, anchor, ropes, food, water, navigation instruments and books, besides fifty gallons of petrol? . . . The experts said "no"; the same model plane and motor to which these floats had been attached in Samoa had refused to leave the water with no more load than the pilot and petrol for only eighty miles. Rumour said it was only through the pilot leaving his vest behind that the plane ever did take to the air.

But to *Elijah* the full load seemed to be as nought. She rose like a wild swan.

I returned jubilant!

"Don't forget", said the C.O. gloomily, "you have ideal conditions at the moment. Strong breeze against you, tide with you, and choppy sea to break the suction of the water on the floats. I'd like to see you carry out a forty-eight hours' mooring test, to make sure the floats don't leak; and also some long flights to test your navigation further."

Reason told me he was perfectly right. "Stay and test the machine," said Reason. But the presentiment had said "Go!" Of course, presentiment did seem to be slightly connected with fate—advance information as to what fate held in store, as it were; and I certainly did not believe in fate. Yet I'd go if I possibly could. This fear of something happening to stop me would be the reason—fear that gnawed away unceasingly at my nerves. I'd throw everything I possessed into the scales rather than be held up now.

Again we worked till midnight stowing the dozens of odds and ends comprising my gear—the wireless operator[1] completing installation of the diminutive set he had built for me. It had been his suggestion that I carry a small set for transmitting only. Including aerial, stretched from wing-tips to tail it only weighed 23 lbs. It could not be of much practical use with no ships on the sea to answer an S.O.S. from it, but he wished to experiment and I thought that with careful organization of my work, I could send a wireless message every hour and thus perform a wireless operator's job as well as those I already had to perform, namely, a pilot's, a navigator's and an observer's.

Going to the hangar near midnight, I took a short cut down the bank. At the foot (as I thought) I stepped off it on to the flat. But, actually, I was still halfway up the bank and seemed to be falling for a long time before I fetched up hard on the gravel below. As I lay still for a few minutes where I had fallen (not particularly hurt), I recalled how the Roman senator, if he chanced to stumble at his doorstep on the way to the Senate, regarded it as an ill omen and would on no account leave his house that day. With Friday the thirteenth twice and then this fall, it boded ill. No wonder I was so terribly depressed! Yet there was some strange force compelling me to go on. To give up filled me with horrid thoughts of unhappy wanderings for ever in search of peace of mind. To carry on seemed so right, even if it meant the failure I thought of. It seemed to satisfy some supernatural command. As if it were my destiny . . . No, that was wrong, definitely wrong. There was no such thing as destiny. And now that I came to think of it the

---

1   L.A.C. Partelow, now (1945) Squadron Leader.

senator did right to stay at home apart from any question of omens. And why? Because his stumbling signified that brain, nerve and muscle were not properly coordinating. Well, I must take double care next day and then it would have proved a good omen.

Chapter II

BEFORE SUNSET

I did not sleep well; it seemed that I woke every few minutes to hear the wind roaring about the house. Yet, on being called at 4 a.m., I found it a calm and cloudless sky. The first thing that I saw was the planet Jupiter, staring me full in the eye, bright and unwinking. Jupiter being the father of Minerva, I took it for an auspicious sign, and the enterprise appeared like the planet—clear, bright and shining; until bacon and eggs showed up for the candlelight breakfast and I felt on my spirit all the weight of all the weariness of my flight from England to Australia, when I had similarly breakfasted for day after burdensome day. My God! Here was I going into it again; and what's more, voluntarily. My God!

Flight-Lieutenant Wallingford[1] helped me swing my compass in the twilight before dawn.

Suddenly, I noticed the time was 6.15 by the dashboard clock, and I had fixed 6 o'clock local time as the hour for starting. I shouted to Wallingford, who was about to check the work, that there wasn't time. Then I remembered having altered the clock to Greenwich Mean Time. So there was still a quarter of an hour to go. But I refused to spare time for swinging the compass on any but the one bearing—that of Norfolk Island from New Zealand.

I smashed the bottle of brandy on the propeller-centre for the due propitiation of Minerva—just as I had formerly done before leaving Africa.

Looking up, I found that Jupiter, as if in direct answer to my

---

1   Now (1945) Air Commodore.

act, had at that very moment hidden from sight behind a dark, heavy cloud rising with the dawn. My spirits sank.[1]

When, on testing the motor, I found it would only give 1,780 revolutions, or forty less than it should, they sank further. I could never take off with the motor like that. But I must say nothing to the C.O. about it—he would immediately refuse to let me even make an attempt. And perhaps it was merely a speck of carbon under a valve which would presently disgorge it.

The plane was launched; I faced her into the wind now blowing up harbour, and opened the throttle.

To my great surprise, *Elijah* left the water as easily as a seabird.

I headed the plane to the grey of dawn until it gained enough height to make the long, low-sweeping turn needed by it, thus heavily laden.

Over the Air Base hangars, I fastened the wireless key to my leg with an elastic band and began tapping out in Morse, "Hullo, can you hear me?" time after time. Now I circled continuously, in tight circles and banked as steeply as I dared, the hangar where the operating-room was. I kept on sending, "Can you hear me?" but no answer came. The set must have failed. I ought to return. No, I couldn't now. Should I leave without the wireless being in action?

Suddenly an Aldis lamp signalled back "O.K." in dazzling flashes. "Good! What a relief!" I turned instantly again towards the dawn and made for the harbour entrance. The water below looked grey, the land looked lifeless and bare; Auckland lay for the most part sleeping in the cold grey light, though here and there, a wisp of smoke, lighter in colour, could be seen slipping away from a chimney-top. Never, shivering before the plunge of a mid-winter bathe in the sea, had I seen a dawn look so grey and cheerless.

I thought of city-dwellers below, oblivious to their good fortune, turning over in bed and cursing the alarm clock. Fools! not to realize their luck. And presently, they would sit down in comfort and ease of mind to fried sole, toast and marmalade.

The plane turned the harbour entrance and settled into the flight

---

1   It was not the planet Jupiter that was observed at the outset of the flight as was hastily assumed. Jupiter had already set some hours previously. It was Venus.

north. 6.45 a.m. It would be sunset at Norfolk Island that night at 6.45 p.m. (it being within two months of winter's shortest day), so I had twelve hours before sunset.

And 700 miles to fly. First 200 miles to the northern tip of New Zealand, where I must take aboard as much petrol as the plane would carry. Then 500 miles of Pacific Ocean to Norfolk Island.

It was not the distance that worried me.

But now I must get to work. Considering that *Elijah* had not been a seaplane longer than seventeen hours, I had to make every possible use of this first easy 200-mile stage. I must check the sextant work, find out the plane's true speed and note accurately its petrol-consumption. For with a great float, two-thirds the length of the plane, in place of each landing-wheel, there was going to be a great change in performance. And, particularly, any defects must be discovered *before* reaching North Cape—not *after*.

I soon found one big difference in *Elijah* as a seaplane. By pumping petrol from the front or back tank as required, I had been able to trim her when a landplane to fly level and steady without my touching the controls. She used to trim so well, that if I were reading something in the cockpit, she dived slightly when I bent my head forward and climbed when I lifted it again. Now, however, the fifteen-foot floats made her unwieldy. She not only pitched, but yawed as well. I could not leave the controls alone for ten seconds without her going into a steep dive or climb. I should have found it out before. I ought to have tested the sextant in a seaplane as well as in a landplane . . .

I settled back inertly in the cockpit. I had a feeling of emptiness inside me. It was a good job I had no physical effort to make, for there seemed no strength in me. It was a cold-blooded job—this. It drove one to a feeling of isolation, of solitariness. When observing sea or promontories, I found it was with a formal, distant regard, as if they belonged to some other life to which I was a stranger. And the grey-green sea below appeared coldly inhospitable and pitiless. We were overtaking a long swell from the south-east; it unrolled softly and smoothly underneath; it bore a threat; there was something mightily indomitable and merciless about it. It needed an effort to shoot straight across the bays and not cling timorously to the land.

On turning Cape Brett, I anxiously observed the lee shore of the Cape. Would it be sheltered from the force of the rollers? If so, I could expect to find the lee of Norfolk Island similarly sheltered. No! like spokes of a wheel, they radiated from the Cape as hub, changing direction and swinging relentlessly round it to discharge on the rocks behind in jagged lines of white surf. Nothing in that to allay my anxiety about Norfolk Island . . .

Past the Cape, I changed course north-westward.

Had the flight really started? Was I at last free from that cankering worry of uncertainty as to whether we ever should start? It had been such a sketchy, indeterminate act, departing, almost I had stolen away. Always waiting up to the last moment for any of the many knock-out blows to fall. But I had started at last, surely?

Yet at Parengarenga, I had still to collect the weather report which the C.O. was telegraphing on for me. It might predict adverse winds making it impossible with my 700-mile range to reach the island. And any weather could be expected, from those heavy-laden clouds pouring from the horizon.

As for the C.O. suggesting I might not find any sun, there was not yet the least sign of any. But of course, it would appear!

A ravening hunger was seizing me—fortunately, because fear seemed unable to contend with it for place. I had the ration of bread, butter and jam given me by the Isitts; but I refused to pacify such a fighting appetite with cold bread, when I could partake of royally hot dishes at Parengarenga—where I had to buy my emergency rations in any case.

8.30. 160 miles flown.

Passing a deserted little island named Mahinepua, which lay a bare, brown rock, with some patches of dull green, I had trouble in locating it on the map. It was small enough on the water, but on the map it was almost too trivial to be noticed. I received a shock when, on measuring it, I found its length was a mile and a half, or a third of the greatest length of my objective, Norfolk Island.

I kept constant look-out for the smallest break in the grey-black clouds sufficient to give me a test observation with the sextant.

At 8.40, a shaft of light pierced them right ahead and cast a small circle of brightness on the dull sea. It was as if the sungod, Phoebus, had stirred an opening through the clouds with his little finger and was peering down to decide whether he should shine through.

At 8.49 the plane struck the edge of the sunlight, and before we were across, I had "shot" the sun four times. This would be the last chance to check my astronomical navigation. I worked out the position-line resultant from the sight: then turned to the chart. The observation was 140 miles out!

For a second panic seized me. I was going to look for a 4½-mile island 500 miles away and here was a mistake of 140 miles. The night before I had carefully checked my chronometer watch with Greenwich Mean Time to the nearest half-second; it was then 10 minutes 55 seconds slow. I had forgotten to apply this correction to the work just done, I found. Then panic gave place to the desperation of extreme helplessness on recollecting the infinite variety of such childish errors it was possible to make. Gradually, I overrode that feeling. The work did require extraordinary concentration. Though I had found it comparatively easy to do in an open car driven at 50 m.p.h. by somebody else, it required a vastly different effort to pilot a plane, attend to the five instruments on the dashboard, maintain a course by compass and take observations with a sextant of the angle between horizon and sun, or work out carefully the resultant problem in spherical trigonometry all at the same time. And to exercise the precise care necessary was difficult in the 100-mile-an-hour blast of wind round one's head from the propeller-slipstream: it tangled up thinking, and the pulsating roar from the open exhausts broke up association of ideas. Well, I must definitely make up my mind to exert the will-power necessary to exclude these influences and supply the required standard of brain-work. There must be no mistake made whatever— there could not be.

Looking to the side, I found I was in the act of passing

Parengarenga Harbour.[1] It was scarcely noticeable, set in a vast expanse of sandhills so low that a large Pacific roller seemed quite capable of oversweeping the whole. But there was a sheet of water lying among the sand, and as the chart showed Parengarenga Harbour to be the only such stretch of water at this end of New Zealand, Parengarenga it must be. So I turned and made towards it, my now voracious appetite inducing visions of crinkled bacon and fat eggs. Perhaps a fried flounder to begin with and afterwards, luscious dabs of butter slithering about on hot toast, a great pot boiling over with fragrant black coffee.

Not that I dared stay long: it was now 9.15. As I depended on finding the island by the sun, I must arrive before sunset. Even so, it was doubtful if the sun could be used for the last hour before setting. But I was prepared to risk that. What I must have was spare time-allowance for a contrary wind, for some unpremeditated event delaying the flight, for drop in engine speed, and for locating a mooring-place at the island. With an adverse wind of 20 m.p.h. (and heaven knows! that was mild enough to expect over the sea) or a drop in speed of that amount, the flight would take 9½ hours. In that case I should need to leave in a quarter of an hour. I could hardly do that. Suppose I set three-quarters of an hour as the longest time I could stay.

However, it would only take ten minutes to fill up the main tank with petrol, and when the agent put off in his boat immediately to enquire how much was needed, I could return ashore with him, pick up my emergency rations, and with the appetite I now had, devour a good meal as quickly as a starving dog.

I must not forget the emergency rations because I should much prefer to have some tins of bully beef under the canvas thwart, if forced down, and rowing about in my rubber boat.

I could see a few houses clustered at the spot marked on the map "Parengarenga", but my petrol was actually at a place named Te Hamua, a mile or two across the water from Parengarenga. I skimmed round looking for this place and finally decided it must

---

1 See route map, at end.

be a group of some three or four wooden huts and fowl-runs. They were located in a small clearing by the shore, with a great expanse of stunted scrub all round, driving them, as it were, into the water. No other hut or fowl-run was to be seen. I flew down low to inspect, the fowls scattering in all directions with furious flutter of wings. On throttling the motor to alight, I was glad to see one or two people waving pieces of white material at me. The seaplane was just about to settle, when pebbles, shell and weed appeared so startlingly clear that I was afraid of insufficient depth. And knowing all this expanse to be dry at low tide, I shied, opened the throttle and went round again. I noted the dark streak of the deeper water in the channel further out and came down to that. The plane alighted with a glorious dragging kiss of the floats caressing the waves, a sheer delight that momentarily elated and made me think of Saladin drawing his rapier across the satin cushion which the heavy sword of the Scottish knight had failed to cut.

On the water at Parengarenga view aft from the cockpit.

Immediately *Elijah* lost way, she began to drift rapidly down wind. There was a snappish breeze now blowing. As quickly as possible, I threw overboard the anchor—it weighed 3¼ lbs. (to the nearest half-ounce) and the chain attached to it 2 lbs. more. I paid out the full length of line to give the anchor the best chance of holding, then peered into the water to see how it did hold. I was surprised at the transparency, though there must have been five or six feet of depth. After watching for a while the patches of weed slipping by like a landscape seen from a low-flying aeroplane, I was reluctantly forced to the conclusion that the anchor was not holding, and in consequence, *Elijah* was now drifting rapidly on to a lee shore. Not knowing what might result from this, I was perturbed. I looked round anxiously for any Te Hamuan resident, but there was not now the slightest indication of life anywhere. I looked at the watch—9.30. H'm.

One or two boats reclined inertly on the beach or lay at anchor close to it. I watched the shore behind the plane; it appeared more distinct every moment, and I was wondering if the motor would start in the hurry that would soon be called for—drifting at this rate—when someone strolled on to the beach and stood looking towards the plane. Presently he turned round, and stood gazing for a long time until another man joined him. After a stately interval, a boy followed and they all sauntered down to a dinghy, which they launched. This disappeared behind an anchored boat. Lifelessness settled on the place again and the outlook seemed black indeed. But suddenly the launch, as it turned out to be, moved from its moorings and the outlook was immediately bright again. Round in a wide arc it swept, dinghy in tow, and arriving at a point some two hundred yards to windward, came to rest there, as if *Elijah* were a mad dog not to be safely approached any closer. At least, it was two hundred yards at the moment it came to rest, but three hundred by the time a man and the boy had dropped into the dinghy and begun to row towards me. And what with the deliberate style of the boy and his father (or maybe grandfather, judging by his display of energy) and the almost scared manner in which they looked over their shoulders every stroke or two, for each yard they advanced on *Elijah*, she drifted away two. I watched with anxiety the shore ever drawing nearer, until in the end I decided I must start the motor even at the risk of hurting

Elijah, a De Havilland Moth with an 85 h.p. Gipsy 1 engine. Total weight empty (with floats) 1,150 lbs., span 30 feet, length 25 feet 5 inches. Note the petrol tank on top, still showing the effects of a night's bumping on the sea-bottom.

their feelings. I did so, and as the plane moved forward, reeled in the dripping anchor-line, precariously standing on a float behind the evanescent propeller-blades. The effect on my visitors was magical. As soon as they saw the plane approaching, the launch moved off at full speed, and the occupants of the dinghy rowed like men possessed—as if terrified of hydrophobia from the snapping tappets of this mad dog *Elijah* rushing towards them. Abreast of the dinghy, I switched off the motor and threw out the anchor again. Re-assured, the rowers rested on their oars, and stared at this strange creature invading their waters. Heavens! they were Maoris.

"I want an anchor," I bawled. "Have you got an anchor? I must have an anchor. Can you let me have an anchor?"

Presently the brown-faced man with a squashed nose turned to the boy and said: "Py Corry, he want te phlurry anchor, I tink, hey?"

"Yes, py Corry," replied the boy, "mine tink he want te phlurry anchor all right."

Without another word, they set off leisurely for the launch, and once aboard, held much discussion. Then the launch set off leisurely for the shore. Now the Maori is a devilish fine fellow, friendly, good-natured, sporting and with perfect manners of a kind: in fact, quite a gentleman. So I suppose one should not blame him if he is a trifle slow in absorbing new ideas. But possessed with impatience as gnawing as my hunger, I waited helplessly, while my dreams of luscious eggs and curly bacon faded and died.

Far worse, the three-quarters of an hour allowed for my stay had also run out. It was ten o'clock.

Well, I must take a risk. Another half-hour of my time reserve must be sacrificed. But I muttered curses; and not to one second after that must I risk deferring departure.

Ten minutes later they returned to the boat and put off again— just as I was forced to restart the motor and taxi back to the channel in order to avoid stranding behind. The launch made its great circular course and slipped the dinghy to wind ward as before.

This time they rowed with their best stroke, and slowly caught up the plane.

"Fasten your anchor on to mine!" I shouted.

"Hey?"

"Pick up my anchor and fasten yours to it."

"Hey?"

"Fasten your anchor to my anchor"!

"Py Corry!" remarked Hori to the boy, "I tink he say 'fasten on anchor.'"

"Py Corry," said the boy, "I tink so too."

They swept about in the water for my anchor-line with an upright oar and after it had eluded three sweeps, caught it and added their own anchor.

"I want the petrol," I shouted.

"Hah?"

"Petrol! Where is my petrol?"

"Ho! Petrol!"

"Yes! Petrol! I want my petrol!"

"Py Corry!" said Hori senior to Hori junior, "I tink he want his phlurry petrol, hey?"

"He! he! he!" said the boy, "I tink that th' very same feller he want."

"Didn't you know I was coming for petrol?" I demanded, in exasperation.

"Ho, we think you not come this soon," he replied, though a second telegram had been sent only the day before to warn him of my impending arrival.

"Well, for the love of Mike, go and get it! I want it at once, immediately, now, on the spot, without delay. *And* hurry!"

He said nothing and rowed back to the launch. Launch returned to shore. Men disappeared. Wind blew, water was flecked with the white tops of waves and time ran on. It was eerie out on those deserted waters in the bobbing plane, with waves softly slapping the floats and salty air blowing into one's nostrils. The seaplane was such a rickety and frail craft, there seemed to be no security standing on a float with the water lapping one's shoes. It was like being in the foretop of a sinking ship when the water was already halfway up the mast.

And there was a strange sense of unreality. It was hard to connect this with a trans-Pacific flight already overdue to start. On the other hand, what I did realize was that I should have to return if unable to get away within a few minutes. Return! my God! and again go through all the nerve-wearing, rasping fear of being unable to attempt the flight! Or if ever that fear were quiet, then the fear of the flight itself hanging over my head like the sword of Damocles! No, I couldn't return now.

10.30.

No! They could not possibly take any longer to bring the petrol. I would use another half-hour of the reserve time. That left eight hours instead of nine and a half. A fifteen-mile breeze or drop in speed would make it impossible to arrive before sunset. A hundred other things could use up the margin. In a flight over land, what odds would it make! But if caught at sea by darkness . . . And with only an hour or two's petrol left . . . Even had I brought star declination and right-ascension tables, there was no light in the cockpit . . . Not even a lighthouse on the island . . .

Meanwhile the hamlet had swallowed up the men, and might have been an old sow that, momentarily stirred by a prod in the belly, rolls over with a grunt and straightway begins snoring again. Time went by, and no sign of life appeared. Were they holding a council of war, or could they be taking a siesta? No, it was too early for that—perhaps they were eating my ham and eggs: in that case, if they ate as much as I felt I could, they would need a siesta of several hours afterwards. "Oh, well, there is nothing I can do to cure the delay, so why turn my hair grey over it?" I fumbled below the seat for the jam and butter and the loaf of bread given me by the Isitts. I cut myself a great slice. Riding astride the fuselage behind the cockpit, I was half through this when the men came down to the beach and the launch put off again. I hastily rammed the remainder of the bread and jam into my mouth and scrambled forward on to a float. The launch came towards the plane. Well, the position was not really so hopeless as I had been thinking. All this fretting and anxiety had been perhaps unwarranted and the difficulties exaggerated.

The launch did not slacken speed or alter course; it shot by and headed for the other side of the harbour. None of the occupants took the slightest notice of me. For a moment the mastication of bread and jam ceased as I stood stock-still, following the launch with my eyes, which I could not at first believe. If thought-transference were a fact, it was a wonder the crew of the launch did not shrivel and fall overboard. On and on it went—not a sign of turning—it became smaller and smaller, and finally disappeared to view opposite Parengarenga township. And, what's more, they must be using my petrol to get there. Or what *had* become of the twenty-four gallons awaiting me?

Eleven o'clock. The last half-hour had passed. I sank into deep depression, stirred now and then by bursts of sullen rage.

"Turn it in and go back," suggested Reason. "It's too late to start now."

"No," said Instinct, "we are going to start. I know it. I feel it. Nothing can convince me we are not. Didn't I feel a week ago that we should leave to-day? Didn't I urge you then to prepare navigation for this day? And at that time the floats were not repaired, they had yet to be rigged on to *Elijah*; you did not know whether *Elijah* could lift enough petrol for the crossing; nothing was finished; you knew nothing. Yet did not I, Instinct, say we should leave to-day?"

Yes, that was true, though the idea had been to come up to Parengarenga yesterday.

"Don't be crazy!" urged Reason. "Of course, I admit you can leave any time if you like to be a fool or a suicide. But we've played this game, about twenty times already, leaving so as to get caught in the dark at the end of the flight, and we shall play it once too often. There was that little crash arriving in Africa after dark. And Africa is *slightly* bigger to find in the darkness than is Norfolk Island."

"I'll let another half-hour go."

Five minutes of it had already gone.

I scrambled back on to the fuselage, sat astride behind the cockpit and cut myself another great slice of bread and jam. But I scarcely tasted it, though swallowing voraciously.

It was extraordinary how desolate it was. Except right behind, there was only a thin rim of distant land all round; and the grey-green sea, whipped into white crests by the stiffening breeze, seemed a deserted waste. The wind, putting a chill into the air, seemed also to put a chill into a man's heart.

The clock showed I had twelve minutes to go. To relieve the load of impatience and anxiety on my mind, I pulled out the wireless-transmitting key, rested it on my leg and, still astride the fuselage, began to send a long message to the Air Base saying where I was and including a few trenchant remarks about Te Hamua and the petrol-providing potentialities of its residents. "And I only want twelve gallons altogether, yet cannot leave without it," I Morsed. In the middle of a sentence, I looked up to find the launch in sight and apparently heading straight for the plane. I broke off the message with a hurriedly sent: "Here comes the launch again," and put away the key.

But now what to do? There only remained seven minutes of the very last half-hour I had said I could possibly spare. The launch could not arrive and I could not refuel in that time. "It's madness not to turn back now," said Reason. "Bet on a favouring wind," urged Instinct. "By Jupiter!" I thought desperately, "how can I turn back now? The wind is favourable at present—I'll take a chance it holds throughout. At any rate, I'll see how long it takes to get the petrol in, and then decide." This time I did not arrogantly assert I must leave within so many minutes or not at all. But I felt desperate, like a man driven back to his last line of defence.

Tense, I watched the white bow-waves increase in size. Would they pass a cable's length away once more? No, it really was petrol this time; the dinghy came down the anchor-line with three cases on board.

"Got a funnel?" I called out.

"No, we not got funnel. Hey, you make us present of this benzine-case, hey?"

"All right, how about opening it first!"

"We not got hammer to open with, hey?"

I scrambled back to the fuselage-locker for my little collapsible funnel, then on to the wing-root to ransack the front cockpit for the tools at the very bottom of it. I passed over the big spanner.

"Hey!" he said, "we got no screwdriver, hey."

My new and only screwdriver followed, to be belted by the spanner into the wooden case. After making a hole in one of the four-gallon tins into which he could have thrust his fist, he handed up the tin to me. From the wing-root, I worked it up to the motor-cowling, clambered up after it, got it on the top tank, and then stood precariously trying to balance myself on the motor of the bobbing plane, my right arm round a thirty-pound tin of petrol and left hand at the collapsible leather and chamois petrol-filter. And, my sainted aunt! how that collapsible funnel could collapse. I cannot imagine a more perfect or more frequent collapse with any collapsible funnel ever made. When it wasn't collapsing to send a surge of petrol up my sleeves, it collapsed to send a surge down my legs; and when it wasn't collapsing at all, the seaplane pitched, and shot a geyser of petrol into my cockpit. And as if that wasn't sufficiently exasperating, Hori chose this moment for a little questionnaire. Evidently, someone at Parengarenga had put him up to it.

Question: "You going far?"

Answer: "To Australia."

Question: "Ho, Australia, hey! You give me that benzine-tin when it empty, hey? How many mile this Australia?"

Answer: "Twelve or thirteen hundred."

Question: "Py Corry! you hear that!" (turning to his young relative). "Twelve hundred mile. Py Corry! that th' phlurry long way to swim, I tink." (Anxiously): "You make me present of that tin, hey?"

Answer: "All right."

Question: "What time you get there? I tink you not get there for lunch, hey?"

Answer: "I'm only going to Norfolk Island to-day. That is to say," I added, looking up at the clouds, "that is where I hope to get."

Question (anxiously): "You give me that benzine-tin when you finish him?"

Answer: "All right."

Question: "Norfolk Island! You hear that? Ho! ho! ho! Norfolk Island; you hear that! He say he go to Norfolk Island. How far this Norfolk Island?"

Answer: "Four hundred and eighty-one miles as calculated by logarithms, but slightly over five hundred by the course I hope to take."

Question (slowly): "Five hundred miles. Why! py Corry, that th' phlurry long swim too, py Corry!"

Answer: "Hand me up another tin, please."

Question: "Where you come from to-day?"

Answer: "Auckland."

Question: "You give me that tin too, when he finish, hey? When you leave Auckland then? I been to Auckland."

Answer: "Quarter past six."

Question: "What! To-day?"

Answer: "Yes."

Question: "What! you come all that long way from Auckland in one morning, in two, three hours! Ha! ha! ha! that the phlurry joke, I tink! You hear that Hori, hey? He say he come from Auckland in two—three hour. I tink he pull our phlurry leg, what you tink?"

"He! he! he!" replied little Hori, "I tink he pull our phlurry leg all right."

I filled up with twelve gallons so that I now had about fifty on board which amounted to ten hours' fuel. I had tankage for fifty-nine, but knew it would be hopeless to try rising from the water with more than fifty.

"Hori," I said, "my anchor no good. How about the swap?"

"Ho, we not got the other anchor this place."

"But you can easily get one across at the store if you want one. You can have my chain into the bargain."

"Ho, that anchor, he belong to my mother's sister's son's wife's brother; that th' very valuable anchor, that anchor!"

"Look here," I said, with great apparent reluctance, but desperately wondering in secret how long it would take to make a deal, "I'll swap my anchor, *and* chain, *and* a tin of petrol for it."

The petrol was worth about three anchors like his, but I must say I did not anticipate having to pay for it, which, I thought, evened up the deal from my point of view. Although it seemed most strange, almost a dream, to be chaffering at such a time, for an article worth half-a-crown, yet I told myself that no matter what I offered him—the seaplane, even—the deal could not be made any shorter than by the customary haggling.

"All right," agreed Hori, rather reluctantly, "you have that anchor then. That very valuable anchor, that anchor."

"Good! Now hurry, please! Lift the anchors, take off mine and bend on yours."

"Ho, py Corry, I forget; they got th' telegram on shore for you, hey!"

I ran my fingers into my hair and clutched two handfuls of it. I started swearing vehemently, though in scarcely more than a whisper, and unloosed oath after oath till presently my anger was under control. Then I laughed, and suggested "suppose he go and fetch it". He sheered off from the anchor-line and made for the shore. "And go like hell!" I shot after him.

As he rowed for the shore every second was now to me like another ant come to devour a man staked to the ground. Still, now that the telegram had arrived I had better see it. Suppose it warned me of an adverse wind!

When the Maoris were halfway to the shore, I saw a lumbering hulk of a boat leave its moorings and start towards the plane. It exchanged shouts with the dinghy, which then turned round again.

The hulking great launch came up to leeward of the plane and a white man stood in the bows waving a telegram. By now I was so ridden with impatience that hot blood seemed to press on the back of my eyeballs. "Stay there!" I roared, "and read it out!"

The boat blundered on towards the seaplane tail.

"On behalf of the residents of Te Hamua . . ." the man began to intone.

"Don't come any closer!" I bellowed, "read the telegram out from there!"

"I should like to say," he continued, "that we wish you . . ."

"I hear you've got a telegram for me," I raged, feeling the heat of a desert at noon in my head. "Read it out! I'm late and in a hell of a hurry. And don't come any closer—you're going to ram me in a second!"

"I should like to express on behalf of the people . . ."

"My God! Read out that telegram and let me get away. And stand off, man, don't ram the tail! Are you daft?"

The man looked excited and scarcely comprehending my words until the last outburst, which he seemed to take in, though barely. He spoke to a man behind him, who then let go the anchor a fathom in lee of the plane's tail.

"Forecast from Dr. Kidson," he read out. "Weather expected fine; fresh to strong southeasterly breeze; seas moderate, becoming rough."

"Rough seas"—h'm—that threatened bad conditions at the exposed island. Well, there could be fifty-foot waves for all I cared if only I could get away!

"And I should like to say . . ."

"Heave up that anchor," I shouted to Hori, back in his former position at my anchor-line, "take off mine and bend on yours. And shake a leg, for the love of Mike!"

"We wish you every-success-on-your-flight!" shouted the white man, triumphantly.

"Thanks," I mumbled, "sorry I'm in this hell of a hurry."

As I watched, Hori got up the anchors and began changing them. Suddenly the idea penetrated my over-hot brain that dinghy and plane were now adrift together, and the hulking launch was anchored in the path of drift. Startled, I turned round to find it looming a few yards from the tail empennage. The sight gave me a shock as if a rock had struck me. One bump on the elevators from that ungainly monster, and the plane would be as good as the hulk itself for flying.

"Let go the anchor!" I bawled at Hori, "let go that—— anchor, Hori!"

Thank heavens, he did so instantaneously—I think he dropped it through fright. And fortunately, both anchors were still on the line. Would they pull the plane up before it fouled, or wouldn't they? They did! Whew! that was a close call. I felt shaken, jumbled, as though my nerves were telegraph-wires, crossed everywhere and tangled. I translated my feelings into nautical language—deep-sea stuff. I think even the chap on board the hulk-launch realized the pilot was upset about something, for he heaved up his anchor, without a word, and moved away from our lee. Hori took up my line again, removed the small anchor, and then rowed clear. I hauled in and stowed the anchor in the front cockpit, swung the propeller, and while taxi-ing the few minutes to warm up, fastened the small barometer and chronometer watch to my wrist. Then I opened the throttle wide.

I welcomed the stiff breeze, for heading into it, the seaplane needed to get up so much less speed on the water before becoming air-borne. With a lopping sea to break the hold of the water sucking at the floats, the conditions seemed ideal.

Elijah threshed through the water, on, and on, and on. She showed not a sign of leaving it. After a run of more than a mile, I had to desist, because another cable's length would have run her aground on the opposite shore.

As I turned *Elijah* back towards the hamlet, I anxiously sought a reason for the failure. At dawn, the plane had taken off with less favourable conditions—less wind, less sea. The motor was no worse now. True, it should be making forty or fifty more revolutions per minute, but if it had taken off at dawn, it should take off again with far greater ease under the superb conditions. Were the floats leaking? No! that they could not possibly be after their thorough testing—when filled right up with water, scarcely a drop had leaked out; and if none could leak out, none could leak in. If she refused to take off, after having got so far . . . A cold feeling spread in and laid hold of me like the tentacles of an octopus.

I turned into wind for another attempt. The sea-plane bumped and porpoised but showed no sign of rising. Desperate, I snatched at the control-stick as at the bridle of a horse, and jerked up the plane's nose. She jumped out of the water, settled back again—with the waves dragging at the float-heels—but not so deep in as before. I snatched again, and again she jumped; settled down after the jump, but held off the water within a few inches of it.

Slowly she gathered speed, overcame the heaviness of her stalled condition, and rose. Ah! we were away.

11.50. I had ten minutes less than the still-air time of flight. It was no longer a case of being able to succeed with an adverse wind—of even five miles an hour—I must have a favouring wind now. Well, it certainly favoured at present.

I looked down at a sprawling desert of deathly-white patches of sand among thick stunted scrub; absently, I mused. Perhaps I had been rough with those poor fellows—probably it was the first plane they had ever seen and the first amusement that had come their way for a twelvemonth. I had been harsh, yet otherwise, I should have been kept there all day. Or was it the truth that I had been exasperated by their complete lack of sympathy with, and understanding of, my task? Now they would be returning to their ordinary, everyday affairs. Was it possible that placid, secure life continued down below? Incredible that they should be going about their peeling of potatoes and gossiping at the door of each other's huts. What a gulf isolated my life from theirs! No helping hand could reach me across it.

Fool that I was to make this venture when not compelled to by material reasons . . . To go through with it only for some indeterminate idea, as if it were a penance . . . For a definite gain, the risk would be easier to take . . .

Well, I had chosen my own course . . .

Pouf! I was exaggerating the risk. The Atlantic, for example, was a flight 800 miles longer. Yes, but no ship passed this way for a month—sometimes not that often. And, anyway, what chance had one ship of finding a minute object on the face of the ocean? But I could row a few hundred miles in the rubber boat . . . Pity I had no emergency rations. Though, why should the plane fail? For dozens of reasons—and one was enough, that each valve was struck open—880 times each minute—and valve stems break. I had wireless. True, but of what use with no ships on the sea?

All this was nothing; the real task was to *find the island*, and before sunset too. It was a fourteenth the size of the smallest compulsory landfall made by an aeroplane. From New Zealand it presented a target half a degree in width. And my compass, recently swung twice on that bearing, had varied 9° during the interval; further, it was nothing to drift 30° in a stiff wind. And since an error in the course of only 5° meant passing the island 50 miles away, it was plain I could only depend on the sun to find it.

Instead of heading direct for the island, I altered course 10° for a point 90 miles to the left of it. Flying towards this imaginary point, I must observe the sun carefully until it gave me the exact bearing of Norfolk Island on my right, and showed me to be on the line through point and island. I must then immediately turn to the right and head direct for the island.

I must make no mistake and turn neither a minute too soon nor a minute too late.

No mistake whatever. . . .

And only a few hours ago I had made an error of 140 miles . . .

They had said no man living could do it . . .

Were they right? Was I wrong? No! I had to be right. And that thought was like a sponge of cold water to stiffen one's purpose and clear away misgivings.

Looking at the air-speed indicator, I found it at zero. What! I leaned forward staring—but zero it was—a splash of spray in the pilot tube must have put it out of action. Well, the more primitive subsidiary indicator out on the front inter-wing strut could still give me a rough idea of the speed. It showed between the 75 and 80 marks—77 miles an hour I gauged.

Ahead, I could see an edge to the layer of black clouds, with clear sky beyond, as if I were under a partly iced-over lake surface and able to discern the edge of ice above and ahead.

I slipped off my goggles, and lifting the helmet flaps, stuffed each ear with a plug of cotton-wool. They muffled somewhat the cracking roar from the open exhausts which beat on my eardrums.

12.00 hours. 225 miles.

The plane shot over the edge of the last of New Zealand. It was Spirit's Bay. I thought of the old Maori belief that here was the vast cavern through which passed all the spirits of the dead when leaving this world.

The plane slipped from under the pall of laden cloud that had overhung threateningly all the morning, and slid into pure, clear atmosphere above the water. The sun shone down staring out of the sky; there was not a cloud or a flaw in its blue as far ahead as the eye could see. Things were going well! Like a butterfly emerging from its chrysalis, I expanded in the sunlight and shed all my miserable anxieties. I was thrilled through and through. Free! free! Away at last! Ha! ha! ha! free from that infernal negative craving to attempt the flight, which, if unsatisfied, would have rotted a man's very soul.

Over my left shoulder, the last of New Zealand receded rapidly. Ahead stretched only sparkling water that reflected a thousand little winks from the eye of the sun. I was thrilled again and again. "Ha! ha! ha! Last of New Zealand!" I thought. "Now that I really have escaped, I've a feeling I shall not see you again for many, many months. Let's be sporting and carry away a photograph of your topknot as a souvenir."

I took out the camera, and working the plane controls with my left hand, brought the camera across in my right, pressed it to my face, sighted and pulled the trigger. Already the tones of the land-colour were merging in the blue haze of distance.

My body seemed to expand with power, vitality and zest in life as I drew in a great full breath through closed teeth. By Jupiter! was there a sport to touch this? By Jove! it was the king of sports! And worth almost any price to play.

The plane was flying 325 feet above a purple-blue sea,

impenetrable in its depth of colour. Thousands of flying fish shot out of the water ahead, flitting from the plane in the form of a giant bow-wave ploughed away before us. It was unceasing. Thousands! there must have been millions of fish. They dashed with a jet of spray into the side of a wave or roller ahead. "Ah! ha!" I thought, "*Elijah* could teach you something about alighting; it's a wonder you don't wreck your undercarriage crashing into the water like that." Evidently, the sound-waves or vibration from the motor must reach and scare them.

I made an inspection to assure all my gear was in order. In front of the compass, the Bygrave position-line slide-rule, consisting of three cylinders revolving one within the other, for working out sextant observations. Under the seat, Roper's *Practice of Navigation* with all the logarithm and other tables in case the slide-rule failed me; chart of the Pacific, another of Norfolk Island, Mariner's description of Norfolk Island, a sadly depleted loaf, butter and jam; my chart in an aluminium case with rollers to turn it on as required.[1] Pasted to the cockpit-side, for quick reference, were: the page of nautical almanac for the week, a scale for converting land into sea miles, and tables for dip to allow for height, for refraction of sun's rays and for rate of change per minute of the sun's altitude with different azimuths in these latitudes. On the shelf above the instruments, three protractors and two rulers (that were apt to fly over-board) and a pair of compasses. Suspended from my neck on cords were sextant, camera, protractor and pencil. In a belt: two spare compasses, spare watch, spare spectacles, indiarubber, films and sheath-knife. Strapped to my wrist the chronometer watch and accurate barometer for measuring height above the sea to within 25 feet. Strapped to my right leg, the wireless-transmitting key; and to the left, my logbook. And in my pocket, the instrument which I had taken the utmost pains to provide—but now, alas! useless—a tin-opener.

I made sure the petrol-pump was drawing from both bottom tanks, then settled down to hard work. I observed the plane's drift when flying straight ahead, changed course 30° to the right and

---

1   See end for photograph of the N.Z. to Norfolk Island flight chart.

observed it again, and a third time when flying 30° off course to the left. I plotted the results on my chart and estimated a 24-mile wind at our back. By Jove! that was good. Next I estimated when the plane should be at the turn-off point 90 miles from the island. At five o'clock, I decided; and worked out what height the sun would appear to be in the sky if the plane were in correct position at that time.

I noticed with keen satisfaction that my brain was now working with cool steadiness—as though it recognized that from then on, success depended entirely on accurate work. It gave me a feeling of power which slightly elated me—that, and the perfect conditions. The sun shone in a cloudless, light-blue sky, and its rays, slanting over the top wing, caught my head and the top of the cockpit. I could feel (or imagine) a warmth from it. The exhausts emitted a steady, rolling roar, with a suspicion of black smoke sometimes discernible in the blast-fumes of the four stubs. The hand of the revolution-indicator might have been the hand of a clock, it kept so steady. I felt braced, keen and powerfully confident about the sextant work on which everything depended. The time for it was rapidly approaching.

I observed the drift again three times and decided the plane would have been pushed off its course 12½ miles during the hour. I therefore altered course another 10° to make this good. And so, actually, the plane was now *headed* to pass the island nearly 200 miles to the left. I had to reassure myself that it was all right—however queer it might seem.

01.00 hours. 328 miles.

Pressing down the wireless key, to make sure the needle of the current-meter oscillated in response, I rushed through a message to the Air Base operator, who should be listening as the hour struck.

"Position by dead reckoning at 0100 hours GMT 33° 15′ South 171° 35′ East Wind 24 mph from 162 degrees true."

I made three more observations of drift at the beginning of this hour and three more at the end. Then I plotted them all on the chart. Everything was still well. The sun shone in a cloudless sky, though it had now dropped from my sight behind the top wing, unless I craned backwards. The motor steadily roared. And the wind, still favourable, had slightly increased. Yet my mood of exhilaration seemed to have worn thin, perhaps due to the critical sextant work drawing near, or to the thought of the mountainous seas which such a wind must be raising round Norfolk Island. I reckoned we had been driven 15 miles off course again, thus counteracting the previous 10 degrees allowance for leeway. But with wind blowing us 26 miles forward, I estimated we had made at

02.00 hours, 344 miles.

I must try a shot with the sextant to find out how far off we were from the turning-point. I must "feel my way". I trimmed the tail for as delicate balance of the plane as possible; but even so, I had to give constant attention to the controls while adjusting the sextant. The plane was as tiresome and restive as a—spoilt dog on the lead. I wanted to adjust the sextant to observe both the sun above the top wing and a piece of horizon showing between top and bottom wings. To make sure I was using the piece of horizon directly below the sun, I had to wipe out attention to the plane's balance and concentrate on that of the sextant. I was just making contact between sun and horizon when pressure of terrific acceleration on my back made me drop the sextant as if it were red-hot. I seized the control-stick and eased the plane from its vertical nose-dive seawards into a normal dive, and from that flattened out. Phew! that was no good. I set the tail trimmer back notch by notch till the plane was bound to climb as soon as I left it alone. I tried again, and this time managed well enough, easing the control forward with my left elbow when the plane climbed so steeply that the wing cut off the sun from view. I noted the time of observation to the nearest second, but when I turned to the altimeter, I found it read 2,500 feet above the sea; yet, looking over the side at the water, I could have sworn we were not above 400 feet. I must be mistaken—had I not bought the altimeter for this work because of its accuracy? and had I not observed it night and morning for six months to grow used to its slightest vagary? My eyes must be deceiving me; but I would quickly prove or disprove that. I dived the plane down to the water surface. The altimeter still read 2,500 feet.

I tugged at the sextant to make sure it was securely held by the lanyard about my neck. For the altimeter to break was bad enough, but if I lost the sextant overboard . . .

I yet had the dashboard altimeter. It was not of much account and had failed me before when over the English Channel at night. But still, I could make it suffice, I supposed, by noting the position of the hand at sea level and then deciding what angle it had moved through on ascending. I flattened out close to the surface and flew along skimming it. I gazed a few yards ahead, fascinated by the heaving water. The shape of every wave was as clear and sharply defined to my sight, as if both plane and sea were suspended without motion. Here the water was beginning to heave up. There it was in the act of leaping high. In another place it had flicked its top into a white crest; while yet elsewhere, I caught sight of a lopped peak in the act of dropping to the foot of its watery mountain. I was past before any had time to move. And it seemed that the plane, too, was dead still, in a world deserted through the death of motion.

Glancing further ahead, I was astonished to notice the plane was below the water level—as though in the vortex of a whirlpool with the rim of water above—until in a moment I realized how, watching the surface close under the plane and flying by it, I had been unconsciously raising the plane to the huge swell, to hug the trough and gently lift to the roller. A long, loping swell was riding the same way at perhaps a third the speed; and the plane seemed a toy thing in the trough.

The rollers themselves had a disturbed look—annoyed by an over-running cross-sea from the south-west—by comparison a mere herring splash on the whale back of the other—though I felt sorry for any seaplane that tried to ride it. How solitary it was down there, as if one's soul were winging through some stratum of atmosphere between this and another unknown world. I felt

47

oppressed by a deathly silence as of illimitable space, and fell into an abstraction. I returned with a start to consciousness of the present. That mighty monster, with its terrible, yet satisfying power, had nearly hypnotized me.

I rose till, by the old altimeter, I judged the height to be 400 feet and then took five "shots" at the sun. Conditions were ideal, with a clean-cut, sharply defined horizon to use. The five "shots" took 6¼ minutes to observe. In another 14 minutes I had the observations worked out in two ways and the result plotted. It indicated that I had yet 230 miles to fly before turning to the right for the island. Another 320 miles all told. *Was* it correct? Now that I had used the sextant, my confidence in it vanished like a pricked bubble, leaving a poison-gas—doubt—which entered me and corroded.

Depressed, I went about the drift observing in a hurry to be ready for another wireless message at 2.30. There then remained four hours before sunset and by the sextant 280 miles yet to go.

I dashed off the message:

"CQ de KK AAA Position by sextant and DR at 0200 hours GMT 32° 17 South 170° 15′ East AAA Wind 30 mph from 152 degrees true AAA AR."`

I rushed through more drift observations, plotted them on the chart, and calculated the wind had increased another 2 m.p.h. Whew! I was getting a favourable wind all right. Through the speed being so much greater than I had expected, I was becoming hard pressed to carry out the work. After the haste necessary to plot the drift in time for sextant work, I felt distinctly hustled.

At 03.00 hours, I secured four observations at a mean altitude of 300 feet. The sun was now dead ahead and had dropped from sight behind the petrol tank between the top wings. I had to work the sextant fast, setting the plane into a dive on purpose to get the sun above the tank. The horizon I picked up beside the motor. At each shot, immediately I had the sun touching the horizon in the sextant, I jerked back the control-stick to climb while recording sextant, watch and altimeter readings. My handling of the plane was already becoming automatic—I was getting the "feel" of *Elijah* as a seaplane. I worked fast at the calculations. 127 miles from the turn-off point, I made it—217 miles to go. I wiped my brow under the flying-helmet peak. This pace was too hot altogether. My brain was becoming jammed with work. And it scared me. With a slow-acting brain, I dared not force it to work any faster than usual, however pressed for time. Especially with the engine roar trying to scatter thoughts. I must have time to collect them and run over the general scheme. No use working out a position accurately by sextant, if I let the top tank run out of petrol or made some other childish error. While thinking this, I became aware of a beat in the motor, a regular muffled knocking. That cursed No. 3 again! Was it failing? At this low altitude, I must turn right about instantly if it did, in order to face into wind before the plane hit.

I must cut that out—I couldn't afford to waste an atom of energy on anything I was unable to help, all thought or worry about the motor must be wiped out completely.

And I dare not let myself become hustled . . . But what to do? Perhaps if I left out the next drift observations and gave up the time to thought? Well, I would.

I let my brain become a complete blank. Then flitted in thought from one thing to another: "Compass, petrol, revolutions, oil pressure, height (damn that motor!), chart—h'm, getting very close to turning-off point now—little more than an hour—probably ready to turn at 4.30 instead of 5 o'clock as expected. Have to work out sun's position afresh—must hurry with it—what's that? Clouds ahead—fleecy—hanging in the air—h'm, not thick, thank heaven!"

03.30 o'clock; three hours before sunset; 153 miles to go according to the sextant.

"CQ de KK AAA Position at 0300 hours GMT by sextant and DR 31° 17′ South 168° 50′ East AAA Wind 32 mph from 143 degrees true AAA AR."

I turned from the wireless to drift reading, made three

observations and plotted them. The wind had increased to 39 m.p.h. By Jupiter! it would be soon blowing a gale at this rate. I rushed through the calculating of sun's position for a four o'clock sight. I must arrange so that when that moment arrived, I should have only to take the sights and no more. I had to fight an intense excitement trying to seize control of me; but it did good in that it keyed me up to a high pitch of alertness and mental activity for the vital work ahead. At 04.00 o'clock, I took four sights at 100 and 150 feet up, turning the plane to the right in a steep bank to catch the sun abeam behind the wings and turning on to course again while recording the instrument figures. (During the observation, the plane flew under balled white clouds littering the sky.) I quickly plotted the result, which showed my dead reckoning to be 19 miles in error. H'm, why was that? A mistake somewhere? Where? And if one, then why not several?

No time to worry about it. I must put my faith in the sextant. It said the plane was only 45 miles short of the turning-off point, and then it should be 75 miles to the left of the island.

This half-gale was making the pace too great altogether. I throttled back the motor until the flying-speed was only 60 m.p.h. Even so, with a forty-mile wind bringing the actual pace up to 100 m.p.h. it meant cutting out the distance to the estimated turnoff point in thirty minutes.

(Of course, that wind-speed indicator on the strut over-registered—that might account for the 19 miles' error. But suppose there was a double error? . . .)

I hurriedly computed the work for another sight at the end of the half-hour. It would be the critical moment of the flight. When I turned it must be towards where the island lay—not towards where it did not lie. Now I had to work fast, but consciously demanded of myself an extraordinary effort, that the work should be accurate as well. And never before had I felt so intensely alive—I seemed to vibrate with vitality—or perhaps it was only excitement. But I felt I was living at the highest possible speed.

The clouds were becoming numerous and beginning to tower.

I calculated what should be the compass bearing of the island when I turned the plane towards it.

The clouds were forming into dense cumulus, and rapidly. I watched with anxiety.

A few minutes before the end of the half-hour it was driven home to me that there would be no sun available for the sextant. I swept the clouds ahead, but could see no opening. And they were darker. What should I do? Of course, if I could depend on the last sight . . . Supposing it were wrong . . . No, I must have another. To turn at the right moment was vital. But I could not heave to and wait for sunlight. I must turn left away from the island, and hunt for some. The clouds looked whiter there.

Yet I kept straight on, hope still alive in me of finding sun ahead. Gradually the hope faded and died in me. Close to the half-hour, I turned my back on where the island should be, and flew away from it at increased speed.

As I flew on, mile after mile, the excitement was too great. I was worked up to such a pitch that I had, consciously, to exercise control over my thoughts to prevent their leaping wildly.

The plane had flown three or four miles when I spotted a round patch of sunlight ahead and slightly to the right. I increased the motor revolutions another fifty.

Life seemed to be standing still while the plane reached for that sunlight; though the distance could not have been above four or five miles more.

The area was small. I set the plane circling and kept it in a steep bank by working the rudder with my feet while I worked the sextant with hands and eye. I straightened the plane's course while reading the instruments and quickly shot out of the patch. I turned and re-entered to make another observation, again circling inside the arena of sunlight. Four sights I obtained, with the plane thus chasing its tail in a tight circle. I adjusted them back to 04.30 hours by the table for the rate of change in sun's altitude according to its azimuth and the observer's latitude; I then compared the result with the calculations already made for that time.

On the line! I had expected to be, yet when the mathematics

confirmed my expectations, it came as a great, fresh surprise. My God! On the line through Norfolk Island and the imaginary turn-off point!

I turned right about and headed for where the island should lie, 85 miles away.

Immediately I swung on to this course, nearly at right angles to the track from New Zealand, desperate misgiving assailed me. All round to the limit of sight stretched nothing—unconfined distance—space—between heaving water and cloud ceiling. Markless and signless for hours had been this desert of air, no one hundred cubic miles differed from any other cubic miles. Yet always I had flown in one direction until the idea had become stamped in my instinct that the island lay dead ahead. And now that I turned almost at right angles to the former course, my whole nature rose in revolt to repudiate such an unwarranted change in mid-ocean. To turn was suicide . . . My navigation scheme was but a flimsy, irresponsible fancy hatched in my brain. I could not have flown so long on the same course without the island lying ahead—ahead—ahead . . . Panic welled up in me. Reason tried to reassure . . . Turn, it said . . . No, I must fly straight on. For God's sake don't let me do this crazy turn! My muscles tried of their own account to swing the plane back on to its former course.

"Steady, steady, steady," I said aloud, "take it steady now!"

Let me be reasonable. Whether the method was right or wrong, I must trust it now. I could not draw back. I could not give in or adopt any other method known to be safer. I must stay with this method as if it were a steel gin that had snapped its jaws on me.

I kept the new course.

But I could not prevent myself from searching the horizon to and fro, to and fro, from the tail of the plane, right round, with an intensity of looking which seemed to burn the back of my eyeballs. "It is useless to do it," argued Reason, "either the island is dead ahead where calculated, or else your system has failed, and then God only knows where it is." "But the island might be just behind us, even in sight," objected Instinct, "and we now flying away from it." I continued searching.

The clouds were darkening and hung above without a break; the wind was dropping; the plane now drifted only 15° to the right, and for that amount I had allowed.

I *must* get another sextant shot. How could I trust those others? I would work it independently. No, I had a sight prepared for five o'clock; I would adjust it to that. But could I possibly secure one with the sky overcast?

I throttled the motor back to 60 m.p.h. and now searched the clouds as well as the horizon.

Suddenly, I picked out the shape of the sun through a thinning of the clouds; but it was covered again at once.

I adjusted the sextant to the angle I expected, removed the shades necessary for strong sunlight, and held it ready in my hand. I waited and waited. Five miles went by. Suddenly again, I could see the rim of the sun through a wraith of black cloud where it had momentarily thinned. I secured a single shot before the thick cloud closed over again for good. But it was a fair sight, with horizon line adjusted in the sextant to make a perfect tangent to the sun's reflection. It was at ten seconds before 05.00 hours. I felt grateful; that saved work—with three complete sets of observations in two hours besides the routine work, my brain was clogged up.

The observation gave the same result as the last—that the plane was dead on the ling to the island.

Good enough! I dismantled the sextant and put it away in its case. I felt like a man so sure he is right that he will stake everything on his conviction, and with indifference—if he loses, it will seem the only possible ending, when after being so sure he was right, he *is* wrong. I was positive I was right. If I did not find the island it would be the island that was out of position.

It should be in sight that very minute. It was said to be visible from a ship 36 miles away on a clear day, and so it should be visible easily from a plane at that distance—in spite of the sky being completely overcast with the grey of covering nightfall.

I searched the horizon from side to side. Nothing! I could do no more work even if I wanted to. I must stand or fall by what I had already done. My God! what excitement—waiting for the decision. How paltry and petty seemed every other excitement in the world! A simple decision—either I found the island or I did not. 05.05; 05.05½; 05.06; I seemed to live a generation in each minute.

The wind was dropping; the drift was only 10° now—that must be due to approaching nightfall.

Down below, the swell might have diminished, but the cross-sea was as strong as ever. Its grey-blue face looked to me cold and hostile. "Expect no pity here for failure," it said clearly. Suddenly fear froze my blood. If I had failed, what could I do? If once I missed the island, I could not find it—for where should I seek? There was no alternative place, according to my calculations, where I could look. Panic! what plan could I adopt? Should I fly north, south, east or west? I had not petrol for more than halfway back to New Zealand. My brain was numb; I could think of no plan. My God! why had I not thought out beforehand what to do in case of failure?

05.08. By my estimate, the island ten miles overdue to be sighted.

Well, there was something grand about this finish. Staking everything on a clear brain, on the cool working of a scheme bred in it and on the scheme being without a flaw. It satisfied the very source of life which desired everything to lead up to a definite, clean-cut ending. And it was I who had set myself the problem; if I succeeded, I was responsible; if I failed, I alone was responsible. What better way to end up? And failure perhaps would not be so hard with it thus.

05.09. Ah! was that land away to the left? Grey, purple crest. It was changing shape. Ach! a cloud lying on the horizon. By Jupiter! the cloud ceiling was dropping.

Why should the calculations be wrong? There was that time I was 740 miles out. Yes, but not with this sextant. How about to-day, 140 miles out—and often, land was not visible five miles away.

05.11. "This twisting my head from side to side makes my neck ache. What to do if I have missed the island? No use flying madly about anywhere. No, I must make the best alighting I can. How much longer shall I give it on this course? I could alight, I think—but the sea is too rough to ride in a seaplane. How long would she last? Blow over at once cresting the first swell? The rubber boat would be my only chance, if I could get it out in time. A pity there is no food."

05.12. Island fifteen miles overdue. Ah! surely that was land to the left front! Two hills raising their cones above a narrow band of grey cloud, and the dark coast purple below. I stared fixedly. By God! it was changing shape. By heavens! it was only another cloud. A wave of anger passed through me at being deceived yet again.

05.13. "What an incredible stretching of time! Well, I must decide soon what to do. Och! blazes! quit this worrying! Haven't I done everything I could have done? By Jupiter! I'll just fly steadily ahead. Why! for half an hour more. Worry can't help. Haven't I done my best? No man can do more than that. If I've failed, then it is fate."

Immediately I let myself think that, my agitation vanished. I felt resigned.

And as if some power were only waiting for me to resign my personal claims and acknowledge that it was only a question of fate, a cloud ahead lifted like a drop-curtain and uncovered land.

Land! staring me in the face.

Land! land! Ha! ha! ha!

I threw back my head and laughed aloud, till the blast of the slipstream drove the laugh into my throat and bellied out my cheeks. Triumphant joy swelled in me and every limb wanted to dance or move violently. Ha! ha! ha! we had made it after all. I seized the wireless key and began transmitting boisterously—uncaring whether anybody could hear me or not—so long as I had the illusion of being heard—only craving expression of any kind as a vent for my emotions.

"CQ de KK AAA Land-O dead ahead 0514 hours GMT AAA Crew excited AAA AR."

I looked up to find a cloud had obliterated the island from view again. No wonder I had not seen it till so close, it must be attracting cloud.

Ha! ha! ha! Ho! ho! ho!

Reason: "What are you laughing at?"

Pilot: "Nothing."

Reason: "By Jupiter! that was dead easy—getting here. That navigation was childishly simple after all."

Wuzzy (the beard): "Personally, my views on astronomical navigation coincide with those of the dear old lady with the knitting-bag."

Reason: "What were they?"

Wuzzy: "'Why!' said the dear old lady with the knitting-bag, what I think is so wonderful, so marvellous, so miraculous about this here h-asteronomy is how they found out the names of the stars.'"

All: "Ha! ha! ha! Good old Wuzzy! No bird's nests in you Wuzzy! Haw! haw! haw!"

Instinct: "Good old Minerva!"

Wuz: "I wonder if we shall meet anyone like Circe or Calypso."

Instinct: "Who was Circe?"

Wuz: "You remember Circe who entertained Ulysses with convivial, connubial caresses."

Pilot (severely): "Wuz! I blush for you!"

Wuz: "Don't! Save it up for Circe."

All: "Ha! ha! ha!"

Reason: "I bet Cook wasn't as excited at discovering this island in 1774 as we are at discovering it now."

Wuz: "Or I shall be if we discover Cook as well as the island."

Reason: "There's no Cook here now, you fool. He died a hundred and fifty years ago."

Wuz (groaningly): "My sainted aunt! No cook here and only two slices of bread and jam since 4 a.m."

Reason: "Don't be childish! I suppose most of the inhabitants will be descendants of the *Bounty* mutineers."

Wuz: "But I thought the *Bounty* mutineers went to Pitcairn Island."

Reason: "So they did, but they shifted to this island sixty-six years later."

Wuz: "All the mutineers?"

Reason: "Well, they had a few arguments so that only one mutineer was left after ten, years."

Wuz: "If only one mutineer was left after ten years, how many were left after sixty-six years?"

Reason: "They took six native women with them to Pitcairn Island originally. And women have children!"

Wuz: "Why! fancy that now! And how many came on here sixty-six years later?"

Reason: "All the descendants—a hundred and ninety-four of them."

Wuz: "By the beard of the prophet! What a survivor that one survivor must have been!"

Reason: "I say, chuck it, you fellows, we're nearly there. And dirty work yet before the night's out, unless I'm mistaken."

I picked out the chart of the island and studied it in relation to the direction of swell, from which Cascade Bay, I decided, was the most likely spot to be sheltered.

The black of the island now lay close in front: a sombre slab, with a thick black edge, moored out in mid-ocean. There was something threatening or fateful about its appearance. The *Bounty* mutineers episode was only what one might expect of such a place. A narrow ribbon of white marked the base of the cliffs where the swell crashed against the rock.

Fifteen minutes after first sighting it we were abreast and passing the only spot round the whole island where the 300-foot-high cliff of rock was low and allowed the land to come down to a small beach of sand. I recognized Kingston, the metropolis, where lived perhaps one hundred of the total thousand inhabitants. I picked out "Quality Row", where the warders used to live; the walls yet standing, and the ruins of the old jail. "Gallows Gate" must be just to the left of the big square. From the air, it might have been an old Roman ruin. Though it was no earlier than 1855 that it ceased to be a convict settlement.

Not a soul was visible. I flew on and rounded the south-east corner. I was just above the top of the cliff, and from here this great slab provided amazing scenery. Tall, tapering firs—Norfolk Island Pines—grew in cluster, and threw deep shadows as dark as night. Little fields lay among the spinneys. It was the toy model of a hilly country. Pretty white birds which I took to be doves fluttered frantically among the tree tops and one or two horses stared up at the plane with mildly disapproving interest, but I had not yet seen one human being. I now turned the north-east point and studied Cascade Bay below. As for its being a bay, it was scarcely an indentation of the coast; though they had succeeded in carving a road in the face of the rock and throwing a small jetty into the water. However, the surface looked calm, though the swell was there, and threatened cold hospitality as it broke at the base of the rocky cliffs. At last I noticed a few people; they were on the jetty, so I shut off the motor and glided low to inspect the water surface from close above. Though the propeller still beat the air like a plover's wing, it seemed an eerie silence after the endless roar. The wind had now died right away. Had I flown to the land of Eolus who had imprisoned all contrary winds in an oxhide for Ulysses? I was just thinking how I had been treated to the best possible weather all day when, below the cliff top, there was a violent bump. With one hand I gripped the dashboard and with the other hung on to the control-stick, feeling instantly hot and damp all over—I ought to have had my safety-belt fastened round me.

I decided to try Duncombe Bay, the other half of this north side—perhaps it would be better.

I thought the water calm enough, but the cliffs looked even higher and more precipitous. There was no road down them and the whole place looked deserted.

I turned back to Cascade and found a boat had been launched and manned; it was moving slowly through the water. I glided down, hanging on tightly for fear of another bump which did not eventuate until *Elijah* plopped unexpectedly into the water and I realized I must have been judging height by a trough of the swell ahead, without remembering the crest behind it. No harm, that!

I switched off the motor and mopped my forehead.

On the water at Cascade Bay. The trees are the famous Norfolk Island Pines.

05.40. I had done it in time . . . but had it not been for the strength of the tail wind . . . and now it had died down—when its force would have been a danger . . .

The boat looked unwieldy, bearing down on my frail cockleshell. The crew of powerful men drove it through the water with great sweeps of their oars. I wondered if just such a crew had rowed just such a boat to Pitcairn from the *Bounty*. Or, could that be Caligula in the stern, and this an ancient Roman galley? In any case, if it became entangled with the wings or floats . . .

"Hey there!" I shouted. "Stand off, you're going to ram me!"

"All right, Skipper, all right," sang out Caligula, "don't get excited; we won't hurt you."

"That's all right," I replied, "but if you touch me with that great whale-chaser of yours, you'll sink me at once. Look out with that confounded oar!" I shouted, my voice rising again as one of them showed signs offending off *Elijah* with his long sweep.

"All right, Skipper," returned Caligula in a boom intended to be soothing, "all right, Skipper."

They were really very patient over my roars considering they must be among the best boatmen in the world; transporting from exposed ships to open shore every ton of cargo that comes to the island. While a man with a sweep in the stern keeps the boat from being smashed against the rock and stone wall, others sling up the cargo as the boat rushes the length of the jetty and is sucked back again on the exhausted swell. And there is always swell; I doubt if these boatmen could sleep without the roar of its bursting against the cliffs.

"You're late, Skipper," said Caligula.

"Am I?" I replied with a look up at the darkening skies. "I'm sorry . . . How about some petrol? I want to refuel to-night so as to be ready for an early start in the morning."

"Petrol's the other side of the island, but we'll ask them to get it for you."

"How long will that take?"

"Ten minutes."

"Very well; and can you borrow a heavy anchor for the night?"

They rowed back to the jetty and sent for the petrol. When they returned they had a stout rope fastened to a number of pieces of iron. I thought, as I watched the boat approach: "Pieces of iron— pieces of eight would be more appropriate!"

Their idea of an anchor seemed rotten to me, and I said so.

"That's all right, Skipper," said Caligula, "you leave it to us; we know all about it."

I heaved at my own anchor-rope. It refused to come. A sharp tug and it came away light. The line had parted on a boulder or piece of coral and Hori's anchor would now rust in peace on the ocean floor. My opinion of Caligula rose.

"Better come ashore, Skipper, till the petrol arrives."

"No thanks, I'd sooner wait here."

"Oh, come on, Skipper! The boys want to see you. They've been waiting for you for hours; you're late."

Was I, in some former life, a slave in Caligula's galley? At any rate I obeyed meekly. Nor was I sorry in most respects to be off the plane. I had been aboard for nearly twelve hours and was beginning to feel like a canary in a cage—only with no inclination to chirp. Hopping from one float-tip to the other by way of under the propeller and across the boom; from float-tip to wing-root; passing doubled-up between the wings to the cockpit or down on the heel of the float; astride the fuselage, or in and out of the cockpit to the other wing-root; from there up to the motor-cowling and so on, endlessly. And I had the unpleasant beat of the propeller always in my head—the grrr, grrr, grrr of the final glide with the motor off. It was peculiar that this pulsation, lasting only a few seconds, should not abate, while the motor's ordinary rhythmic roar lasting the whole flight left no noticeable effect. I jumped into the boat and Caligula caught me in his great arms—a gorilla and Caligula ought to be a good match.

"Here he is, boys!" he boomed, "all the way from New Zealand—isn't he a little French gem!"

The first sensation I had on jumping ashore—I stood poised on a thwart and jumped on to a low rock as the boat surged past—was of the air's having a strange quality. It might be an explosive quality as if it would be dangerous to strike a match. This puzzled me till I learnt more of the island habits. If you want a bottle of whisky on Norfolk Island, you must have a permit from the Administrator. These he issues once a week. I had arrived on "issue" day.

I was offered and gladly accepted some tea.

When the petrol arrived and I returned with it to *Elijah*, the "fun" began. Riding the swell, she had a twisting pitch. This made it quite impossible to stand on the narrow motor-cowling to fill the top tank, so I sat astride and concentrated on the 20-gallon tank in the front cockpit. In the opening to one side of this, the collapsible funnel developed a fresh type of collapse. It would collapse on itself near the bottom end and then no petrol could get through. The top would fill up and the petrol spill on to my leg. However, I coaxed quite a lot into the tank. When it came to the second tin, the "fun" became fast and furious. Petrol and sea-water on my shoes, the floats and wings, made them all as slippery as a damp glacier. As the plane pitched and tossed, I slithered and skidded about with the tin in my arms, trying to get it up on to the motor-top. At each slip I spilt more petrol, which made the float-top or wing-root more treacherous, and I was quickly saturated up to the knees with salt water, and from the waist downwards with petrol. Some of the petrol must have been stronger than the tea, because it burnt six inches of skin off my left leg. I soon had a feeling of utter futility. The parting of the anchor-rope had brought home to me my helplessness to prevent the plane's destruction if the rope parted again at night; how should I always prevent the plane's being rammed? To fuel a lively craft like this was an impossibility for one man—it was a three-man job. To work spanners and the 15/1000-inch thickness gauge for tuning up a jumping, kicking, bucking motor was another impossibility. Yet the sea was comparatively calm now—God help the plane, and me too, when it grew really rough! And what with the darkness of fallen night, and the ugly threat of the black cliffs towering above me, I realized in despair that I had undertaken an impossible task. "Bah!" I thought, savagely, "don't be weak! You're just not used to it. After the first seven years you probably won't find anything difficult about it."

The rest of the fuelling would have to be left; I unpacked the engine and cockpit covers and fixed them on with the aid of a torch.

Well, I had covered the 718 miles before sunset, at any rate.

Chapter III

NIGHT

On shore, the Administrator's secretary invited me to the Government House, and drove me across the island. On arrival, the first thing I begged was a half-gallon of water, which I promptly quaffed. After that, a hot bath. This was not so easy because the fire was out (as well as the Administrator and the cook). However, a Mrs. "X", who was another guest there, somehow obtained a can of hot water and I laid aside my petrol-soaked clothes to dry, while I washed off the acid, or whatever it was in the petrol that was burning my leg. "Now," I thought, "I know why a bluebottle expires so quickly when it falls into a tray of paraffin." The secretary lent me some pyjamas and a dressing-gown; after that I was offered some supper, which I enjoyed heartily, in spite of being plied with questions by Mr. and Mrs. "X".

After supper the secretary left to play bridge, so the other two guests and I had the place to ourselves. Everybody had been most kind to me, yet I could not help feeling that there was a nasty little nigger in the administrative woodpile concealed somewhere. The atmosphere had not that warmth which you might hope to meet on a sub-tropical island. Perhaps it was affected somewhat by the nature of the house we were in. This Government House was the old Prison Governor's house, or chief jailer's, with high ceilings and great stone walls so thick that just outside the room assigned to me was a sentry-box cut out of the solid masonry of the wall. Here a sentry, with loaded rifle, had stood at all times of the day and night. I take it those prison governors were not over-zealous of their charges' welfare, and that their charges shared the same sentiment concerning them. Eventually, I ferreted out the little devil in the woodpile: the Director of Air Services, New Zealand, had asked the Controller of Civil Aviation, Australia, for permission on my behalf to fly to Australia via Norfolk Island and Lord Howe Island. Knowing that Norfolk Island was under the Authority of the Australian Commonwealth, I had never given a thought to obtaining special permission from that island to fly to it. In this I think I was totally wrong, and that I should have asked the Administrator of Norfolk Island for special permission to fly to his island. In short, I had flown to Norfolk Island without the correct permission. Fortunately, the Administrator did not take the drastic steps he might have, the seaplane regulations of the island were waived in my favour, and I was not, I am glad to say, ordered to return whence I came. Nor, once ashore, was I refused permission to land. "However," I thought, "next time I fly here, I shall know better, and will take great pains to obtain the necessary permission first."

When I did get to bed, I could not sleep well, and had scarcely dozed off before again, becoming sufficiently awake to be conscious of my thoughts.

Reason: "As a piece of co-ordinated brain work, to-day's flight pleases me singularly."

Instinct: "'Let another man praise thee, and not thine own mouth,' Proverbs XXVII, 2."

Reason: "'Speak not in the ears of a fool: for he will despise the wisdom of thy words,' Proverbs XXIII, 9. I meant I was glad to-day's navigation proved so easy. We should find the rest of the flight child's play, because it cannot be anything like as hard as to-day's. I feel strangely confident all of a sudden."

Instinct (groaning): "Oh, heavens!' How often have we got into trouble immediately after a fit of cocksureness! As if the powers decide on something unpleasant at just that moment."

Pilot: "Can't we eliminate these condemned conversations in the middle of the night? It's already half-past two, and we have to turn out at four."

Nor did it seem ten seconds before Mrs. "X" was knocking at the door to warn me the hour had struck.

As I wearily dressed in sticky, cold clothes, I groaned within me at my abject foolishness in proceeding with my project without being forced to it by a brigand with a loaded gun, and at the thought of the millions of men with some sense, still lying in bed and able to sleep for hours more, with nothing to disturb them.

"You should feel sorry", said Reason, "for all the other poor wretches you are turning out at this ungodly hour—people without the pleasure of a nice seaplane flight to compensate them for the unnatural rape of sleep."

"I'm not," I snapped, "they should pay entertainment tax for having their monotony of life broken for them."

As it turned out, I really might have slept for another two hours because, after stowing away a breakfast of bacon and eggs with the aid of a strong whisky and soda, I received word from the secretary that it was no use starting before dawn. I could have slept on and breakfasted with him. Then, just as dawn was breaking, and the secretary was ready to leave, the Administrator arrived and requested me to carry a letter to his wife. Naturally, I was delighted to do so; after that, he proposed a second to the Governor-General of N.S.W. which I was also delighted to carry, and that in turn suggested a third to the chief citizen of Lord Howe Island. By this time, dawn was well broken—in fact, my private opinion was that it had crashed badly.

We now set off in the secretary's car—but not straight to the jetty. We had to pick up some boatmen on the way. They lived in thick-walled, squat, stone cottages that once housed prison officials, and before our knocking had ceased to echo, the door would open and they would come out, one hand rubbing eyes, and the other chasing elusive buttons. At each cottage I waited in the car in the dull twilight of dawn, in a state of mixed impatience, anxiety and weariness—I had had only four hours' sleep last night, three and a half hours' the night before and four hours' the night before that. Yet the weariness was not so much through lack of sleep as from the nature of the work usurping its place—and yesterday's share of that seemed the least heavy of the past three days.

We called last at the house of one "Martin", a merchant, but after some delay, a member of his family came out to inform us that her father had left for the jetty two hours ago.

Chapter IV

AT SEA

My first act on boarding the plane was to try the compression by swinging the propeller. No. 4 cylinder was bad enough, but No. 3 had none at all—was quite dead.

My brain seemed to clarify in a flash, and sum up my position without illusion.

In front of me was the prospect of trying to get off the water with a full load, and if I could succeed in that, of starting on an eight-hour flight across the ocean with a defective motor. I knew exactly what to expect—attempting a flight like that.

Behind me . . . a small hard stone jetty with rollers surging against it and leaving a white smother; a few yards of steep boulder beach, one moment bare and shining, the next covered with boiling white surf as, deep as an oar on end; otherwise a stark face of black rock rising perpendicularly from the ocean. There could hardly be a coast more hostile to a small seaplane.

It would be unable to leave; it was impossible to get it ashore; the seaplane was trapped.

And so was I.

I felt some inexorable power had determined I should not cross this sea. And to carry out that determination, had trapped me here . . . Fate?

Bah! man was master of his fate. I must get away somehow.

On thinking this, I felt guilty, as if I had decided to attempt some forbidden thing. Then I seemed to divide in personality. My mind withdrew itself as if hurt by the vulgarity of futile striving and kept itself detached and disdainfully aloof. It seemed to take with it all sentiment. I was no longer able to feel anger, fear, impatience or annoyance . . .

The other half of me seemed to freeze to my purpose. For all it cared, reason, sentiment, any thing or everything else could go to hell. The plane must leave the water . . . and it was going to . . . unless something completely failed.

I proceeded to carry out my work with the cold soulless efficiency of a robot. I checked the tappet clearances, inspected the petrol-filter, replenished the oil, completed loading the petrol and packed away my tools and gear.

When I hauled on the anchor-line, it parted and. came away empty in my hands.

Why had this not occurred a few hours earlier in the dark, to send *Elijah* adrift on the rocks? What use was my striving when a mere chance happening could thus have wrecked the whole project?

"Bah! Get on with the job."

The boat towed *Elijah* out somewhat from the cliffs and cast off the rope. I reeled it in and swung the propeller.

At the anchorage the breeze had been off-shore, so I made out to sea in order to fly back into it. *Elijah* rolled and wallowed a good deal. When in position for the take-off, the breeze appeared to be from exactly the opposite quarter. This must be an incorrect observation, I decided, so I opened the throttle wide to take off in the direction of the jetty. The plane bumped and ploughed towards it, yet, though I kept her going until the last possible moment—till perilously close to the rocks in fact—she did not attain anything like enough speed to become air-borne. As I throttled down the motor again, I decided the breeze out there must have been from the other way after all; so I turned about for another attempt—this time headed out to sea. I kept *Elijah* at it in a long effort. Towards the end of the run, hitting a succession of swells larger than their fellows, she swerved off her course to starboard and I felt her beginning to capsize like a fast car skidding on a sharp bend, I closed the throttle again quickly, mopped the sea-water off my face and wiped my goggles clear of water and evaporated salt. With the motor just ticking over, I let the plane continue slowly seawards. Everything needed a spell. The pounding on the rollers must have strained *Elijah* at every joint. The prolonged threshing of the motor at full throttle and under the violently changing stresses from the bumps was the harshest treatment it could receive. Turning, which was strangely difficult—perhaps because of the humpy sea[1]—necessitated bursts of motor at full throttle. During these bursts, with the floats settled in deep, the propeller repeatedly encountered heavy spray—almost solid water. The crack, as it smashed through this, was heart-rending. How it stood the strain without breaking was a mystery to me, for even at lower speed, each smack slowed and nearly stopped the motor, while the plane quivered from end to end. It was hard work for me too, craning to watch for rough water, hand on throttle, slowing the motor each time a curling crest rose against the propeller; and with the motor dead slow, hurriedly wiping spray from my goggles after each manoeuvre. I reached down for the navigation volumes on the bottom of the cockpit and sat on them to obtain a better view; in doing so, I found the inside of the fuselage streaming with water, which was not likely to enhance the plane's airworthiness. Steadily ploughing through the waves, I reviewed the situation. I had to force myself to do this; I didn't want to reason; only to burst into the task of getting off . . .

Somehow, I had now quite ceased to worry about the motor—perhaps I sensed it to be no worse than when in New Zealand, where *Elijah* had managed to take off all right. I did not actually *know* what revolutions the motor was giving at full throttle, not daring to take my eyes off the water long enough to look at the instrument-board. But no, I did not think the motor was the trouble; the plane itself felt peculiarly heavy, lazy in the water like a log of wood. Something else was wrong; what was it? Could the swell be the cause of the sluggishness? *Elijah* would get up speed on the crest of a roller and perhaps shoot off it, only to strike the rise of

---

1   Actually because a starboard float-bilge was half full of water, for the reason given in the footnote to page 82.

the next; the floats would plough in deep and *Elijah* slow down again. The same thing happened at each swell. With the plane at rest, this was hard to understand, for, although she tossed and wallowed on the lopping waves of the surface, she seemed to be unmoved by the swell; only the island rose and dropped from view, as the rollers, perhaps a hundred yards or so from crest to crest, stole up, raising the plane, and slid away, imperceptibly lowering it again. But immediately *Elijah* began hydroplaning fast, she was striking the crests like an automatic hammer cracking concrete. Isitt had said I should never leave the island because of the swell, but I had refused to believe him. An awful thought—could he be right?

Perhaps the floats leaked? No, because they had been tested at Auckland and when filled with water there, none had leaked out; if none could leak out, none could leak in.

I must get off.

Yet, how could I? Should I make an attempt along the swell instead of across it? What were the words of the *Seaplane Training Manual?* "A cross-wind take-off along the line of swell is an extremely hazardous proceeding and should not be attempted except by the most experienced seaplane pilots and only then in cases of emergency." I looked round. Clear skies. The weather was perfect; yet bad weather, I knew, was brewing to the west. Then I looked at the precipitous cliffs; to-day in the sunlight they were black, sombre and forbidding like the walls of some rocky fortress prison; with here and there white flashes where a swell burst at their feet, a cascade of spray falling back. In one place, owing no doubt to some peculiarity in the rock, I saw it burst like a depth charge and shoot thirty feet into the air. And to-day, it was fine. What was it like in rough weather! Nothing was more forcibly apparent than that of all the deadly places in the world for a seaplane, this island could hardly be eclipsed.

Heading the plane along the line of swell, I pushed the throttle wide open again.

If only the surface were smoother! The plane attained more speed than before; it swayed and rocked, knocking the waves.

Difficulty in controlling it was very much increased. It would jump, yaw to the right, and come down slightly across its course.

A bigger jump and a worse yaw compelled me to realize that a very little more would sheer off the floats or capsize the plane.

I slowed the motor and leaned back in the cockpit seat, relaxing the tenseness of my muscles; I looked about at the bare expanse of water and at the land away behind. I was now well out to sea and picking up rough water of a deeper purple-blue colour. It was very solitary out there. The seaplane, with its frailty and flimsiness, was the cause: it was like being left on the water astride a bird-cage. I had the distinct feeling that some part of me was standing aloof and refusing to take part in a futile struggle against fate. If so, the other part was equally set. I was going to get this plane off or . . .

But I had an unutterable weariness, and an almost overpowering lassitude, bred no doubt by the constant joggle and toss of the plane on the water, the smacking of spray in my face, the blast of wind, the roar of the motor, and the constant effort of extreme concentration.

I tried again along the swell; this time toward the shore. The attempt was a failure.

I decided to make for Duncombe Bay, 2½ miles further on from Cascade. The water there might be smoother. Anyhow, on arrival, I would first try the bilges; not that the floats could have leaked, of course, but merely as a routine job.

It was dreary, hard work getting round. The cross-sea off Bird Rock and the other rocks between Cascade and Duncombe was particularly troublesome. I had to nag at the controls the whole time to negotiate the waves at a safe speed. Suddenly above the noise of the motor, I heard a scream behind my head. I started in my seat and twisted round as if expecting a stab in the back. If there was one place where I thought myself alone, it was out on these waters, and besides, had I ever before in the plane heard any noise above that of the motor?

A great bird with spread of wings like a vulture, outstretched neck and pointed bill, was swooping at my head.[1] I ducked instinctively, but it turned and swept round the plane to fly straight at the propeller. I slowed the motor at once and anxiously watched the bird, wondering if it would see the flying blades. It spun round when a few inches from them. After that came another and another until dozens had dashed and whirled, screeching about the plane, and then flown away. Perhaps they thought it a giant marauding bird, in which case I ought to have admired their gameness; but I could only curse them in sulphurous terms as I was forced, perhaps fifty times, to throttle right back and wait till they had left off flying within a few feet of the propeller. If they were not aware that contact with the propeller meant the end of them, I certainly was aware it meant the end of the propeller. Well, they had the laugh of me, swooping about up there.

I thought we were never going to reach Duncombe; each half-hour in the seaplane seemed longer than a whole day in a boat. But when we did, the water was certainly smoother and I decided I must try once more before testing the bilges. The breeze, which came from a different quarter everywhere I went, was parallel with the cliffs. In order to fly into wind and as close under the cliffs as possible—where the water surface was fairly calm—I threaded a way to the far side of Duncombe through the craggy rocks rising above the surface.

The attempt was a failure.

I switched off the motor and considered the problem of how to test the bilges.

I had no bilge-pump, having considered it unnecessary when the floats were proved watertight; and then again there was the extra weight to be considered. If I removed the "manholes", the floats would promptly be swamped by the waves. I remembered a length of rubber tubing on board. I must see what I could do with that. Jumping out, I unpacked it and pushed one end down the pipe leading to the bottom of the bilge. The other end I inserted in my mouth and sucked. There was no water in that bilge. I tried the next with the same result. The third also was dry and I was feeling

---

1   A mutton-bird.

confident that this unpleasant task would soon be over, when I sucked a mouthful of water in the fourth. I began drawing it up the pipe by the mouthful—a height of three or four feet—and spitting it out. I squatted in my socks with one knee on the float. My feet were awash, and waves lapped me to the waist. Every now and then the float submerged with a gurgle, and broke surface again like a toy submarine with the water streaming away either side. The water was not really cold, but it felt clammy. It was surprisingly hard to suck the water such a height and draw it through the small pipe. My mouth ached, and my cheeks grew sore where they were drawn against the teeth.

In time, my jaw muscles began to cramp, and I had to rest them. I listened to the strange silence after two or three hours continuous engine roar. Really, it was not silent with the hiss, slap and gurgle of waves about the plane. But the birds had left me alone after passing Bird Rock and I could hear no noise of surf. The swell rose at the steep rock face, and fell away again silently, as though sucking at it for a hold which failed.

Soon, the pores of my tongue and mouth began to feel as if they had been dragged inside out.

After half an hour, I estimated I had drawn up four gallons of sea-water: my jaws ached as if they had been struck a blow with a wooden pole. When I took a mouthful away from the pipe—nipping the end to prevent the column of water from dropping back again—I could no longer spit it out, but was only able to open my mouth and let it fall.

But I was just thinking that a man could draw up a pondful of water, if given enough time, when my mouth jammed altogether as though through lockjaw.

I rested for a while, rubbing my-jaws till they moved again. Then I pulled up the pipe to stow it away. Apart from ordinary relief—for I think the brine was working into my flesh, and I should soon have been sick—I felt a spirit of contentment, as if to give up the task were a virtuous deed—as if I were obeying a master's order not to drain the floats.

"Damn that!" I thought, unpacked the pipe, inserted it and began again. But my mouth cramped almost at once and I was compelled to realize that it was physically impossible to obtain any further practical result that way.

I racked my brain to conceive some way of improvising a pump: I could think of nothing on board that could possibly serve as one. I replaced the cap on the bilge-pipe: as for the four bilges in the starboard float, they must remain an unplumbed mystery.

10.30. It was too late to start for Lord Howe Island. Well, I must have one more shot. I started the motor afresh and taxied inshore, where it was calmer. There was a rock ahead; I would turn this side of it. There was plenty of room to turn. I put on full rudder and more engine. The plane was slow in moving into the turn. I opened the throttle wider. Still she lagged. I increased the revs, to 1,500. Suddenly the plane was right on top of the rock—I found myself staring at the black stone crown of it showing six feet above water, dead ahead. The plane had refused the turn. Even as I looked, the rock disappeared in a seething boil of white water, which eddied and swirled over the crag as if making every effort to suck *Elijah* to destruction. The only hope was to do something instant and drastic. For some reason, she had refused to turn left . . . I must take a risk . . . I thrust on full *opposite* rudder and maximum engine power.

The plane lurched round, heeled over, and the off wing dipped into the white water. I dared not slow the motor, I must risk the plane's tripping on the submerged wing to capsize. I kept the motor full on, easing the rudder to nearly fore and aft. She dragged clear. I laughed—not from amusement—but it seemed to me that I had escaped something I was not intended to.

I manoeuvred for position to take off: in the ensuing run, during which I had to keep a sharp look-out for the rocks, *Elijah* made some pronounced jumps out of the water before I was compelled to stop in the cross-sea off Bird Rock. "By Jupiter!" I thought, "we'll do it yet!" and returned once more. The plane started, gathered speed, was hydroplaning. I kept down the nose to get up as much speed as possible while still hydroplaning. Then, as soon as I considered the utmost had been reached, I jerked the stick back to pull off suddenly. The plane jumped from the crest of a swell and was in the air. But she had not the speed to remain air-borne; sank back and plunked into the sea. Once more, by Jupiter! But the result was only the same; with this exception that, as the plane hit the water, I saw a wire flicker like a rapier blade. One of the twelve inter-float bracing-wires had snapped under the strain.

That definitely settled the question of getting off. I must give up even trying. I at once felt like a schoolboy doing something right for which he knows he will be commended. And that part of me which had dissociated itself from the attempt to get into the air, seemed to return; I was once more capable of feeling emotion, though I did not—only intense weariness.

The question now was—could I reach Cascade? At each wave, with the bracing-wire parted, the floats spread like flat feet, and in the troubled sea off Bird Rock, I waited every minute for them to break up. Proceeding at dead-slow speed, it was a wearisome anxious passage. But the plane held together and at last we were off the jetty again.

I found myself surprised, as well as relieved. I had been expecting something to happen; I had been sure it would; then it had not. In some strange way, I had escaped.

Chapter V

A LANDING

And now the plane *must* come ashore, impossible or not; it could never fly until the bracing-wire had been mended, the floats drained, the motor repaired. It was obviously useless on the water—once a wind arose, total loss was certain. It must come ashore immediately, even if it had to be dragged up the rocks and were crushed and battered in the process.

How could it be brought ashore with the least damage?

I looked at the jetty. With the swell lifting and surging against that solid mole of rock and stone, with the plane's wing-spread of 30 feet and length of 24 feet, what chance was there of bringing it up without crumpling the wings at least?

Could it be coaxed up the little boulder beach? Possibly, if a railway could be laid far enough through the surf and a heavy iron trolley or truck used. Something in this scheme appealed to Caligula's sense of humour—I'm not sure if the idea of finding the rails, finding the truck, or laying the railway; however, it was abandoned.

Any other way but by the jetty I could not conceive, so turned back to that.

It had a pair of rails laid along the top for a hand-winch which could be wheeled out and clamped at the end to lift cargo. When finished with, this was wheeled back to the cliff, to escape being blown or washed away. It had a short fixed arm, not long enough to reach over the plane. Caligula maintained it would easily reach—his idea of landing a seaplane was to hook it in the gills and lift it out like a fish, I think. "You leave it to us, Skipper," he stoutly asserted, "we know all about it." Well, if he knew, I didn't; I knew nothing about this aspect of seaplane flying except that it was definitely not provided for in the *Seaplane Training Manual*. But I knew the matchboard-and-thread construction of the wings. I had felt the float-shell between finger and thumb, and I knew that, once caught by a roller and banged on the jetty or a rock, the plane would be crushed like the top of an egg by an iron ladle.

Well, come ashore somehow it must; I personally favoured trying the beach but reflected that adoption of the boatmen's method would enlist their help.

They entered into the game with great zest, regarded it, I think, as an unexpected jaunt, and had none of my qualms about the plane's frailty. Watching it charge about the sea at many times the pace of their own boats, they probably thought it many times as solid. Mr. Martin, the merchant, offered to help and drove off for materials. He returned with some wire rope to sling the plane, two small lengths of wood to spread the sling-wires and prevent their crushing the top petrol-tank, also a saw for cutting the spreaders to the right length. The saw looked as if more used to cutting down Norfolk Island Pines of six-foot diameter.

I noticed a chap with thin features and thick eyebrows; he never spoke unless spoken to, and when he did, his replies were scarcely audible—but they were always worth listening for. He was quiet, almost timid.

"Looks to me like a crack mechanic," I thought, and asked him if he would help me. " Yes," he replied simply, and stepped into the boat.

He climbed on a float—and carefully, as if it really were a seaplane and not a traction-engine. He peered at the vitals of the motor, softly touching the control-rod, a magneto, or other parts of the mechanism, as though making friends with them.

With a bootlace, we measured the lengths required for wire ropes and wooden spreaders. It was splendid to see (and hear) Caligula in the boat cutting a notch in a thin board no wider than his palm with a saw as long as himself. I think he finished it off with his pocket-knife after all his known language was used up.

I found myself beginning to enjoy the organization of the show. I no longer stood alone; the plane had become cargo, and the responsibility appeared to be shared.

But the two hours that followed were quite sufficiently nerve-racking. However, at last the plane was gaffed by the crane-hook, lifted from the water, lowered on to a truck, and wheeled in against the cliff. And on inspection, I was astonished to find no wings or elevators crumpled. Only the port float-tip stove in a few inches. My spirits rose like the mercury after a typhoon and even when Brent let about ten gallons, or a hundred pounds' weight, of Pacific Ocean out of the starboard float, I felt that, for the rest of that day, I was not caring two straws about the cause of it. It was three o'clock, so I greeted with deep-seated pleasure an invitation to lunch with Mr. Martin, the merchant.

Elijah, riding the swell, is brought to the hook.

Chapter VI

ON LAND

Mr. Martin also invited me to stay with him. I told the secretary of this. "Naturally," I said, "he had not anticipated my being on the island more than one night . . ." He thought it would be a very good thing for me to accept—in fact, they were expecting a visitor at the Government House next day in any case.

Martin took me up the steep track hewn aslant the cliff side and we motored across the top of the island. This was my first view of the country in daylight; I was very disappointed. It had appeared so beautiful from a height. We moved steeply up and down a narrow road surfaced with several inches of yellow dust like soft powder. Martin told me the roads were maintained by every islander working at them with pick and shovel for so many days a month. I was much intrigued by the thought of my companion working in a road gang—he was genial, good-natured, urbane and bland, reminding me of a chap at school of the same name and with round, chubby cheeks, known to us as Fatty Martin. But he added with a trace of satisfaction in his voice (or so I thought) that there was now a rule by which a man could pay the price of a day's work instead of doing it himself. Here and there were clumps of huge Norfolk Island Pine, which grew to a height of 200 feet; but seen close to, their great boles looked crude and bare; and the little patches of banana plantation fiddling. The number of small cultivated plots suggested the grounds of some "Institution". There was not a square inch of privacy; in fact, most of the allotments were overlooked by at least twenty neighbours. I thought it tame and dull. Martin told me that up to £200 an acre was paid for banana-growing land: which completely upset my expectation that it would need to be a present to induce most men to settle there. I mentioned my surprise at finding a motor car on an island only 4½ miles wide. "Why," he replied, "we have more than a hundred." I pictured them at the weekends, roaming the island in a follow-my-leader procession, head to tail, like a hundred ants on a bad plum. Yet I must say that I, myself, never saw more than four at any one time.

The "Maison" Martin had a wide veranda and was built high off the ground on wooden piles.

It was a rambling house of generous proportions, and, I thought, just suited the Martin family's character. For a more hospitable house I never was in. After some lunch and a bath, I had a few minutes' sleep, and it seemed no time before dinner. What a feast that was! We sat at a very long table with a tablecloth of big red-and-yellow check (Mrs. Martin was a Frenchwoman, dark and generously built). At the other end sat Martin's charming step-daughter, Simone, who looked after his store or some such thing (and, very astutely too, I expect, whatever it was). Then there was a step-son who spoke only French, and a brood of young Martins.

Those omelettes! And what a prodigious havoc I wrought among them with my black, wooden-handled fork! As for the Burgundy— well, Martin had sold French wine to French people in French New Caledonia for twenty years! I had not spoken the language since I was in Tripoli, and the struggle to express myself took me right out of the present and into a different, mighty pleasant atmosphere. The Martins were most polite about my howlers—that is to say, they all roared with laughter in a most polite kind of way. I enjoyed myself enormously. "You know," said Martin, as we sat drawing at cigars equal in excellence to the wine, "it is a refreshing sight to meet once more a man with a beard. I must say I do like to see a man with a beard. Now, naturally, you will disregard what I say if you find it impolite, but I should very much like to know what motives actuated you to grow it [les motifs qui vous ont promptés le faire croître]."

"Well, you see [voyez donc]," I replied, "it's like this: it helps me. I, in a seaplane, shaven, would be oppressed with thought of the dull money-making life I ought to lead. Whereas, with a beard, the pound-dispersing propensities of aerial peregrination appear more appropriate."

"Ah! [ach!]," said Martin, reflectively.

I confided in him the great fascination of Lord Howe Island for me; of how I felt I should have no rest or peace of mind until I had flown there; of my great desire to fly rings round Ball's Pyramid; and of how I had been looking forward for months to a day's rabbiting on the gentle slopes of Mount Lidgbird.

"Rabbits!" he exclaimed; "rabbits! Ha! ha! ha! what a joke! Why! there aren't any rabbits there—only rats, millions of rats."

Great Scott! What a blow he dealt me! I asked how the rats came there.

"The island steamer, the *Makambo*, ran ashore one night," he explained, "and the rats deserted. They increased till the island was overrun by millions and at one time they feared the islanders would be driven out."

"I don't care," I maintained stoutly, "I feel in my bones that it is an island paradise and that I shall fall in love with it."

"I'm afraid you will be disappointed. It's so small, for one thing."

"That's pretty good coming from a Norfolk Islander," I remonstrated.

"Why, Norfolk Island is four miles across, while Lord Howe is only half a mile; and think of all those rats!"

"Well, I shall look forward to a day's ratting on the gentle slopes of Mount Lidgbird, that's all."

"Ha! ha! ha! you won't like that island, I'm sure. Do you know," he added mysteriously, "it's a place where the birds live in holes in the ground and the rats live in the tree tops!"

"Really!"

"It's a fact!"

"Well, at least, they must be rats with high aspirations. And, at any rate, they don't reside at an island with knobs on."[1]

"You're wrong there," he chuckled, "because Lord Howe Island has Nobbs on too. One of our own Nobbs became a nob on Lord Howe Island."

A more genial or good-natured man than Martin one could not wish for; but after a while, I began to suspect hidden depths in him and a carefully concealed core of determination. For one thing, he made up his mind to help me in every way he could, and later I came to think that nothing could have shaken his resolve.

My first concern next morning was the weather. *Elijah* was precariously perched on a small rock platform at the base of a great rock cliff, and about as safe—if a wind got up—as a sheet of notepaper fastened to a flagstaff by a pin.

Though still dark, I could see it was so far a perfect day, with not a cloud in the sky, nor a breath of wind. Truly Æolus must have bound the contrary winds in an oxhide for me too.

Soon after daybreak, Brent and I set to work on the machine. To begin with, he fixed the new shackle made for the bracing-wire. Then I started him dismantling the motor while I turned to the floats. Presently, with a detached cylinder-head in hand, he turned his pale face towards me and made a speech that must have been his record for length.

"You're lucky, aren't you?"

"I don't know. How?"

"I mean, you are fortunate to be alive?"

"I don't know. Why?"

"Look at this!"

I looked and saw the inlet valve was in the exhaust valve's place. They had been replaced wrong in No. 3 cylinder-head.

"And just look at this!" he exclaimed, pointing to the phosphor-bronze seat of the exhaust valve. It had begun to unscrew and was already a third of the way out.

---

1 The Norfolk Island population seemed to consist chiefly of Nobbs, Quintals, and Cornishes.

"It's a wonder it did not come right out, once it started," he said.

"H'mm."

"And jam the valve port open or shut."

"H'm."

"And the motor break up in either case."

" 'm."

So, after all, I could not say that success in reaching the island was due to me. In fact, had that bronze seating come out all the determination in the world would not have got me to my destination. Could there be something in this "fate" theory after all? No, certainly not—for how should I ever fly away from here if I waited for fate to get me into the air?

No. 4 exhaust valve was pitted where the explosion flames had blasted through an irregularity in the valve seating. I let Brent give his genius full rein at the valve-grinding. I did not dislike the interminable twisting of it when in a mechanical mood, but when in piloting mood it was an unpleasant labour.

I considered the floats. Undoubtedly there had been a lot of water inside them. Therefore, as Socrates would have deduced, the water must have found entry somewhere. How? They had been proved watertight at Auckland. Well, they must be tested again.

Martin went off, and returned with two large, wicker-covered beer-jars. The boatmen watched them with the aspect of a pack of terriers who observe a bone in a nearby hand. When we lifted one on to the top of an empty barrel, the atmosphere was charged with expectancy. When my rubber tube was inserted and Martin sucked at the other end, the expectancy threatened to become excitement. When Martin lowered the pipe and mere water siphoned out, I fancied I heard a hollow groan. Martin filled up the eight float compartments one by one. There was no sign of a leak—only a slight weep in one place. But that wouldn't let in ten gallons in a month. Brent and I examined them carefully all over. After much discussion, we decided the only possible entry was between the covers and rims of the inspection holes (manholes, I called them). These float-top openings were large enough to allow an arm entry into the float. There were twelve, and a separate cover to each was held down by eight screws. Some of the screw threads were worn out and we decided the covers must have lifted and the water crept in when the floats were submerged.[1] Brent tapped out the worn threads and fitted larger screws. I considered the trouble disposed of.

It was a flawless day, and hot enough working in shirt-sleeves—the rock an enticing seat when doing any small mechanical job. The sea sparkled and flashed to the horizon under the line of sun; there was not a breath of wind. Ideal for our work, it would have been useless for flying. Even had there been no swell at all, I did not think the plane would have risen in such calm air and from a too smooth water surface. It was almost uncanny how the weather had favoured me. But I must not be lulled into feeling falsely secure. The cyclone centred in the north-west Tasman off Australia, was travelling this way. There was only one thing to do with regard to Norfolk Island—to leave it at the very first possible moment. The plane on the island was like a spider on a rock in midstream, with the tide turning and a storm approaching. If the wind rose, it would be blown into the water; if the sea rose, it would be washed away; if there were a swell rising to the rock it would be unable to spread its gossamer sails; if there were no wind, it could not sail away once they were spread; and if the wind came from the wrong quarter, it could not reach land.

Even to-day, perfect though it was, a slight swell was coming in. And I was thoroughly frightened of that swell by now. It was trouble. It was (I now felt convinced) the cause of my failure to escape. Could I avoid it anywhere round the island? Or could I devise some scheme? I began racking my brains for an inspiration, every now and then studying the chart of the island. *How* could I get off with a swell running? *Where* could I get off with a swell

---

1 Actually, the rivet-heads holding the keel to the float-bottom had corroded away or worn off. When water pressed from outside, it pushed the thin float-bottom away from the rigid keel and let in water. When water pressed from inside, it pushed the float-bottom against the keel and stopped the leak.

running? If I felt like a rat in a trap, let me imitate one and range the island in search of a way of escape.

Consider the east coast. I had flown along that; it was precipitous, with craggy rocks in the sea; and as it caught the full force of the swell coming in from the south-east, I could not hope to get off from that quarter. The south coast was exposed as much to the south-east swell as was the east. The north coast I was on, and knew only too well by now. There remained the west coast. The chart showed a small bay there, Anson Bay. That should be protected from the rollers, if anywhere on the island.

Mr. Leonard, another great supporter of mine, drove me across the island with Martin. All the way—except for one level avenue with a line of towering firs majestically guarding it on each side— we moved continually up and down short hills.

From the edge of the almost sheer cliff at Anson Bay, I stared down several hundred feet at a perfect little crescent of yellow beach, diminutive, at my feet. The dark blue of deep water came to its edge, and the rollers, scarcely perceptible as they smoothly glided up, humped suddenly near the steep beach and struck it with a sudden short surf.

That was no better than Cascade; and besides, it was tiny for a seaplane, inaccessible and with no boat.

While there, we entered the relay cable station at the top of the cliff and asked Sydney for the weather forecast from Dr. Kidson.

"Northerly winds, freshening near Lord Howe, cloud increasing, weather becoming unsettled."

"Come on!" I said to Martin, "there's no possible place on this coast from which to take off."

On the way back, I suddenly thought, "Why not look at Emily Bay?"

Along the shore in front of the old prison ruins, the chart marked "coral reef, uncovers at low water". In New Zealand, I had hunted out the captain of a ship which had run to Norfolk Island several times. I asked him if it were possible to alight behind this strip of reef. "Useless to consider it," was his reply, "a strip of water only a few yards wide and full of coral snags. At the end of it, a small basin, Emily Bay, which [he thought] dried at low water; and anyway, no one kept even a dinghy there."

I suggested it to Martin.

"Emily Bay!" he exclaimed, "why! it's not much bigger than a large swimming-bath."

"I can't help it; I'm growing desperate."

The reef ran along parallel to the shore and certainly not many feet from it; but I found water lying between reef and shore.

The shape of the water was that of an ancient war-axe with a bent handle. The axe-head was Emily Bay and faced inland. A splendid little beach provided the edge. The axe-head was 150 yards across. I might get into Emily Bay, but I should never fly out of it again.

Then I studied the handle of the axe. This strip of water had clumps of coral encroaching on it from shore and sea. Where the axe-handle joined the axe-head beside the old prison salt-house, I stood on a brown pile of jagged dead coral—I could feel its sharp scratch at my sole-leathers—and studied the water. I estimated its span from shore to reef could be no wider than the span of an ordinary seaplane. Besides its narrowness, two or three foot waves escaped over the reef and made steep ridges and furrows along the line of a plane's alighting. More unpleasant than any of these drawbacks was the fact of the bend at this narrow place. A seaplane taking off along the strip would have to turn in its course at the narrow gut, with coral waiting a few inches under the surface on either side (yet invisible to the pilot) to rip off the float-bottoms. At the other end of the axe-handle was a jetty used for cargo, with a passage blasted to it through the coral from the open sea on the other side. By Jupiter! this was no place for a seaplane.

There was only one course open to me; I must get off from Cascade somehow or other.

On return, we found Brent had nearly finished; he would have before dawn, he said.

I spent a wearisome evening at the "Maison" Martin attending to fifty details, trivial, yet not to be neglected. His step-son made me a bilge-pump by reversing the valve in a bicycle-pump. He then borrowed a forge and made me a new anchor. Martin brought down a mail of one hundred and forty letters for Lord Howe Island and Australia. People came in and discussed things interminably. My last thoughts before going to sleep and my first thoughts on waking were: "Can I escape from this island?" "How can I escape from this island?" and "When can I escape from this island?"

Chapter VII

IN THE AIR

On setting out for Cascade at dawn, I found it was another perfect day as far as the weather was concerned. The skies were cloudless: but when I wetted my finger I could not detect the slightest breeze. And there was a quiet swell gently heaving the ocean against the coast.

I felt about as enthusiastic as if preparing my own funeral. The enterprise was too big a task . . . inadequate equipment . . . hopeless conditions . . . I might as well admit I had been too cocksure in saying I could carry it out. Better give it up while there was a chance . . .

As soon as the dozen odd mechanical jobs were finished, my gear all stowed aboard, and another tinful of petrol added, the crane was wheeled back and the plane launched with comparative ease. The sea was quite calm on the surface of its swell.

I detected a puff of wind from seawards and headed into it. The attempt was futile. I switched off the motor and waited for it to cool.

The sun put a sparkle into the water, which out here in the open sea was of a violet tinge and danced with liveliness. It would leap to a peak, to subside in the same place with a quiet "chough".

There came a puff of wind from the island. I restarted the motor and headed in the direction of the jetty. The plane bumped hard as if the floats were iron bars and the waves concrete. Every thump I felt and it seemed a blow at my own vitality. The strain on the machine must be terrible.

It was no good: I should never get off like this. I must think of some new scheme.

I signalled the boat and unloaded into it my collapsible rubber boat, the oars and pump, my shoes, overalls, and everything I could possibly do without. My heart sank in depression to see my beloved boat jettisoned. Every pilot draws his line about risk. As at one time I drew the line at flying out of reach of a forced landing-ground in case of any motor trouble, was braced by or tolerated any risk less than that and hated any risk greater; so now I drew the line at ocean flying without a sound machine, or without my rubber boat. With them, I felt it an ordinary risk to fly any ocean; without, I both hated and feared the thought.

I turned seawards and tried again. Smack! smack! smack! she struck the rollers. For over a mile I held on vainly hopeful at each leap, despairing at each bump. The motor was heating up: I switched off and let the plane ride. I opened the cock of the top petrol-tank and jettisoned petrol till only nine hour's fuel remained.

This was terrible! They had said I should never be able to take off.

I turned about and headed again for the jetty across the line of swell. It was the closest yet to getting off.

At a bump, I saw the bracing-wire flicker.

Brent came aboard and surveyed it, then left for an hour while he made a new eye for the bolt. It was calm enough to fit it while the plane rode.

I tried again—and again—and again. The more I tried, the stronger the plane seemed to be fettered to that island prison; and the more set I became—now angrily, now despairingly—to tear it away.

How that seaplane stood up to the battering, heaven only knows! Each time it survived added severity on my part, I at first marvelled, only to grow accustomed to its survival and again increase the harshness of my treatment.

But the machine was drawing near to its end.

I jumped her fifteen feet into the air off a roller: hope leaping in me with her; but in reality, it was hopeless. The bracing-wire snapped as she struck the water.

I taxied back very slowly.

I must get off somehow . . .

It looked as if Brent were unable to repair that wire—and how should he considering it was of high-tension steel especially built for the purpose?

"If I'm going to get off, I must not become fanatical about it. There's a way to do everything if only it can be discovered."

I went ashore and strolled about until my brain was empty of thought. An idea then came almost at once.

That wire could not be replaced on the island.

Yet the plane must break up without it or any other of the lateral bracing-wires. They were diagonals keeping a four-sided figure rigid.

But surely, the plane would still be structurally rigid without the fore and aft bracing-wires. If only one of them would fit in the place of the lateral wire that was broken. Though it was unlikely, because, for example, it was of different construction. However . . .

Brent and I returned to the plane.

The wire fitted.

It was now too late in any case to start for Lord Howe Island, so I went off with Martin for something to eat, the whole time turning over the situation in my brain. I had a strong feeling that *Elijah's* end was approaching rapidly at this place and that my only chance of saving her was to escape immediately. But I was becoming cooler-brained and beginning to realize this was not to be done by the mad rushes and angry snorts of a bull—only by some subtle, foxy scheme.

A weather forecast which arrived from Dr. Kidson nearly had me in a ferment again by presenting the thought of bad weather. "Conditions rather uncertain. Desirable get Lord Howe Island report by wireless."

"By Jupiter! by hook or crook I've got to leave here before bad weather arrives!"

I began circling the island again in imagination. Surely there must be some part free from the swell! But when it reached the island, this seemed to part, only to sweep round the sides and join again at the back. Certainly the force was diminished for a space, but only as the flow of a stream is diminished by a stick held in its current.

But every time I went over the problem afresh, it grew clearer.

Suddenly I decided the strip of water with the narrow gut behind the reef was negotiable.

"Look here," I said to Martin, "I'm going to try Emily Bay."

"What!" he exclaimed.

The first question was how to get the plane into the lagoon. Martin took me off to find Caligula and discuss ways and means. It was a long way round to taxi, with the propeller chopping spray the whole time. It would never stand it; already the fabric was stripping off and the wood itself chipped at the end of one blade. However, Caligula settled that question: there was no opening in the reef even if I could reach it. I suggested the crane might pick her out of the passage blasted to the jetty and set her down in the lagoon the other side. No; bare coral lay against the jetty in the lagoon—and coral, as I knew, would rip open the floats like the tusks of a thousand wild boars. I suggested mounting her on a lorry and taking her across overland. To this it was objected that: firstly, it was doubtful if a lorry with the plane on it could pass the cliff overhang by the track; secondly, the plane would have to be slid off the lorry on to the beach at the other end—a manoeuvre unlikely to leave her intact; thirdly (as if to drive home with incontestable force the first two objections) there was no lorry on the island big enough to mount the plane fore and aft.

"Why not fly her over?" suggested Caligula, amidst applause from the bystanders.

"Well, Caligula," I thought, "I believe you are right. Though, God knows, it is not so lightly done as you lightly suggest." I should have to remove every drop of petrol except the bare sufficiency for getting aloft—forty gallons, quart by quart, slowly and laboriously—and every ounce of gear, tools, and spares. Even then, I doubted if it could succeed. I was beginning to wonder if the plane would take off under any circumstances with a swell running. But it struck me that I had better fly round if I could—for quite another reason. People, after seeing their first plane flying close to, could be relied on for enthusiastic assistance of almost any kind for three days before they and their enthusiasm faded away. But scarcely anyone had seen my plane fly at all: it had slipped in quietly and quickly at dusk. In fact, Cornish, the oldest inhabitant, when taken to see it, was reported to have exclaimed: "That thing flown from New Zealand! Impossible! Don't believe it!" Already they were losing interest in me. I must get into the air somehow, for, with a seaplane to handle and my wealth in cash only amounting to £2, I should be in a truly awkward position without plenty of voluntary assistance.

We rushed back to Cascade and arrived to find the boat towing *Elijah* by the nose. She looked like a large silvery bird with spread wings and grotesque great feet waddling along.

"Just in time, Skipper," said one of the boatmen on stepping ashore after re-anchoring the plane, "we was working on the road, keeping an eye on her as you did ask, when suddenly we noticed her just about on the rocks. Cut her line again, she did. Close shave that!"

What! Again! If it had happened at night! . . . Was it a hint that any effort on my part would be futile if fate were against me? No! it was not. It was my fault for not calculating that the coral would cut the rope.

I went out in the boat and tediously unloaded all my gear, piece by piece. When Martin returned with empty petrol-tins, I suspended one from the back locker hasp, inserted half my rubber tube into the back tank and sucked till petrol ran into my mouth and started siphoning, when I slipped the tube end into the tin. I repeated the manoeuvre with the front tank. Every time the plane rolled or I pulled out the tube to see if the petrol still flowed, it promptly ceased to flow, so that I tasted petrol a good number of times before ten four-gallon tins were full. My tongue seemed to be made of fibre cells, which had been dragged inside out; or I might have been sucking a lemon full of corrosive acid.

Elijah succeeded at last, when empty. She left the crest of one swell, hit the next, and sprang off it, 40 feet into the air. She looked like settling again, but gathered speed before the floats touched. I had no feel of the controls at all and was as much at loss with the plane as if I had not flown for a year. I put this down to the continual snatching, jerking, and coarse manipulation of the controls while riding at sea. The feel soon returned to me, until in a few seconds, I was once more using the plane with no more consciousness of effort than a pen.

As I flew level with the top of the cliffs in Duncombe Bay, I felt triumphant. I had escaped from Cascade.

I turned the point and rose a hundred feet to overlook the cable station in the clump of tall pines and peer contemptuously at piffling little Anson Bay. Inconceivable that I should have allowed myself to become concerned about paltry things. How people down below do worry about trivialities! When they should let themselves respond to the thrill of life. Ha! ha! ha! Flying through space, devouring distance like gods—speed—up in the clouds with life-force dominant and throbbing in heart and veins. 3,000 feet; touching stray clouds. I could see the ocean reaching in every way for perhaps a hundred miles under its cloud ceiling of warm deep blue faded at the rim. What majesty! By heavens! what an intensity of living. Poor wretches below that had never touched the heart of living! Down under was the round blot of the island all in green of every shade, brightened by the sunlight except for a few packed cloud shadows dawdling across—the black of the cliffs tucked away out of sight under the edge. Oo—oop—I pulled up the nose till the plane stood on her tail; made her topple slowly over the right wing to drop nose first like a stone and gathered speed with an acceleration which had my cheeks lagging and vitals thrusting backwards against my spine. Ha! ha! ha! what intoxicating existence! At the end of a 500-foot drop, I pulled out of the vertical dive—gently, so as not to tear off the wings with their whining, shrilling wires. I turned and swooped and cavorted till back at 1,000 feet, barely able to restrain myself from looping the loop in spite of the strange things told me of what can happen to a sea-plane in a loop.

I picked out Martin's house and the cars crossing to the lagoon with the Cascade party. They were halted in the middle of the island, and white dots marked their upturned faces thrust out of the cars.

I made for the lagoon. Ugh! Now I had to come down to earth again—and cannily, too. At once, all my fatigues and worries settled back on me like a swarm of wasps.

I studied the lagoon while circling. The longer I looked at it, the less I liked it. Sprinkled with dark blobs of coral from end to end, with only a thin stream of dazzling white sand twisting through at the Emily Bay end. It was over that narrow brook that I must alight. I tried to fix in my memory the lie of it and of the coral clumps darkening the edges. I knew I should be able to see nothing ahead when close to the surface. "If I look much more," I thought, "I shall get stage fright." I swooped down, forced myself to put the plane on the surface at high speed, and hydroplaned fast through where I judged the narrow neck to lie expecting every instant to feel the jar and rip of coral at the floats. But we passed the neck and I let out my held-in breath in a burst. By Jupiter! mighty fortunate there was no wind today . . . the least cross-wind . . .

Emily Bay, with its few yards of flawless, easy sand-shelf, was a picnic ground after Cascade; and so thought a few hundred onlookers, who quickly arrived to bask in the sun, loll on the beach, and watch the new vaudeville performance, "Fun with a Seaplane".

However, it meant plenty of assistance for me. Young fellows dived about the plane like porpoises. But my chief assistant was Mr. "X" from the Government House. He was already bathing when I arrived but for another hour continued to fetch and carry thirty-pound tins of petrol through the water up to his shoulders. And when a large anchor weighing at least twenty-five pounds arrived, he swam out with this, towing the seaplane as well. In deep water, he dived and planted the anchor. The fact that he was sixty-five years old increased my admiration for this Australian from Melbourne.

Work kept Brent and myself busy till the cool of the evening. I went ashore and sorted my gear, leaving behind everything possible. It was a wrench leaving the boat—with it, though it was only of rubber, there was always a chance in the event of coming down in the sea and, in any case, one would have hope to the end instead of being left to swim about futilely for perhaps an hour knowing there was none. But, with oars and pump, the boat weighed twenty-seven lbs.; it was a big inflatable rubber tube with canvas bottom secured to the tube. Its length, equal to that of a man, was twice its breadth. I persuaded Brent to accompany me in it for a row down the lagoon, so that I could inspect at close quarters the coral obstructions to the channel I must use for taking off. Brent said nothing, but his look spoke a volume when he stepped into it. I think he would not have minded had there been something mechanical about it—if only a piece of clockwork. Rowing through the narrow neck, I was so busy explaining how safe it was if you rode a wave properly, leaning first this way and then that to balance the boat over the crest, that I momentarily forgot to do so, and a two-foot wave breaking over the top of the reef, broke over the top of the boat. However, immediately I saw the spray as it struck Brent's back, I carried my theory into practice and, by the way I myself escaped a wetting, demonstrated how true and correct, not to mention efficient, the theory was. But, after that, I noticed a disquiet in the look of him, as of a bird, sitting on a clutch of eggs, that begins to suspect they are broken.

I made as careful an inspection of the channel as I could.

"I think I can do it with a bit of luck," I said to Martin, who was waiting on the shore for me.

"You won't attempt it to-morrow, will you?" he asked. "Surely you will rest for a day or two first?"

"Look here," I said, "I could not get off this strip except with a wind from one quarter—straight up and down it—about north-easterly. Even with that, I shall be jolly lucky to get off at all. As for rest: I can see I shall never get any rest while the plane is anchored out. I must make an attempt the first moment possible." "And", I thought, looking at his face, "the sooner I go, the better for you, my friend." I never saw such a quick change in a man. He looked haggard, as if his face had been lined with a sooty finger. He had been "on the go" for me every day from dawn till eleven o'clock or midnight, and I think, felt just as much, if not more anxiety for the plane than I did myself.

On the way to Martin's, it suddenly occurred to me that the nautical almanac I had brought with me ran out on March 31st, so that I must find another for to-morrow, April 1st. To my surprise there was not one to be found on the island: in fact, the idea seemed to prevail that a nautical almanac was a calendar which you hung on the wall beneath the smoked hams, with a picture of old Sam, in a blue jersey with VICTORY in white on it, standing beside a lobster-pot. True, that had been exactly my own idea of it until I began to study navigation ten months before. Well, I must have one if I wished to find Lord Howe Island; I should never be able to do so without sun observations—in fact, I had not even my compass swung on the bearing; and compass deviation might easily amount to 10° either way. I felt checkmated, until I suddenly thought, "Why not construct the information myself?" Why not? Somebody must always do it! As soon as I had the idea, it was simple enough. I needed the sun's declination, right ascension and semi-diameter for every hour of Greenwich Mean Time. I took the figures of several days previous, made them into a mental graph and thereby assessed the values of right ascension and declination for the morrow. In spite of the fact that this would not have presented the least problem to any student of astronomy, I was jubilant about it. I think it was that I had been at last able to surmount decisively an obstacle.

When Mr. — of the cable station arrived late in the evening with my chronometer watch which he had checked for correct Greenwich time, I arranged to send a wireless message every hour of the flight if I could take off on the morrow. His set was the only one on the island which could pick up a 44-metre wavelength.

My waking thought next morning was the weather. The wind

must blow from one direction—and one only—for the plane to take off behind that reef. Furthermore, it must blow a pretty fresh breeze against the plane for it to succeed in the limited stretch of water. I stepped outside in the dark.

Against the starlight, I could see the fringe of a tree top on the stir and swaying. For the first time since I arrived, a fresh breeze of 15–20 miles an hour was blowing. Excellent! I turned each cheek to it until it blew evenly on both, and I knew I was facing whence it came.

South-easterly!

As I motored to the lagoon, instead of a load of depression weighing me down, excitement kindled within me for the first time. I ought to subdue it—the wind-direction might be changed by local layout of the land in the middle of the island. Not it! I had suddenly come to life again; something in my blood or in the air subtly whispered of action.

On arrival, I found the wind blew from 10° south of up and down the water. That would do: and the strength of about 20 m.p.h. was ideal—rather, it was marvellous. On my first night at the island, a wind was likely to have sent *Elijah* to destruction on the rocks after cutting her anchor-rope; on the second, it would have been impossible to swing her ashore with any wind; on the third, any strong puff must have blown her off the rock platform; on the fourth, any cross-wind would have made it too risky to try alighting behind the reef; to-day, there blew the strong wind with which alone I could hope to leave the lagoon, and from the only direction from which a take-off could be attempted. Could there possibly be anything in this "fate" theory after all? Well, I couldn't start thinking about that now, though of course, my reason knew there was no such thing. Man took decisive action to decide his own destiny.

I hurried on with preparations for fear the wind should drop or change. Martin's step-son worked with his pump at the bilges. Meanwhile, I had to resolve the problem of getting *Elijah* down to the far end of the lagoon.

Of the water shaped like an axe, the handle strip was 480 yards long. I had taken off in less than that at Auckland. At Parengarenga, on the other hand, I had taken over a mile. There was Emily Bay at the end of the strip, but I must be off the water before reaching that, otherwise it would be impossible to surmount or circumvent the low hill on the promontory in face. And I must be exceedingly careful—the narrow neck lay at the end of the run; waves were coming across the reef there, and consequently one float might be in a trough while the other was on a crest, and I was not sure about the effect of that; and then, with only a few yards to spare at the narrow neck, I must watch carefully to be certain we had not drifted to one side or the other. In the neck I must make instantaneous decision if the plane were not off by then. And in the neck was where the channel kinked and where I must change course at the correct instant.

As for getting into position down at the far end, it would be impossible to taxi slowly through the channel with such a breeze. A puff on the tail would swing it round to head the plane into the coral one side or the other. While, if I taxied down fast, the same would happen when the plane had to be slowed or else it would dash into the coral at the end.

Martin drove Brent and myself with the rubber boat and big anchor down to the far end of the lagoon, where the boat was launched and I dropped the anchor as close to the coral as I dared. I paid out the anchor-rope to the beach, where I left it in charge of Brent with the boat.

Martin had a dinghy carried overland into the lagoon.

This towed the seaplane to the neck and then let it drift downwind. I sat on the top petrol-tank, conning the boat, an act which seemed to annoy the boatmen; but I continued because I could see better high up, and besides, they had not been in the lagoon before. Although a good breeze blew the plane along and the boat let it drift freely except when it approached the coral, it seemed to move at an incredibly slow pace. At first, I observed and memorized as well as possible the lie of the channel. At the narrow neck were quick, short waves. A few yards further down, the reef bellied towards the shore, and I tried to determine whether this would necessitate another change of course when taking off, but could not tell if it were in the line or not. A few yards lower down again another clump of dead coral projected into the passage on the shore side and would have to be avoided. It seemed a horrible zigzag for a seaplane to thread. The intensely clean-looking patches of clear sand that I had noticed yesterday were scarcely apparent to-day. For one reason, the water had a slight chop on its surface, and for another, a grey haze hung in the sky above.

Soon, I became so impatient of our funeral pace that I shouted to the boatmen to row on and tow *Elijah* downwind. But, when broadside on, the wind caught the tail and pushed it as hard one way as the boat could pull the nose the other. The plane headed straight for the shore and I had to roar like the bull of Bashan for the boat to return urgently, head the plane, and let it drift backwards again.

At last we reached the end. Brent passed the anchor-rope twice round the inter-float boom and held the loose end in the rubber boat. *Elijah* was now tethered to the anchor behind and haltered to the dinghy in front. I started the motor and as soon as I was in the cockpit with the rudder under control the dinghy slipped its line and cleared off. I could not see the place where the reef bellied shorewards, nor where the clump of coral jutted out. I should have to look out on both sides for them: it would be a tricky piece of work—steering straight for the narrow neck at the same time. Checking the direction of the wind, I found it had backed some 10° and was now blowing clean up and down the waterway. It was almost eerie.

Looking over the cockpit rim, I found myself staring at the lively, perhaps excited, features of a swimmer. He was balanced half out of the water, with his wrists on the extreme end of the float. The propeller-tips, invisible to him, were cutting past his brow at almost half the speed of a rifle bullet. If he swayed forward an inch, he was a dead man . . .

Darting my finger at him as though a dagger, I shrieked.

He slipped back into the water with a sheepish expression on his face. Probably having no idea of the death he had narrowly missed but affected by my screaming before the people on the beach. I slumped back in the cockpit seat, my blood feeling momentarily turned to water—it was not so much the shock at the thought of his death, for after all, it would be an easy end, but the idea of my killing him. And every time I began to feel confident about overcoming obstacles, there arrived some event out of the blue like this, which might just as easily have ended otherwise, and definitely stopped me.

But this was no moment for weak thoughts. I must bestir myself and concentrate on the affair in hand. Brent was obviously freezing in the propeller blast blowing the water flat behind the plane.

I gave the motor full throttle and signed him to slip the rope. *Elijah* shot forward—like a straining hound slipped from its leash; she gathered speed quickly. I pressed back in the cockpit, my head as high and as far back as possible. I darted quick looks from side to side, at the reef, at the shore, and then at the narrow neck. I was not aware of the plane at all, and must have gone through the various manoeuvres instinctively. At the narrow neck, about to shut off for having failed, I found to my surprise that we had not only left the water but were a few feet above it. Yet there was not height enough to turn properly without the wing-tips striking. To avoid the hill in front, I slithered round in a flatskid—flying abhorrent to a pilot. I swept by the promontory, now flying again with true balance, in a wide sweep back to the lagoon. I deeply regretted leaving my boat. I could have carried it easily. Should I return for it? It was terrible to face the distance without it in this battered and strained machine. No! My God! *No!!* Return after I had escaped at last and with the plane still in one piece—heaven only knows how! After it had escaped destruction, escaped being dashed-to pieces on that horrible rock, black as the rock of Scylla! Not I!!

Chapter VIII

FROM SCYLLA

I swooped down, flew along the lagoon and saluted the crowd. Then headed west.

I noticed great lag in the compass; the needle would not travel when the plane was in a turn and I had to straighten out where I guessed the course to lie, allow the needle to swing free and then turn again, until I found I was on the right course.[1] It was 10.50 (22.50) Greenwich Mean Time, or 10.02 hours local time.

A mile out the plane flew from under the grey overcast sky above the island into sunlight unmarred by a single cloud. The blue stretched clear to the horizon, except in the south, where at immense distance, it lost colour and faded into white. The sun was behind my right shoulder, and the aluminium-painted lower wing was dazzling bright with strong sunshine except where a strut shadow lay across it like the arm of a pendulum and travelled to and fro a little as the plane swung about its course. During the time of the flight I could expect the sun's path to take it from behind the right wing, over the wing-tip and down in front of it. At the time I hoped to be near Lord Howe Island it should be in front, nearly dead ahead. The navigation was, therefore, fly to the right of the island. I altered course 10° to the right. This should take me to a point 109 miles to the N.N.E. of the island. When sextant observations showed the plane had reached a line drawn through that point and Lord Howe Island, I must then turn left.

---

1 Because the compass was built for the northern hemisphere, and the magnets were counterbalanced for north magnetic dip instead of south magnetic dip.

It increased the length of the flight to 600 miles but was the only scheme of navigation that could find me the island.

I looked back for a last sight of Norfolk Island, but was surprised to find it already hidden in a faint purple haze; yet a mental calculation showed it was only 15 miles away. It seemed as if its guardian, disgusted at my escape, had covered it up and put it away, determined at any rate that I should never return. Well, I *had* escaped, and was flying towards Lord Howe Island; so what did I care if I could not return—knowing I would have paid any price and sacrificed everything rather than give up the flight at Norfolk Island.

But by Jupiter! how the plane was vibrating. I could scarcely form figures in the logbook as I worked with slide-rule and my sheet of nautical almanac to calculate the sun's position for the time I hoped to reach the turn-off point.

I made three observations for drift, and forty minutes out from Norfolk Island slipped the wireless key under a band round my leg for the first hourly message I had promised to send to the cable officer. But when I looked at the battery current meter, I found the pointer dancing about the zero mark, starting away from it as if in fright; yet the current was not even switched on. The infernal vibration must have short-circuited it somewhere. The set was useless . . .

But perhaps he would hear enough to know I was transmitting. I had undertaken to, so I would carry on just as if the set were in order.

I sent the message, made another set of drift observations, and by the time they were plotted, the second half-hour had run out. I found the vibrations interfered with my work and slowed it up. The wind had backed from E.S.E. to E. by N. I was elated to find it had added 20½ miles to the hour's run. Thank God! it looked as if I were going to have an easy, unadventurous run across. The plane had been blown 9 miles off course to the right.

1 hour 10 minutes out.

107 miles flown.

I wished I did not feel so drowsy; my head seemed heavy as if all the blood had been pressed into it. It must be the sea air; or was it through sitting without movement in the strong sunlight and the blast of air? Or just the weariness I seemed unable to shake off? I must overcome it somehow—there was intense and hard work ahead.

I must have everything prepared to swing the compass by a sun observation immediately it was abeam. A task of vital importance with the compass not swung on this course. It might deviate any angle up to 10°, and 10° meant throwing the plane 100 miles off its course in 500. I made a guess the sun would be dead – abeam when 3 hours 20 minutes out. I worked out its position for that time; but found it would then be too far west, so tried again for 15 minutes earlier. Again, at this time, it would be too far west. However, it would have to do—any earlier would bring the sun too close to its meridian for the observation.

It was very difficult to work. The plane had never before been so hard to control. It totally refused to trim on an even keel. However carefully I adjusted throttle and tail-trimming gear, it pushed its nose into a steep dive or climb immediately I left the controls alone for a second.

And apart from the inconvenience of having to nag continuously at the controls, it meant something was wrong with the rigging. It was hard to say what that might be unless a float had been knocked out of trim during the plane's terrible battering. If one float pointed downwards, even with the plane otherwise level, its top surface might catch the air-flow and drag it into a dive. And the speed-indicator which still worked—the one on the strut— showed the plane's speed had dropped from 77 to 72 m.p.h. By Jupiter! a few months ago, I wouldn't have flown such a plane over the safest route in the world. But now, with *Elijah* a seaplane, one's humble aspirations seemed to rise no higher than to get her off the water, even if she were to fall to pieces when once up.

With a stray glance to the south, I noticed a billowy black cloud rising out of the horizon like the genie of Aladdin's lamp. But even as I watched, it changed shape, one billow rolling and folding on another. Cloud! that was no cloud. It must be smoke! It must be the *Makambo*, the monthly steamer, nearing Norfolk Island! I waggled the plane's wings in salute, as excited as if I had seen a vessel after clinging to a spar in mid-ocean for three days. I seized the wireless key and tapped out an exuberant message that I could see her, that her bearing from me was 170° true. As I finished, she belched out a prodigious smoke which warmed my heart as a signal that they had heard me on board or seen the plane. I myself could not see the ship. I was still looking at the smoke when a whale, like the side of a vast grey-black egg, broke surface just below me and spouted. I could see the wind catch its spouting and scatter it briefly into a white feather. Instantly, I had the plane steeply banked to swoop down close to it, but with a slight shock, I realized I was in the middle of the Tasman and must not do that sort of thing; I banked steeply the other way and swung the plane back on to its course.

When making observations for drift it occurred to me that the slow old *Makambo* would certainly be stemming direct course from island to island. I looked at the chart. That steamer must have been 30 miles away when I joyously waggled my wings in salute. I might as well have been in the South Atlantic for all they could have seen of me! Curious how plain the smoke was when the island had been lost to sight at only half the distance.

While recording the drift observations, I had taken the logbook off my knee and was holding it in my hand with my little finger crooked round the control-stick. My right elbow, touching the fuselage woodwork, made it impossible for me to write figures. All of a sudden, the fact was driven home to me that the vibration was not only extremely severe, it was also decidedly dangerous. I felt the throttle-rod and the woodwork in other places. The whole fuselage was shaking with a quick, short period. And the rigging-wires, which should be taut, were vibrating heavily with a slow period. I could imagine how they must be strumming. What was the cause? Not the motor—the exhausts were firing with staccato bark, the general roar was steady and even. It must be the propeller, damaged by smacking through water and wave crests. The strain on the machine must be terrific. If any weaknesses had developed in it! . . . What a fool I had been to leave without the rubber boat! Thank heaven for a following wind and perfect weather! If the plane struck any bumpy air in such a state, God help it!

But the sun still shone untouched by any clouds—just behind the top wing—and some of its rays found their way into the cockpit, lighting up the far side of the instrument-board and a patch round the throttle lever. At half-past the hour, I transmitted as agreed. Somehow, I felt I was getting the better of the set by ignoring the possibility of its being useless:

> "CQ de KK AAA Position by DR at 1200 hours GMT 29° 23′ South 166° 03′ East AAA Fine weather wind 19 mph from 85 degrees true AAA AR."

I turned at once from that to drift readings and the plotting of all six observations. But I found myself in difficulties. The three drift lines of the first half-hour should meet in a point; so should those of the second half.[1] Neither set did. An error somewhere—but where? I racked my brains. Some simple, trivial mistake, no doubt. Yet I could not perceive it. The exasperating thing was that I repeatedly felt just about to do so, when it slipped from the clutch of my thought and eluded me. To see more clearly, I marked the first three lines (1), and the second three (2). It would be some ridiculous little error that a child on land could detect; but it was not among the stock ideas of the routine associative thinking I had trained myself to; a new idea must be conceived in the brain to trace it, and the brain utterly refused to conceive that idea. Whether the vibration kept it in a state of oscillation so that no new thought could form, whether the hurricane of wind playing on my head dulled it, or the roar of the motor, or my weariness, or the salt air, I did not know. At last a glance at the clock drove me on, the delay was crowding me for time. I used my own judgment as to the wind, basing it on previous observations.

---

1   See photograph of Norfolk Island to Lord Howe Island flight chart, with the description of the navigation, at end, reprinted from the R.A.F. training magazine "Tee Emm" (August 1944) by courtesy of the editor.

I decided the plane had covered 83 miles in the hour, for 11 of which the wind was responsible.

2 hours 10 minutes out.

190 miles flown.

Glancing down, it was as if a pailful of icy-cold water had been thrown suddenly over my head—I received such a shock. The whole compass was loose in its bed and had turned from the lubber-line until the plane was now on a course that would have taken it some three hundred miles to the north of Lord Howe Island. The vibration had rattled the screws out. I twisted it back to the lubber-line and rammed wads of paper down the side to keep it in place. Held tight by these, it was now subjected to the full force of the vibration and the needle shivered violently on its pivot. That, too, would presently break. I felt with anxious fingers for the pocket-compass in my belt. Thank heaven I had not left that behind! Then the idea of finding Lord Howe Island with a loose miniature pocket-compass in hand made me smile; but the smile only made me feel that my lips were without "give". That scare had jolted me—the plane was beginning to break up.

But presently I rose to the surface of my fear again, spitting it out, as it were, and throwing it off. And was left feeling hungry. Well, let us eat, drink and be merry . . .

I worked a fat tin of pineapple from the front cockpit through the hole cut in the back of the seat and scarcely large enough to let the tin through. My mouth watered as the top curled away from the opener. I drank the juice with unparalleled zest, laughing aloud after it. Nectar for the gods! I cut the round slices across and across with my big sheath-knife, eating the chunks with a pair of dividers. By heavens! it was good! I threw the tin overboard and watched its smooth, backward, curved drop, turning and twinkling, down, down, down . . .

I found myself even more pressed for time. I had to hurry with the drift observations to be in time for transmitting at half-past the hour and I hurried with the wireless to finish with the compass-swinging sextant work. But I could see it was impossible to catch up with my tasks: I decided to abandon the hour's second set of drift observations and calculate wind-speed from those of the first set only. Even so, I only just finished estimating the hour's run—making it 74 miles, and the total 264 miles—in time for the sextant shot. Looking at the dashboard altimeter preparatory to reading it at the time of observation, I found its pointer travelling round the dial in endless jerks like a full-size second hand on a clock face. It turned evenly and steadily clockwise. The propeller revolved anti-clockwise. It looked as if that was the source of the vibration which had broken it loose. I was thrown into an abyss of depression. Wireless broken, speed-indicator broken, compass broken, both altimeters broken. How long could the machine stand this strain? It was breaking up . . . breaking . . . breaking up . . . But as for that pig of an altimeter, it had always tried to fix me. And now I must have the altitude for sextant work. Well, it shouldn't get the better of me. I'd judge the height for myself. It had waited too long before breaking—my eye had become practised in telling the height above water.

I secured three sights with the sun just behind the starboard wing-tip; I took them without changing course, the horizon was clear and hard—I felt they were good ones, and obtained clear satisfaction at the thought of my work being good. The plane might be breaking up—I could not prevent that; but if I could carry out my own work efficiently, I felt I could bear the thought more hardily; I felt that somehow I might still be the winner in spite of it.

The mean of the heights I judged to be 450 feet; the mean of the times, 22½ seconds past the time calculated for, but I made an adjustment to bring that back. I had the maths, completed by 3 hours 20 minutes "out", so decided to make another observation. It would be a check in view of having to guess the height. I made three more shots and completed the working independently of the first. The results showed the plane to be 25 miles south of where I thought. In the distance flown of 264 miles, this represented a compass deviation of about 5°. I altered course 5° to the right in consequence and then a further 10° to make good the 25 miles of leeway. The plane was actually headed 20° to the right of Lord Howe Island.

I only just finished these calculations in time to send a wireless at half-past, so was again forced to cut out the drift observations. I ignored the probability of the wireless being out of action, and gave position by sextant as well as position by dead-reckoning. From transmitting, I turned to drift observation in haste, and then to plotting the hour's flight. I slowed the motor a few revolutions; it eased the vibration—at least, so I imagined. The wind had backed with sudden rapidity: it was now almost from the north, and the hour's flight totalled only 73 miles.

4 hours 10 minutes out.

337 miles flown.

The wind had already backed enough to throw the plane 10° off course the other way, *to the left*. If it backed any further, it would mean beating into a head wind. And with the plane's speed cut down, and with only 5½ hours' petrol left, beating into a head wind meant . . .

At least, the weather was still good. The sun, in front of the right wing-tip, still shone in a cloudless sky, casting the top wing's shadow on to half the lower wing surface. And the sea, with purple tint hinting at its profound depth, was yet all of flashing facets to the limit of sight, an unceasing sparkle, ever changing, always the same.

Yet the sunlight looked somehow weaker.

I wrote in my logbook, "Expect propeller or structure break up any moment." Also, the vibration was making it hard for me to think, increased the difficulty of grasping the significance of events, and caused every operation to take longer. I was feeling rushed and that was a danger to the efficiency of my own work. With a brain so slow to take in new ideas, I must have enough time to perceive mistakes. It was no use working out drift to a mile if I left the compass pointing 30° away from the course at the end of the observation. I must sweep all detail work from my brain and give it a chance to perceive any such error. Time! time! time! I must have time! I rushed through the drift observation, plotted the results, worked out the whole hour's flight, all in the first half-hour of it; and dashed off the wireless at my fastest speed:

"CQ de KK AAA Position by DR at 1200 hours GMT 29° 23′ South 166° 03′ East AAA Fine weather wind 19 mph from 85 degrees true AAA AR."

I had now twenty minutes of the hour remaining. I took several deep breaths and relaxed, letting my thoughts dawdle.

"Compass—was it set right? Let's see—direct bearing of Lord Howe Island from Norfolk Island 251½°; add the 10° aimed to the right for sextant navigation purposes; add another 10° drift correction; another 4° for compass deviation; subtract 11½° for magnetic variation—net-result 264°. Compass all right—until it breaks finally. This vibration . . . devilish hard to think . . . if the propeller breaks . . . h'm . . . if only I had the rubber boat . . . what's the time? Nearly 5 hours out—ought to reach turn-off point 6 hours out. Must get position-line from the sun at end of this hour. Too much work—brain feels ready to sweat blood."

In the distance ahead, I could see a line of gathered clouds—long, low and white, like scrolls of parchment suspended in the sky. That did not disquiet me at the time; it was exceptional to fly as far as I had without any cloud. And the wind had veered again to N.E. by N., which was good. Yet the sea had a checked appearance, like a restive horse only letting itself be held back while making up its mind which way to break. The S.E. swell was now nearly countered, its surface all broken up, leaping to toss crests to white foam, subsiding to leave patches of white water.

I spurred myself away from contemplation of it to concentrate on a position-line sight.

5 hours 10 minutes out.

417 miles flown.

I secured three observations. Leaning well back, I worked with the sun across and above the right wing, the horizon below it in the wing bay. I proceeded immediately with the mathematics. I had to read the telescoping slide-rule sideways, as, pulled right out, there was not otherwise room for it in the cockpit.

The result showed the plane to be 26 miles short of where I had estimated. Suddenly there was brought, home to me the possibility of mistakes and their consequences. Possibility—no, probability rather—the dim spectres of every mistake I had ever made paraded through my brain—I always had made mistakes, copying figures down wrong, or subtracting wrong, or adding wrong.

I remembered the strut speed-indicator; it over-registered four or five miles an hour. How stupid of me to forget it! So now, I had only flown 391 miles instead of 417. But had I forgotten it? I thought I had allowed for the error in the speed-indicator each time I read it—I had meant to anyway. Was the sextant wrong? Certainly an error somewhere. Dead-reckoning made it 74 miles from the turn-off point, sextant made 100. Which was wrong? I could not tell until the end of the hour. I could only wait till then. But I must make an absolute certainty of the shot when the time came. It must be decisive and precise. I must force the working to be without mistake. I went over again the work already done for it. Further, there must on no account be any delay.

The plane had flown under a scattering of voluminous white clouds, with edges turned in like rolls of parchment. Well . . . but looking ahead, I found pieces of the horizon cut out by dark grey rain clouds; they squatted on the sea surface like shapeless fungus on top of a log. Bad weather! My God! that was too much. I suddenly felt emptied of all courage; I touched the utter depth of cowardliness. I was so terribly helpless, totally unable to lift a finger to keep off the death I could see inexorably closing in on me. Wireless gone, compass, instruments breaking one by one, navigation 26 miles out somewhere—perhaps double as much, plane gradually breaking up, propeller so strained by its out-of-true wobbling that it was bound to collapse sooner or later—it was only a case of time, and now, my God! bad weather.

I turned to the wireless transmitting; useless it might be, but as a routine act to which I was accustomed, it seemed the only thing I could lean on; it gave me support like an old friend.

Before the end of the message, the plane struck rain; its stinging cold chilled the outside of me—but not as much as it froze me inside.

Emerging from it, I found the sky with an aspect of oppressive weight, and though the sun still shone through the cloud gaps, the water had lost its sparkle, only glistening in patches on an otherwise dulled surface. Streaking the space between clouds and ocean were now many slanting columns of rainfall from leaden cloud bellies to grey blotches of sea; I hurried through my drift observations and plotted in the hour's flight. Halfway through the work, I noticed the slanting pillars of rainfall were now squat and many, whilst those of sunlight were only, slender and few. I made sure there were still one or two sun-shafts ahead—otherwise I must use the sextant at once—and continued the drift plotting. I found the wind had backed right round to west of north. So now the plane must begin to beat into a head wind. I glanced up at the petrol-tank—3½ hours' left. At the end of the hour the position should be:

6 hours 10 minutes out.

Miles flown 491 or 464, I could not tell which till the next shot.

Looking up, I found that the sunlight, which I had made sure of being ahead only a few minutes ago, and which I depended on for the sight, had all disappeared. I peered round—there was none to be seen. Only a low cloud ceiling with rain squalls bulging from it, and threatening to form a solid mass to fill the whole sky. I looked behind. There was none there, even. The cloud openings had everywhere shut against me. I could not get the sight. I could not tell where I was. "Steady!" I said aloud, "take it quietly! Don't get excited!" At this moment, the plane flew against a rain squall. The heavy drops struck my forehead, stinging like hail. I was chilled to the bone, desperately helpless: to be flown into heavy rain, and cut off as by a grey curtain, hanging intangible yet impenetrable, from sight of sun, of the island, even of empty space. But the squall only covered perhaps a mile, and breaking through the far side, I found a patch of wintry sunlight lying away to the right. It scarcely seemed real; indeed, in that rain squall I seemed to have flown out of touch with ordinary existence. Both sky and sea had now a scurrying air as if fleeting in a dream. I swung the plane away from its course and set off in chase through spits of rain, the plane now labouring dead into wind. The sunlight, which had appeared close enough at the start, seemed to keep its distance. Fearful that it, too, would disappear before I could reach it, I increased speed and sat tense all over—even ear drums stretched tight by some jaw movement—waiting for the explosion of propeller flying to bits and the runaway roar of the motor. Gradually, I relaxed as nothing happened.

The plane seemed scarcely to draw any nearer to the sunlit edge. Suddenly, I perceived the reason—the patch of sunlight was moving away as fast as the plane approached. Impossible! How could it move against the wind? I must be suffering from a delusion. I could soon test that. I looked down, fixed my eye on a wave touched by the edge of the sunlight, and watched it. Jupiter! there was no mistake: the sunlight was gliding away into wind and at racing speed. The plane was now on the edge—but there it stayed. Cloud must be forming above at a furious rate. Amazed and agitated, I found the plane was not now gaining at all, could only just hold its position, flying beside a ghostly cliff where the beginning of sunlight lighted the end of rainfall.

I must have that sunlight! Thought of the rickety old plane and of everything else was blotted out; I thrust open the throttle wide, leaping for it madly as a stranded fish leaps for its life-giving water. Several times I had a glimpse at the cloud edge. At last I thought the plane in position and turned sharply to secure the sight broadside on. But as I lifted the sextant, the shadow raced over the plane and on again. Angrily, I turned about and renewed the chase at full speed. Nothing else in the world counted. I adjusted the sextant to a rough guess of the angle between the sun and horizon, then held it ready. I inclined the plane seawards, the speed rising steadily till the wind made a shrill note in the rigging. How it was standing the strain, heaven only knew. I turned with a vertical bank, and had a single shot while still in the turn, pulling the plane out of a crashing dive just above the surface. The next instant it was in dullness and rain; I flew on westwards. The observation was minutes late but I corrected it for time from the altitude-latitude-azimuth table. I quickly made allowance for estimated height above the sea, sextant index error, for sun's semi-diameter, and compared the result with the calculations done in readiness. It said the plane was 21 miles short of the line down which it must turn.

Now the sea was dark, and the grey of rain-sodden clouds was subtly changing to the blue-black of impending storm. The wind was rising fast and the S.E. swell below overrun by a stronger from the opposite quarter of the compass. The waves leaped up angrily and lashed sheets of spray southwards.

I flew on: helpless, hopeless—in the first sextant work at least one error, perhaps several. And what trust could I put in that last miserable observation, only one sketchy shot with the plane mid-way between vertical bank and crashing dive, worked with brain dulled from hours of shaking rattle, clogged with fatigue? And I could do no more to find my position—there was no more sun. The very sky seemed to be lowering on me to force me down. Fifteen minutes had passed since the last sight. I turned S.S.W. There was nothing else I could do.

The clouds were becoming darker, heavier, lowering. The plane was scudding over the rising, roughening seas at great pace, with the wind nearly behind. The drift of 15° showed the alarming, rapid increase in force. The very fact that clouds spilling rain were now fewer seemed an added threat. They were massing above and presently the storm would burst to complete my desolation, so that if I passed within a stone's throw of the island, I should catch no sight of it through the downpour. What a hopeless task, flying over mid-ocean between two specks of land; as hopeless as if I were flying through space from planet to tiny planet, lost control of direction and were shot away into nothingness.

Dully, I stared at every sullen low-lying cloud on the horizon, each a possible concealment of the island: and slowly traversed the stormy ceiling in vain search for a glimpse of the sun.

At last I gave up all hope.

Almost at once a break appeared in the clouds dead ahead arid sunrays shone down. I opened the throttle and raced for it, leaning slightly forward, too intent to feel grateful. I secured three sights while crossing the lake of sunlight. Deafened by the incessant roar, nerves burning with slow fire under my skin through the endless shaking vibration or because of the strain of it, brain doped with fatigue, I laboured heavily with figure after figure, not using any of the data employed in the previous sight, but working the whole entirely afresh. The result gave the island dead ahead. And when I comprehended it, I was exalted with confidence. Of course the island was dead ahead, of course my navigation would take me to it—hadn't I schemed and planned and plotted for months to make sure there was no flaw in my system—hadn't I tabulated every error in every observation and altered the system time after time to make it infallible? I had done my work; it was good; the island was there ahead. I closed up the sextant and stowed away all the instruments.

Looking over the side at the tumult of waters, crests torn off in showers of spray, I found the drift had increased to 20°. A 40-mile wind! But it was the rapid change in the force which caused the greatest anxiety. And the whole sky menacing. What did it mean? What had I struck?

As though hunting a ship with a searchlight, I unceasingly swept the sea to and fro, to and fro. Where low cloud cut off the horizon from sight, it was difficult to tell the visibility. 6 hours 35 minutes out. Where was the island? Minute after minute dragged, itself by. 6 hours 40 minutes. Had I miscalculated? An error in my chart or in the reading of it? A mistake recurring in the sextant work? A defective compass? My God! I had always made mistakes; 100 miles—140 miles of error. I had none of the feelings of a hunter, only of the hunted, twisting my head from side to side as though in search of escape. Escape from this helplessness. I glanced at the petrol-tank—2¾ hours' petrol left. What a terrible weight the atmosphere seemed, or was it the silence of a bad dream in all this desolation of space between grey sea and dark ceiling? Here and there, heavier blue-black clouds were dropping on to the water surface; squalls with their hearts thinly concealed in purple haze, were massing all round the horizon to hem me in. I looked over and found the drift had increased again, was now nearly 25°. A gale! What had I struck? 6 hours 50 minutes. I had missed it! My blood turned to water and ceased to flow. I was bitterly excluded from life, without help, without hope. I had not even a boat. I never realized before what safety it seemed to offer. The plane would not last five minutes in that sea. 2¾ hours' petrol left. It was the utter inability to help myself that bred terror. My brain was numb, and refused to work. What could I do? I must decide on a course of action. I must force my brain to work. If I once let myself get into a panic, I was done. 2¾ hours . . . 2¾ hours . . . very well, on for half an hour, then west for half an hour, then north till the end . . . That last splutter of the motor, the final glide with empty beat of propeller.

I felt a rush of heat through me. Away to port—a long island in purple haze? Hope fired up while I stared. No, curse it! It changed shape! A black, lowering cloud. The flame of hope died out and I sank back again into the depths of depression. Still 6 hours 50 minutes. The clock had broken now! Supposing my watch had been two minutes out all the time, making an error of 30 miles—the discrepancy between sextant and dead-reckoning! 30 miles' distance from the island in this storm . . . as well be 300. The hand had passed 6 hours 50 minutes; the clock could not be broken after all.

With another hot surge of hope through me, I looked to port and found a long line of black cliff, land behind, rising—the top hidden in cloud . . . It lost its outline. Oh hell! a distant squall. It was as though first hot and then freezing water were dashed over me. 6 hours 53 minutes. How incredibly weary I felt. Why could I not just fly on and on for hours and hours with nothing to do but fly? Well, I was tired of worrying. What was the good of it? If I'd failed, I'd failed. And as for that, did it really matter one way or the other? How intolerably stupid to worry about the future—about something one could not control! I would eat something, I thought; at least that could give some sort of tangible pleasure in the present.

I was stretching out my hand to feel what there was, when distinct clean-cut land showed ahead, a few degrees to the left. It stabbed the air like a broad, primeval dagger of grey stone thrust through the surface. Land! My God! Land!! A hot flood of triumph and excitement swept irresistibly through me. I drew in breath till my lungs were tight stretched as if to hold out against the rush of excitement and to prevent myself from smashing things. But what a triumph! Ha! ha!, this was no debatable verdict on a work of art or judgment—it was decisive success of co-ordinated brain work and science. There it stood—the sign of my scheme's success— unquestionable—small, that blade of land in this vast space of desolation—but pointing to an incontestable triumph. Ha! ha! ha! Well, I never had had any doubt about finding it if the plane held together. Jupiter! how easy. I knew all along that the island's position must be wrong before mine could be. Ha! ha! ha! Roll out, ye wireless waves, and tell the skies.

"CQ de KK AAA Land-O right ahead AAA Not the least like my concm ... (erase) ... concp ... (erase) ... conceps ... (erase) ... conception of Lord Howe Island but no other land within 400 miles so must be it AAA Right in great storm AAA Last Signal AAA AR."

That this was literally the last signal the wireless set would ever make, I did not know.

I subsided in the cockpit in a torpor of weariness.

Great Scott! what's that? A vast side of black like some distorted whale in a nightmare showed vaguely broadside on, under dense shrouding cloud as though some foul vapour brooded over it. I stared, and felt that my eyes were starting from my head. That was land under the lifting cloud! Huge black bulk of it. Enormous. Australia! Steady, steady! No panic! How could it be? Australia is 500 miles away ... It looks a continent. Yes, but let me be reasonable—it's because I'm right alongside it. By Jupiter! Lord Howe Island! Good God! to think I had not seen it till right alongside. No wonder that grey land seemed so small—Ball's Pyramid, the solitary rock twelve miles beyond Lord Howe Island, and only a quarter-mile wide!

I swung round and headed for the middle of the island. I sat back in the cockpit, my brain again a blank except for a few idle reflections. I laughed to think how always I had planned to go and photograph the Pyramid before alighting at Lord Howe. As if I cared two straws for all the photographs in the world!

Looking up again, I found the plane was headed for the open sea past the south end of the island. By Jupiter! this was a storm to blow the plane off its course like that in a mere minute or two!

Again I stirred myself from my lethargy to concentrate on the task in hand: the plane beat into the teeth of the wind, seeming to crawl at a snail's pace. I recalled the warning of the Admiralty, sailing directions, that ships passing within a mile and a half of the island during a north-wester, ran the risk of being dismasted by the violent squalls of wind. I fastened the safety-belt; even that was a weariness to the flesh now.

The actual sight of the island close up gave me a great surprise. How many times had I visualized it, imagined, pictured it from constant study of the fascinating chart. But now I could see no resemblance to a Cupid's bow in its shape. It looked so huge, seen close to, compared to its littleness on the chart. Where I had pictured smooth, close-cropped pasture sloping up the sides of Lidgbird and Gower, and their tops a pleasant wood, I found myself flying at twin black trunks of mountains which rose straight from the sea floor; all but their very base thrust into a heavy roll of dark cloud—I could fancy it growling and muttering, angrily. For a few yards above the line of surf thundering at their base, solidly packed palm trees jostled each other for root-hold on the mountain side. Above these, the bare rock face rose almost sheer till lost to view in the vaporous cloud. To the right of the northernmost mountain, Lidgbird, I saw the flat of the island. This I had pictured a rolling pasture, a setting for a farmhouse or two, each with a ring of detached shepherd-huts. I was astonished to find solid, dark-green, tropical foliage and a sea of palm trees. Palms! they upset my whole idea of the island—sprinkling the land below like innumerable stars of gunshot on green glass. As for the close-cropped pastures where I had fancied stalking rabbits, nothing could be more foreign to such an idea than the few cleared patches of vivid, exotic dark green tightly squeezed against the packed trees. Only the lagoon lived up to its name, stretched below with tropical generosity of colour: vivid light blue or bright green, inlaid with patches of sand on the bottom, startling in whiteness where unmarred by coral or marine growth.

I decided to cruise around and pick the best place for alighting. But at that instant, with a whizz of air, the plane was suddenly hurled vertically downwards at the lagoon. Camera, sextant, protractors, pencils and chart flurried round my head like a whirl of autumn leaves. Only the safety-belt held me in the plane, though I clutched frantically at control-stick with one hand, and instrument-board with the other. At the bottom of several hundred feet, the plane fetched up with a bump that jarred me back into the cockpit seat. "Whew!" I thought, passing my hand over my forehead, "how the plane survived that without the wings being torn off, passes my comprehension! Cruise round the lagoon? Not likely!" Right there and now, I was going to alight. I dived straight down, only taking one glimpse at the water ahead for obstructions. The distance between crest and trough of the waves showed me there was depth enough; yet, at the last moment I thought I must have made a mistake and that not an inch covered the vividly shown lagoon bottom. I jibbed, but the thought of another bump brought me to my senses in a fraction of a second and the throttle was shut again almost at the same instant. *Elijah* plopped down on the surface like a duck and at once began drifting backwards at a great pace. I jumped up, freed the anchor from the tangle of gear in the front cockpit, and heaved it overboard. As soon as it "took", the line wrenched at my arms and nearly tugged me overboard. I clung to a float-strut with one hand while the line scoured through the other, until I could get a turn round the mooring-ring. Then the anchor ripped and jerked along the lagoon bed, only the two fathom of steel cable that I had fastened on saving the rope from being cut instantaneously by the coral snags.

Lord Howe Island, taken from *Elijah* looking south on a fine day. Compare this photograph with the chart of the island. The white patches of surf behind Goat Island on the right are the coral reefs, the most southernmost living coral in the world. Note the shark fishers' hut on Goat Island.

Cloud-capped Mts. Lidgbird and Gower with Goat Island on the right, where the shark fishers' hut can be seen.

Chapter IX

TO CHARYBDIS

I was relieved to see a launch making for me, its bow throwing off twin white waves. A second followed and they began circling the plane. The men and women aboard stared as if a live specimen of the dodo had been found, and I were it. Hands to mouth, I bellowed into the gale: "Where's the best place to moor?" They waved handkerchiefs, pointed blind camera-eyes, and all shouted at once. My testiness became edged. I roared the same question again and again. At last it dawned on them that I sought an answer and was not just buzzing with pleasure at their welcome. Every voice gave tongue at the same moment. Some of their words came on the wind, most died before reaching me. There was only one man, sturdy, short, thick-set and powerful-looking, whom I could hear. Yet, where they shouted, he seemed to be only talking. I had to concentrate on him, though chary of such a loud-speaker's opinion. But I gradually found he was interested without being excited, and confidence in him took root.

It was decided I should moor in the boat-pool, a hole of deeper water. I asked him to tow me there. "Why not move across under your own power?" he demanded. I shouted that the plane would be blown over immediately in this wind if I taxied across it. He said nothing to that, but I fancied he thought my explanation old-maidish. However, he picked up the anchor-line and began towing aslant the wind. I crouched on the motor-cowling and braced myself against the top wing petrol-tank. I was in very low spirits and jaundiced with apprehension at mooring out in a storm;

firstly, I had no experience of it; and secondly, I thought of the countless mooring accidents related to me by seaplane pilots. But what else could I do save moor out? I could not get the plane ashore, and even if that were possible, there was no shelter on the island.

Halfway across to the boat-pool, a gust of wind caught underneath the port wing. The plane began to mount in the air on the other wing-tip preparatory to smacking over on its back like a book cover. I was off the cowling on to the wing-root in an instant and ran out on my toes along the narrow spar of the wing. My weight at the end brought it down again.

The boat-pool lay in a corner between the flat of the island and a steep hill with thick scrubby vegetation growing right down to the water's edge.

The plane was moored by stout ropes to two great anchors, while the other launch travelled round in circles and the man directing it—he had a touch of ginger in his moustache, a suspicion of freckles and a suggestion of red hair—pointed a camera—though it was nearly dark—at each circuit. I thought, as I struggled with the wildly flapping cockpit covers: "Of course, it's a jolly fine picnic for you, my friend!" But personally I felt isolated; having to make contact with so many people who wanted a share in the fun while the difficulties seemed to remain exclusively my own property. A violent gust swept down on to *Elijah*. The rush of wind gave the wing enough "lift" to make the plane air-borne. Though weighing three-quarters of a ton, and moored to two anchors, she pig-jumped clean out of the water under me. "What could you do if I were against you?" the gust seemed to say, and any pride in performance that remained with me shrivelled like a piece of orange peel thrown into a fire.

By the time the launch disembarked me on the little wooden jetty, night had fallen. I had arrived none too soon, though, curiously enough, I had never once during the flight considered the risk of being caught by dark. One P. J. Dignam, in charge of my petrol supply, was waiting for me; he asked me when I was leaving this island, what time I had left the last island, and a string of similar questions. For the life of me I couldn't remember what time I had left Norfolk Island. Nor later, did I remember snapping at him: "Don't ask so many questions!" as he declared I did. But the fact was I had seldom worked at a greater mental pressure for a period of eight hours less twenty minutes than during that flight.

He invited me to his house; I gladly accepted and walked along beside him, absorbed in my problem. What more could I do to safeguard the plane? Perhaps if I stayed on board it all night? No! It might serve no purpose and would certainly result in a poor sort of flying next day. No, ocean flying definitely entitled a man to some sleep the night before. I thought of asking someone else to stand by, but did not like to suggest it on such a night; and in any case, a man who had never seen a plane before might be only another potential danger hanging on to a seaplane in a storm. There was nothing I could do, I finally decided, the plane must take its chance.

After a meal, P. J. Dignam took me off to fix up my mail. Between his house and the road, the long, slender young palm leaves brushed their edges across my face. On the island highway, wide enough for a single horse and sledge, my soft shoes padded along on the sand, and the low-slung lantern threw grotesque leg shadows before us, cast its ghostly glimmer on tree trunks or palm stems. At first it was dead calm—and sometimes I could distinguish a palm tree's crest like a bundle of sword blades hung above. But we had not walked more than a few yards when the tree tops sprang to life with a sigh which instantly changed to a roar as the foliage was tortured by a furiously turbulent whirl of wind. P. J. Dignam informed me he had seen water snatched off one end of the lagoon and thrown back at the other, four miles on . . .

I delivered my mail at the little tin-shed Post Office, through mail for Australia was stamped and a mailbag prepared for more. On return I pleaded weariness and went to bed.

For a while I read, trying to obliterate the throb of the motor pulsating in my head. At last I dropped into a fitful sleep, only to awake in terror to find myself drawing back from the path of an express train which. I thought had rushed for me at full speed. But it was only a blast of wind furiously flogging the tree tops. While the squall lasted, I lay tense on the bed, as anxious for my plane as I might be for a delicate favourite child exposed to a storm. An uncanny silence, followed—a deathly stillness—and I fell asleep again. This time I dreamed that a tornado had swept every tree from the island, and that palms, scrub, bush and seaplane all disappeared over the horizon in a black cloud of whirling confusion and left the island as bare as a bald man's shiny skull; only a few humans left crawling about its stark dome. For a second, when I awoke and heard the gale thrashing the trees, I believed the dream. As the night wore on, thoughts became dreams, and dreams thoughts. When awake my brain held fantastic, nightmarish things, whereas when asleep phrases from the Admiralty sailing directions kept running through my head. "When north-east and easterly gales blow . . . anchorage on west side unsafe . . . squalls come down with violence. During winter months anchorage only to be used with steam ready at short notice . . . Sudden and violent shifting gales . . . Caution—squalls—sailing ships run a risk of being dismasted . . . gusts come down from the mountains with great violence . . . alternating with dead calm . . ." At about six o'clock the most violent squall of all awoke me thoroughly. I expected the roof of the house to be stripped off at any moment and pictured the palms bent double with their tops turned inside out and lashed with fury by the mad gale. "Nothing can stand that," I thought. I lay awhile longer in the darkness, and then got up, feeling as if my very bones had known no rest for a week. I dressed in the dark and went to call young Dignam, but found him already awake. I asked him to take me up to the plane, and we moved off under a heavy grey sky of dawn. At the moment, as if the storm had spent itself in that last fierce blast, there was not a whisper of wind.

On passing from under the trees, a stretch of water lay before us, fetching up against a steep black hill.

"Isn't that where we moored the plane?" I asked him.

"Yes!"

"I don't see her," I remarked, trying to penetrate the dull gloom of dawn, straining my eyes to discern the surface scarcely yet disclosed by day.

We continued walking.

"Ah, there she is!" I exclaimed; but yet not certain.

When a little closer, I added: "She looks queer to me."

"She looks queer to me, too," said Dignam.

I could not make out why she did look queer; however, day was breaking fast.

"Sunk!" I said, yet not believing it myself.

We walked on; I could have sworn I carried sixteen stone, of weight, rather than eleven.

At last we could see clearly; like a big fish diving into the water, only the tail of the plane slanted above the surface; and the float-tails, like those of two young fish diving with their dame. Upside down!

We dragged out a boat and rowed across. It was cold and bleak. Again I felt divided into two personalities; one, numb by reason of a heavy weight pressing it down, and the other, a dispassionate observer of the damage. Every thing but the tail and float-heels under water; except that a bigger wave brought the bottom wings (now the top) to show soggily at the surface. The ailerons, had already gone soft, were now twisting and writhing with the movement of the water surface. The sunk wings must be a colossal dead weight, and would soon follow suit. I went round in the boat, slitting the bellies of the fabric between ribs to let the water in and out with the least resistance. I took a certain pleasure in making a job of it; the fabric tore open with a harsh rip.

"Queer", I remarked, "how that storm only blew up an hour before I arrived and ended immediately the plane was wrecked. Do you often have them?"

"That's the first for months," replied my companion.

"It's amusing that the only parts undamaged and which will be of any use again," I remarked, "are those that don't belong to me—the floats. Oh, well, 'Bang goes saxpence,' as they say. Let's go and have some breakfast—I feel devilish hungry."

We rowed ashore from the boat-pool under the hill with the

scrubby trees overhanging the water. Was one a withered fig tree? It would complete the suggestion that *Elijah* had only escaped the rock of Scylla to fall a victim to the dreaded pool of Charybdis.

I balanced precariously, fixing ropes to the tail and other parts.

Chapter X

SALVAGE

On return, Mrs. Dignam, whom everyone (seemed to call "Auntie", produced a feast of boiled salmon and kumeras (sweet potatoes) which would have made an epicure's tongue melt.

"How is the plane, Captin?" she asked. "Done for?"

"Completely, except for the floats," I replied, unable to decide whether the fish was more delectable than the kumeras or vice versa.

"Oh, dear, dear, dear! What a shame! And I did so want to see it rise from the water. Have some more fish, Captin?"

After breakfast, young Dignam rallied a salvage party. I think I only coaxed myself into it by promise of a sleep for seven days and seven nights afterwards. Everybody else, though, seemed as keen to help me as hounds to hunt, and three launches put off to the wreck. For the next hour or two I balanced precariously on the plane, fixing ropes to various portions of it. It depended on where I was fixing the rope whether I was standing ankle deep, knee deep, or waist deep in the water. Sometimes I crawled up the bottom of the fuselage on hands and knees like a fireman seen in pictures rescuing a cat. Gusts of wind spat rain and spray into my face when least desired. The plane was now bumping upside down on the bottom and my scheme was to right it by pulling the tail over the nose. In theory this seemed childishly simple to do, yet each time a brace of launches made fast by a rope to the tail churned up the water to pull the tail over, it slued round either to one side or the other, but never came over the top as required. We paid out a very long rope to the hillside, trying to exert a steadier pull on the tail, but still it refused to do anything but swivel in a most exasperating manner. Finally, they broke a stout rope on it. How it could stand such a strain without breaking in half was a mystery to me; since it was only made of three-ply wooden skin covering a slender frame in which the thickest piece was no more than an inch square of spruce. In the end we towed it by the tail, bumping and dragging along the bottom, as far inshore as possible, and there left it till it could be approached from the land at low tide.

On our return we found it lay on greenish slimy mud in which one's feet were apt to slide away unexpectedly. A few shallow little craters, with pure sand in the bottom, pock-marked the mud, but to my surprise there was no coral there; even so, the wings looked as if they had been crushed through a mangle.

She lay on greenish slimy mud.

A quarter of the island's total population of one hundred and twenty were splashing through the inch or two of water round the plane. And, by Jove, they were efficient! I expected men who had never seen an aeroplane before to feel bamboozled if asked to unscrew rigging-wire turnbuckles, and wing-root bolts, or slack

Finally we towed her into the Boat Pool and left her till the tide was out.

128

away control-cables and air-speed indicator tubes. Not they! Whether the enthusiastic audience of three girls, in shorts and thin jerseys—which adequately failed to conceal the fact of their possessing remarkably handsome figures—had any effect, I do not know; but it was the quickest salvage job I ever conducted. Like ants, one stream of people carried pieces to the shore, whilst another returned empty-handed. The plane was dismantled in twenty minutes, and the only parts lost were some shackle-pins that I myself pocketed previous to discovering the hole in my borrowed shorts. We rolled the carcase, stripped of wings, on to its side, and then righted it with floats on the mud, when it was led round the shore by a party splashing knee deep through the water and near the jetty, swearing vehemently every time they kicked a piece of coral with their bare feet. The rest of us finished dumping the bits and pieces in the old boat-shed under the ancient and tired great banyan tree which, by dropping roots to the ground at intervals along every low branch, gave the impression of being only kept from falling by countless props.

I went round to the jetty to dismantle the motor. Many parts of it ought to fetch something if salvaged quickly before the salt water ate into the aluminium. Standing in water up to knees or waist, some islanders held the floats in position with the motor under the hook of a fixed hand-winch, while I worked with numb hands to unfix petrol, oil, electric, throttle and other connections between motor and fuselage, previous to securing two wire ropes under its paunch. Gusts of wind tried to snatch the tail round, waves tried to wrench the floats away, showers of rain and spray drove at their faces: it might have been a large, flopping shark not sufficiently gassed that they were trying to hold while I operated with pincers, pliers, and spanners to extract its teeth. The rest of the carcase we carried up bodily and dumped behind the cargo shed.

Two men, one of whom, Kirby, with ginger moustache and reddish tinge to the hair, was my photographic friend of the day before, helped me to dismantle the motor and strew a hundred parts about the cargo-shed floor. It was as good as a conjuring trick, the way everything we touched could produce sea-water from its interior.

As I went off to bed that night, Phil Dignam asked me: "What are you going to do about the plane, Skipper?"

"I suppose I must take it all to pieces, save everything salable, and remove the relics when the boat calls."

I felt depressed. In the first place because I had failed; in the second place because I had a secret feeling of resignation over the wreck which was suspiciously like relief and made me despise myself for harbouring it; and thirdly because I knew I should now have the flight hanging over my head for perhaps years, until I could take another shot at it.

Next morning, I dragged up to the cargo shed, where Kirby and a visitor named Keith helped me continue dismantling the motor. It was astounding with what zest they attacked that engine and scattered it in a thousand pieces till the cargo shed was covered from side to side with nuts, bolts, screws, washers, pins, valves, tubes, plugs, pistons, tappets, magnetos and all the other different parts.

A quarter of the island's total population, with amazing. efficiency, dismantled *Elijah* in 20 minutes.

It submitted to being pulled to bits till we reached the crankcase. This resisted every effort, although only the last few threads of a bolt or two prevented it from coming away. The fact is, that before this crankcase could part from the rest of the motor, the propeller-boss had to be drawn off the propeller-shaft. To do this required a special tool; and with it the job would have been finished in a few minutes. Here, however, with no motor cars on the island, and consequently no tools except those for one or two motor launches, it was quite a different question. By Jove! how we did get worked up about that crankcase, each man giving vent heatedly, in rising tone of voice, to his own pet theory for getting it off, punctuating his hot arguments with periodical blows on the propeller-shaft with a sledge-hammer. In the end, Kirby, whose moustache bristled in a way that made me suspect that he never needed much to urge him into battle when a boy, stalked away because we two scoffed at his particular theory. I said to Keith: "Let's leave it for an hour or two, when another way to attack it will occur to us."

However, presently, who should stride in again but Kirby; holding an apparatus which consisted of two iron strips linked by long bolts. He had made it himself to fit the propeller-shaft (and his theory). Keith and I watched in silence as he drew off the propeller-boss and freed the crankcase. Instead of sharing his patent joy at the triumph, I found myself irritated—with absolute unreason and ingratitude—and then grew more irritated at the thought that I was irritated. As for the crankcase, a gallon or so of Pacific Ocean ran out of it.

"Now," I said, "I vote we knock off; there does not appear to be anything likely to suffer damage if left till to-morrow."

"You ought to polish those dirty valve seatings and clean the carbon off the cylinder-heads," said Kirby.

"But they won't hurt now, if left for a few days," I objected.

"I think you ought to finish the job thoroughly, once you have started it."

"No fear!" I replied, "it's against my principles as a member of the Ocean Flyers' Union."

"All right," he said, "then give them to me and I'll do them," and with that he strode off, carrying a sackful of pistons and valves; while I went to buy some tobacco, still more irritated at being made to feel a slovenly workman. I failed to buy any tobacco, because the island had run out of it and would not have a fresh supply till the boat returned from Sydney a month later.

All the time, thought of my failure was biting deep into me.

After starting off for Sydney by aeroplane with such a flourish, the idea of sneaking in behind the deck-house of a miserable steamer was humiliating.

I'd sooner try and sail the rest of the way in a dinghy, I felt. It would not matter how long it took, or what means I employed, if only I could complete the crossing as I had started—solo.

In the middle of the night I was woken up suddenly by the thought: "Why not rebuild *Elijah* here?"

Pouf! Impossible! Wings all smashed, ailerons smashed, instruments ruined, float chassis bent, fittings torn, tanks crushed in and full of salt water, fuselage soaked in brine for hours, propeller chewed up, motor corroded by salt water—besides, the very idea of building an aeroplane on a coral island with no tools or facilities! Impossible!

"Well," I thought next morning on my way to the cargo shed, "emphatic use of that word 'impossible' arouses suspicion; come to think of it many people say there is no such thing as an impossibility."

I decided to inspect afresh the relics.

There had not been room in the shed for the fuselage and it still stood forlornly on the grass behind, with rudder occasionally flapping in the wind. It looked naked, almost obscene, stripped of its wings, motor and fittings—like an old plaster torso stripped of the frock it displayed in a shop window, and lying discarded in the corner. I examined it carefully.

First the plywood which covered the fuselage. It was that thin material, by itself easy to break between finger and thumb, which yet imparted the great strength to the fragile wooden frame. Tacked on and glued, it must prevent the framework from spreading abroad. If the salt water had destroyed the grip of the glue, then the plane might as well be made of brown paper. But as far as I could tell by feeling with the point of my knife, it was unweakened. Perhaps the careful varnishing and enamelling of the fuselage at Auckland had achieved its object and prevented the woodwork from becoming waterlogged. True, it was somewhat cracked where I had clambered up with a rope to the tail. Next, I inspected the framework of the fuselage; in form it resembled that of an oil-well derrick, though the four corner pieces, the longerons, were only inch-square pieces of spruce. The particular importance of these was that both lower wings and float-struts were secured to the bottom two.

And as two of the metal fittings which joined the float-struts to them were torn in half, I feared the more frail longeron of wood must inevitably be smashed. I climbed into the cockpit and scraped away the silt. To my amazement, I could find no sign of a break, though they were bruised—badly enough, no doubt, to expand the spleen of a government inspector, were he there. Eighteen months previously, one had stopped my flying *Elijah* in England. The whole longeron had to be renewed because he could detect in it by the aid of a powerful magnifying glass an otherwise invisible fracture. Poor fellow, not to have a branch office at Lord Howe Island; I must deputize for him. On his behalf, I passed the longeron as good enough.

The fuselage, I decided, could be used again if every bolt, wire, fitting and tube were removed, cleaned of rust, and painted. Two of the six duralumin float-struts were broken and one inter-float boom bent. The petrol-tank battered in.

Now I began to look at the motor from a different point of view. It seemed to me that it had been attended to in time, and that, with care, it could be coaxed into functioning again. This did not cause me totally undiluted joy when I looked round at the crop of bits mingled with old tins, pieces of wood, bags of cement, and stray articles of cargo. A nice greasy jigsaw puzzle to reassemble all those parts, dismantled by three amateur engineers working at full speed.

"You know," I said to Phil Dignam that night, "I could make

that fuselage and engine serviceable again. With some new struts, bracing-wires, and fittings. I could do without wireless but should need a new revolution-indicator, oil gauge, air-speed indicator, clock and magnetos. Of course, I should want four new wings and a pair of ailerons; and the work of stripping the fuselage and renovating it would be a big job."

"What do you figure on the cost of it all, Skipper?"

"About £300 to £400, I suppose."

"I thought you said you had no money in hand!"

"Of course, that is rather a drawback."

At one o'clock in the night I woke up with the thought: "Why not extract the spars from the broken wings and send them to the mainland? The new wings could be built on to them, and that should prove a big saving."

That seemed to me a stupid idea, and not worth being woken up for—the spars were sure to be fractured at their roots. However, next morning I padded up to the boat-shed under the old banyan tree, and the intuition proved correct. Every spar was intact.

On the way back I met Kirby. His voice, which was rather throaty and slightly nasal, suggested the possibility of adenoids past or present. He was about twenty-nine (my own age) and had been on the mainland for a time as a salesman. I remembered how I myself, when a land salesman, never could sell anything to men with a reddish tint to their hair. He asked me of my plans and I told him I was going to attempt restoring the plane on the island and send the wings to be rebuilt in Sydney.

"Why not rebuild the wings yourself, man!" he exclaimed, never for his part having seen the inside of an aeroplane wing, I imagine.

"Pouf!" I retorted, "hopeless, ridiculous! You have no idea of the intricate construction of a wing. Thousands of different pieces in each, nearly all of different size, only half the thickness of a lead pencil—yet all having to be in exact position. All the fabric has to be sewn on, not to mention half a dozen coats of dope! And no tools here—no place to work in. Pouf! Ridiculous!"

And I stamped off. The truth was I myself had no knowledge of wing construction. My experience of it being limited to once repairing an exterior rent made by a cow's horn—which I performed by means of a brown-paper square stuck on with seccotine. But I found myself back in the boat-shed, where I stripped each wing and re-examined it. I studied those wings for hours. Coming away, I met Gower Wilson, the man with the boom in his voice.

"What are you going to do with the plane?"

"Rebuild it here!"

"And get new wings, I suppose?"

"Och! No. Rebuild the wings here too."

"Why, what do you know about wing construction? They look to me pretty intricate. And besides, there are no tools here, and there's no place to work in. It seems impossible to me."

"Oh, that's nothing. I'll just watch how they come apart, and rebuild them the same way."

"Well, I must congratulate you on the idea, at any rate."

"It's not my idea, dammit! It's Kirby's."

I set to work and prepared a list of material and replacements I should need. It filled fourteen pages, though a lot of space was taken up by my having to describe articles of which I did not know the technical name. My hope was that De Havilland's in Sydney would send the materials first and raise the question of payment afterwards, by which time I felt confident some raven would come to *Elijah's* aid. Then I began work on the plane. It was dreary enough, too—always taking to pieces and cleaning wires, bolts and fittings. I was astonished at the number of fittings on that body— angle fittings, joint fittings and hinge fittings. And all the time, I'd know the sun was beating on the patch of sand outside the door, that the lagoon wavelets danced and flashed in its light. I would hear Gower's voice as he emerged from his door with a party of fishermen, his words growing plainer as he approached. Talk of boats, bait and tackle. Then he would pass the cargo shed, launch his boat and the voice die away over the lagoon. On the return, I could hear them scaling fish and would emerge to help them heave their boat up the beach on log rollers, going back to my own task with a sigh.

After work I'd return by way of the lagoon beach, scrunching underfoot the coral sand, so gloriously white and clean-looking. At the rocky point, there lived a big pink crab, which used to scuttle into its cave-like crevice on my approach. A cunning old crab, which on my drawing yet nearer, clattered back into the gloom of its rocky fortress whence it glared at me from behind its great claws held at the ready, and bubbled with rage through the front of its cuirass when I made a pass at it with my long knife.

Then I'd think how glorious it would have been, out fishing or shooting instead of toiling at a miserable machine, product of zestless civilization.

Chapter XI

THE LURE OF THE LOTUS

From now on was added another temptation to give up my project: the lure of the island was there to entice me. The sun and the warmth and the sand and the hearty natural island life began to cast their spell. The charm crept through my veins, then ran, then raced.

In the morning I used to set out barefooted to pad up to the cargo shed (my shoes had come to pieces through the action of petrol, salt water and rough wear; though in any case, the island custom was to go barefoot); stepping softly under the arch of palms and dark-leaved, evergreen native trees, now and then halting a tread when the sole of a foot met the bite of coral among the sand. And how friendly the sand felt as my toes displaced a little at each step. Cool to the touch where the pathway lay under the trees; but in the open, where the sun had worked at it, the heat made me step quickly from one sole to the other. It was hard after that to bury myself head down in the cockpit of the plane, scraping at dirt and rust.

And also, I had met Frank.

Frank Pay ten could divide his countenance in two with an amazingly infectious grin. For thirty-five years or so, he had been growing and growing up without decisively completing either process. He was as broad in mind as in body. An ardent fisherman, as far as I could gather this is how he began his fishing career:

They were out in Middle Reef Passage. It was night, with a moon. After sitting for two hours with his line down, Frank decided to haul it up and take a look. But he could not. It was fast! Yet not to coral, because it gave slightly at each pull. With all his brawn he hauled (and I should think it would take the *Aquitania's* bow anchor to resist Frank's brawn). The line yielded—but reluctantly, as if fast to something not quite dead, and yet hardly alive. Frank was puzzled. What could it be? Not the carcase of a goat—because when, rowing round the foot of the cliffs, they once shot a goat, and it fell into the sea, there was nothing but a wisp of blood and a whirl of sharks when they pulled to the spot. No, it could not be a dead goat. He peered over the side into the murky depth. Suddenly, the water surface broke. A cold and clammy "thing" reached up, enwrapped itself round Frank's neck, sucked and pulled. The position was now reversed and from being a puller, Frank had now become a pullee. Straining against the boat side, but giving slightly at each pull, he found himself looking into the cold, malignant eyes of a huge octopus. He spat into the octopus's eye. The octopus at once squirted a pint of dark ink into his. The liquid dripped from his face back on to the octopus. Frank was sick! The octopus was sick, and disgorged a small herring which had evidently been resting on the end of Frank's line. Then, slipping its mooring from his neck, it moved back two yards. Frank says it winked one eye, which, he swears, gleamed pink in the moonlight (but his vision may have been tinted by the ink in his own). It vanished. Frank, I imagine, was so excited on at last catching a fish, that he fumbled it when detaching the hook. And it is that herring (I assume) for which he has been fishing the last twenty years. Or failing that, for any other fish definitely prepared to commit suicide on his hook.

My first expedition with Frank was sharking. I heard the boo-boo blow three times at breakfast. "Auntie" told me all about it with her good-natured tolerance for a stranger's abysmal ignorance. The "boo-boo" was a conch, and the "blow" was an explosive noise put into the conch by the human mouth. It could be heard for miles and three blows signified "Man the boats for sharking!" Naturally it was impossible to work on such an occasion, so "Auntie" went off into the garden to cut me some bananas; then "put up" some sandwiches, and I rushed to the boat-shed, securing a place next to Frank. It was warm and sunny, with a slight breeze. The boat made the lagoon passage in silence but for the "chuck-sizz, chuck-sizz" of the rowlocks, the "chough" of six blades dipping and the swish of the bows spurting through the water. I sat quiet as long as I could, but finally had to ask for an oar. "Take mine!" exclaimed Frank, almost before I had finished speaking. It was a big oar, and I needed all my strength to keep up with the islanders; but what a sensation of power and vitality to feel the strain on your muscles while the sun beat down on your face! To feel the tang of fresh salty air in your nostrils! To hear the surf booming on the coral reef! Round Finger Peak, the skipper, Kern, conned the boat in near the rock cliff, which rises in one place 700 feet sheer from the water. He wanted to catch fish for bait. "Salmon!" he would exclaim, or "Bluie!" (bream) "Trevalli!" "Brownie!" indicating a school quite invisible to me. Several times he fished, while we lay on our oars close to the towering cliff and rode up and down on the swell, watching it dash against the rock and fall away again in a white smother, the floating seaweed dropping back and streaming after. But the fish would not bite, "there was too much brit in the water for them to feed on," he said. He gave up trying, hoisted sail, and we made away north till the island lay in miniature behind. Here we let down a bag of sand for anchor and baited lines with goat's flesh. I fished away, greatly excited at the number of twenty-foot sharks I was going to catch, while Frank lay on a thwart, his head on one side of the boat, his feet on the other, until gently rocked to sleep in the warm sunlight with a heavy shark-line between his big capable-looking toes. I almost prayed that a monster would take his bait on the run; but from a fishing point of view, the day was not a success, and on our return to the island, I had caught every single shark in our boat. Frank very rudely held it up between finger and thumb for the people on shore to see. Kern looked suspiciously at me when the other boat turned up with a catch of sixty-five. He demanded if my middle name happened to be Jonah.

However, Frank and I were more successful one night when we

launched a boat at dark. And as soon as young Dignam arrived—with a bag containing the bare old wild goat shot on North Peak—sailed away before the wind to the reef passage below Goat Island. Kern, standing in the bows, conned the boat through the passage in the dark. We rode the swell to westward until the island lay like a long dark blot five miles behind. Frank and I had the bows to ourselves and settled down to a night's fishing. Our lines, strong enough to hang a man, were attached to hooks, as wide as an axe-head, by a short length of chain to prevent the shark biting through. Kern fished with a hook and line three times as big again, and must have baited with several pounds of meat at a time. He was only interested in big game; and we had not been fishing for long when his line, without any warning, began cutting through the water at great speed. But immediately he took the strain, it parted. The shark had swallowed bait, hook and chain while on its way to Cape Horn or somewhere, and took no more notice of the line than of a piece of thread. The three men in the stern caught sharks steadily; it was always an excitement, hoping each would be too big to manage. Then would follow the thuds and the mad threshing of the water as they clubbed the brute beside the boat. If I disliked killing every other reptile in creation, I think I could still hunt shark relentlessly—a creature so cold-blooded, that if its side be ripped open, it will turn, rend and devour its own self. The bottom of the boat was soon filled with sharks of every size, lying on their white bellies and occasionally smacking a tail to right and left, writhing like an eel. One had to step carefully in the boat with bare feet. Meanwhile neither Frank nor I had caught any. Not that I cared much as we gently rode the swell, while the dark mass of the island lay black away to the east with only some solitary light briefly twinkling now and then; while the stars slowly rocked to and fro above the mast, and a lantern slung to the masthead threw a feeble light round about amidships—the changing slopes of the water surface offering it back to us as a pale glimmer.

After fishing till midnight with his customary degree of success, Frank declared his line fast. He tugged at it for awhile, then let it alone and went to sleep for another half-hour on the plea that he would ruin his hook by pulling too hard. When he woke again, the hook had undoubtedly freed itself, so perhaps his philosophy had something in it after all. At this point a shark began to bite at my line. It took bait after bait and though I struck with all my force and seemed to have it hooked on each occasion, the pull on the line presently slacked off and the hook came aboard empty. The shark seemed to hang on like grim death until it had chewed off the meat, when it spat out the hook. "Why don't you catch him?" complained Frank, "instead of waking me up every time you nearly capsize the boat." At last I grew cunning and let the shark have the line all its own way when it worried at the bait. And not till I thought it had had nearly time enough to digest it, did I strike. "By George! I've got him, Frank," I shouted. "All right, land him and don't make so much noise," replied Frank, unappreciatively. Every time the shark flashed past the bows it left a spreading track of white phosphorescence like a comet's tail. I played it to the side of the boat with conspicuous success and had it nearly aboard when, with a jar that threatened to dislocate my shoulders, some monster of the deep seized it by the tail. A terrible tug-of-war ensued. Panting and straining with all my might I strove to wrest my catch from the audacious thief. At the same time I began to realize what a giant it must be to seize half my shark in one bite and I thought of the magnificent coup for me if it could only be speared. "Frank! Quick! Lend a hand!" I gasped. The water around us was threshed into a turmoil white enough to read by, as though a liner's propeller had suddenly reversed there. Frank bestirred himself and joined forces with me. But, for all the effect of our united efforts, it might have been a killer whale that had seized my shark and was furiously lashing and flogging the water for yards around. "Hi, Kern!" I shouted, "bring a spear! Quick! There's a colossal brute that's caught mine by the tail."

By Jove! it was exciting.

They crowded down to our end of the boat till it threatened to capsize.

Kern looked over the side.

"Ha! ha! ha!"

"What is it?" the others cried.

"Ha! ha! ha!" roared Kern, "the skipper's—ho! ho! ho! the skipper's caught—*ho! ho! ho!* the skipper's caught the boat!"

"What!" I cried, as they went back to the stern, making hideous noises they fondly believed to be laughter, while that slippery fox, Frank, gave vent to what I can only describe as a succession of guffaws—pretending he had been merely looking on, and not pulling for all he was worth. But, by Jove! it was only too true—the shark was a four-footer, and the hook, passing through its jaw, had caught in the side of the boat as the shark was being hauled aboard.

On the way home, the carcases were thrown over by Goat Island, and two of us, barefoot, waded about collecting and dragging them up the beach. It was eerie work, feeling around in the dark for dead bodies with the oily glimmer on the water only further concealing its hidden depths. Kern's thirteen-footer suddenly lurched against my bare knees from behind and rasped the skin with its side, harsh as a wire brush. I was quite glad we had only caught fourteen instead of sixty.

I always imagined the shark to be, of all creatures, the most useless to man, and was surprised to find they wasted less of it than of a sheep. The flesh was dried for brown-skinned nationalities (I fancy they even eyed me as a possible consumer, coming from Maoriland). The fins and tails were a particular delicacy for the Chinese. The vertebrae became poker chips. The skin became shagreen, and ended up as anything from a boot to a handbag. While it was said that shark-liver oil was indistinguishable from cod-liver oil, even to the taste of the most inquisitive invalid tongue.

Although it was four o'clock before I reached bed, I was up betimes next morning to relate the true story of how Frank had been hoaxed into mistaking a boat for a shark. But for once the scoundrel must have got up early himself, for I discovered the people's mind already polluted by some cunning, distorted tale of his own concoction, and everybody began laughing as soon as I came in sight.

Some nights I went up to Frank's house. At first I too was in awe of his "missus" and sat on the chair edge like a truant schoolboy. But after the flowing bowl had made a round or two, we warmed to our topics. When I said to Frank that I considered a test for an air-pilot was to stand on one leg and pick up a handkerchief on the floor with his teeth, he insisted on trying himself. Every time he fell over, the house shook with the blow as much as I shook with mirth. But, to my surprise, he refused to give in, and to my astonishment finally succeeded.

We were always devising schemes for raising the *Makambo's* anchor, which lay in sixty-six feet of water. He suggested I should jump overboard with a heavy weight and a line, sink to the bottom, pass the line through the chain, and return (if lucky) to the surface. He said he wouldn't like to do it himself but thought I should be quite safe—my beard would frighten away the sharks. What did I grow a beard for, anyway?

"Well, you see," I replied, "it's like this; lots of men in history, whom I admire, wore beards, and I find myself inclined to attempt emulation of people I admire."

"Oh, you mean Henry VIII!"

"No, no!"

"Bluebeard, then?"

"No, no, no. I was thinking of men like Drake and Raleigh, and of course, Ulysses had——"

"H'm," said Frank, rubbing his broad chin slowly. "Perhaps a feller wouldn't have to get up quite so early—it would certainly save that bit of shaving time."

When I asked how the *Makambo's* anchor came to be there, he explained that the ship went aground a few years ago.

"It was some time before the War—say twenty summers back." The skipper, it was said, enjoyed his dinner but failed to turn the corner Wide enough after. There wasn't a rat on the island before then; they deserted the ship when she grounded. But a tug was brought from Sydney, and kedging with all anchors, the ship was fetched off again—and is still plying the same route. But one anchor was left behind, and the owners offered £30 reward if it could be moved into deep water and buoyed for the ship to pick up again.

The young sparks got together and manned two boats. They slung poles across both, and at low tide made fast the anchor to the middle of the poles. The rising tide raised the anchor and they moved it out to eleven fathoms of water. Here they fastened a buoy to the anchor-chain, and proceeded to cut the lashings which held it to the poles. When half the lashings were cut, the whole weight came on to one pole. This began to give at the middle, and the boats to fold inwards like the two shells of a giant clam closing. I could imagine poor slow-thinking Frank's bewilderment to see the boats beginning to shut over him and the water welling up as the inner sides were crushed together and dragged under. I asked what were his last thoughts as they were snapping to above him.

"Thoughts!" he exclaimed, "you don't imagine I stayed to think, do you? As soon as I saw that, pole beginning to bend, I realized at once what was going to happen to the boats."

"And so?"

"Why! I got out of them, of course. By the time I had come up from my dive, the whole outfit—boats, men, anchor and chain—had gone straight to the bottom."

He was alone, and there might never have been a boat there. He swam about for, so he reckoned, five minutes. No one appeared; he concluded they were all drowned, and began swimming shorewards. But he had not swum twenty strokes when up shot Roly Wilson, breaking surface like a rising fish. Then, one after the other, they all bobbed up, gasping for breath and coughing up water. But still were in an awkward plight, a mile from shore, in a strong current and a shark-infested sea. One man could not swim, so they found an oar and passed it to him. He was panic-stricken and tried to climb up the oar hand over hand. Every time he reached halfway, it naturally overbalanced and ducked him again. Frank said he remembered what a ludicrous thing this seemed at the time. The man cried out for them not to swim away, but they reckoned he was as well off with an oar, even though unable to swim, as they were without. Each (with true island independence) chose what seemed to him the best objective, and swam for it. Meanwhile the current had them in its grip, hurrying past the island. Realizing the futility of swimming against it, they had all set out for the group of rocks a mile to the north. Three men landed on one rock, and one on each of two others. The man with the oar, by extreme good fortune, was carried on to the last rock half a mile further out again. Later, they were all rescued by a boat.

After hearing Frank's story of the anchor, I posted hot-foot to Roly. I must know how it felt to be sent to the sea bottom like a cat in a bag with a brick tied to it. But he told me little.

It was pitch dark. He was jammed between somebody's leg and a thwart. It seemed an age. Everything was in confusion. He was often touching woodwork or part of some other body. He felt suffocated and made sure he was drowned. Then a crack of pale green light showed to one side of him. He moved his head and found the crack opened and closed with a motion like weeds waving in a river. Each time it widened further, and he was moved closer to it. He then realized it was above him. Finally he was thrown out as if disgorged by a giant clam.

All this time my job was to work away at stripping and cleaning the fuselage. Then I began to paint the inside of it white. First, because this insured inspection of every square millimetre of surface, otherwise no easy matter owing to the hundreds of dark, inaccessible spots, corners, hidden crannies—whereas the least patch of dark old paint cried sullen protest if left uncovered among all the white. Secondly, because the white would soon disclose, by tell-tale brown dribble, the presence of any internal rusting. The islanders visited the cargo shed in a stream, particularly when I was at work on difficult portions. As I supported myself with chest on the bottom of the cockpit, feet projecting over the cockpit edge, and arms fully stretched somewhere beyond my head underneath, they would take pains to tell me how badly I was doing it. At first this used to upset my pride as a workman, but soon I learned to pocket that and ask to be shown the correct way, thereby squeezing two hours' work out of my critic before he could escape.

At nightfall I returned to P. J. Dignam's. His was one of the large houses on the island. Built of wood, with about eight rooms and a wide veranda encircling the whole. He told me what it cost him; I only remember the sum was big—all the timber coming over from the mainland, as the native trees are preserved. It had no fireplace apart from the kitchen stove. He explained that the weather was never cold enough to need a fire—the island was kept warm by an ocean current sweeping down from tropical New Guinea way; year in, year out, the temperature never dropped below 50° (or rose above 80°). On three sides the house was set against a thick wood of palm and native trees. If "Auntie" wanted fruit to cook, she usually picked it as required, with the following degree of effort: for a lemon she reached up her arm at the back door, where the branches of that tree tapped the house side; for figs she reached up with a stick from the front veranda, where the fringe of fig tree brushed the edge of the veranda; but for the bananas it was necessary to walk quite ten paces to the east to cut a bunch; however, the pandanus tree was not so far away (even if it only flowered and yielded its nuts every seven years); pomegranates in profusion with rosy checks as red as those of a Devonshire girl—forty yards' walk; oranges—fifty; pears—as much as a hundred; red guavas, however, were a lot closer—which I thought very fortunate, because combined with cream they made the most succulent dish imaginable; yellow guavas were nearly one hundred and fifty paces off. I never came across the loquat and persimmon trees, so imagine they must have been a long way away—two hundred yards for all I know.

Phil Dignam had a grown-up family, with two daughters married; he told me that on first coming to the island as a young chap he lived in a hut with palm-stem walls, palm-leaf roof and beaten earth floor. He was one of the first settlers; "Auntie's" father, named Thompson, was actually the first—he remained ashore when a whaling vessel called at the island. "Auntie's" mother, I was told, came from the Solomon Islands, or one of the Polynesian group.

I began to think the island the most attractive spot imaginable. The islanders formed the most independent-minded, thoughtful and happy community it has ever been my fortune to know. I put this down to the natural life they led, to the absence of civilization's mechanical products and particularly to their not being overeducated. They had developed a habit of thinking for themselves, and I noticed that a scanty education did not prevent their being all great readers (the free library was in Phil Dignam's house)— especially of travel and biography. Their individuality was so strongly marked that I wondered if all individualities were more colourful in the days of small villages where every man had his own job to do or craft to work at.

Although Australians, their build was not tall and spare, but more like that of a New Zealander—short and thick-set. Their voices, except for those of a few who had lived on the mainland, were soft and pleasant to hear. They were extraordinarily gentle and easy-going in manners—I never heard one speak rudely; and, though they had every chance to be indolent with mild winter, easily grown food, plenty of fish and few luxurious cravings—yet they seemed to work very hard.

With Phil Dignam, for instance, work was almost an obsession. He was full of a force always driving him on. He might almost be afraid that laziness was latent in him, and that if he once stopped work, he would never want to start again. A garden was the chief scene for his relentless pursuit of toil. It was big enough to tire three men, but he kept it in perfect order, working from dawn till dark. As the household, even with the generous islander's appetite, could only eat about a fifth of the produce, he gave the rest away, or fed it to his beloved pigs. So that, actually, he was working at something which was not essential to gain a livelihood. Yet if anything interrupted his gardening work, his spirit seemed to explode and inwardly rage. After working till nightfall in his garden, he would then sit at a desk for several hours and draw up documents to do with the shipping or landing of cargo, which had all to be attended to by him as agent for the shipping company. Or he would spend hours entering in a card-index the books returned to or borrowed from the free island library in his house. After that he was ready to play billiards with me. At least one afternoon in each week, he played bowls. Whenever the Steamer called, he must be on deck all day checking cargo—very thirsty work this—but he liked cargo day as much as "Auntie" disliked it. He was a soloist and all his jobs were set for himself by himself to be carried out by himself. He liked neither to work under anyone else's direction nor to have anyone else work under his. And not only did he work with this driving energy without necessity—he actually had to pay for doing so. In this way:

The seed of the island palms, I was told, was the only kind that would germinate in cold countries. So I imagined that every potted palm seen in an English house originally came from Lord Howe Island, and for a moment was agitated by great excitement—had I at long last traced to its lair the maiden ladies', dream plant? Or, in other words, run to ground the famous aspidistra? No, Phil Dignam told me, he would scarcely like to call that a palm—he referred to the Kentia palm. And all orders for its celebrated, much-desired palm seed were taken by the New South Wales Government, which owns the island (no one can buy land there, and the islanders only occupy theirs by permission). The Government instructed the islanders to ship the requisite number of bagged-up seed each time the steamer called. The profits were divided amongst the islanders, each man's share being in proportion to his age and residence. If he earned other money by doing other work in addition, his share of the profits was cut down correspondingly. So that Phil Dignam, whose share was cut down because as shipping agent he earned extra money, therefore actually paid for the privilege of working.

His was a generous nature: when I decided on the attempt to rebuild *Elijah*, and realized it could not be done in a day, I suggested that I had better go and stay with Kirby, who kept a boarding-house.

"What!" he said, halting in the pathway, "don't you like staying with us folk, Skipper? I'm sorry to hear that."

"Good Lord!" I exclaimed, aghast at his thought. "Why! I've never been made more welcome. But when you first invited me it was only expected I should remain on the island one night."

"See here, Skipper," he replied, planting his forefinger on my chest, "as long as you are on this island, I want you to stay in my house, and what's more, sleep in my room. I don't mind if it's a year."

Chapter XII

DESIRES TANGLE

I did not think the work would take so long as a year, but I soon realized I was likely to be caught by the gales and storms of late winter. The only chance of escaping them was to give up the idea of doing all the work myself. I found Roly Wilson and asked him to help me. Certainly he would. I asked him how much I should pay him, and he replied that he would gladly do it for nothing. That could not, be, so I demanded how much he was paid if working for any other islander. "So much for ordinary work, and then again so much more if working with a horse." I told him I thought it should be worth as much to work with me as with a horse, and away we went. He was a great craftsman, and, more important still, always agreed with every method or scheme I proposed—a splendid man to work with. In character, he was quite different from his brother, Gower "the Boomer". Roly's mind worked quietly inside him, while Gower's schemes manifested themselves noisily outside. Yet, they were alike in one respect, for it was difficult to say which was the pleasanter.

Roly began by painting away at the floats. Tricky work, because an arm, inserted up to the shoulder, completely filled a manhole, making it impossible to look into the float, and necessary to paint by touch or memory. "Hey, Chick!" he called one morning, "just look at the keel of this float. Someone has plugged the crack between keel and float-bottom with putty. I can dig it out with my knife."

We thought it a queer thing for anyone to do, but Roly picked out the putty as well as he could and painted the seam with especial care to ensure its being watertight.[1]

One morning Roly called me out from the shed.

"What do you think of that?" he exclaimed.

Although we stood in bright sunshine—in fact, so did half the island—the two mountains, Lidgbird and Gower, had their heads in a great black thunderous-looking cloud, as though brewing some evil deed. Out of the cloud on top of Mount Gower, like thin silvery wisps of hair draggling from some witch's poll, shot streams of water to curve outwards and fall downwards. They dashed themselves to pieces on a projecting ledge a thousand feet below, but instantly recovering to become again a body of water, bounded off and poured another thousand feet on to some rugged rock. Once more dispersed, once more they gathered together again for a final 500-foot leap in an arched cascade for the sea. Evidently a waterlogged cloud had collapsed on to the top of the mountain, and the majestic sight before me was a number of falls 2,800 feet in drop, issuing from the dead cloud.

Roly told me there was almost a flat platform on top of the mountain, perhaps two hundred acres in extent. It *must* be *strange* after climbing that height of nearly sheer rock and precipice to come on a plateau of dense vegetation—of thick tree-fern and stunted scrubs, all hanging with long, bedraggled moss incessantly soused in moisture. A lot of the shrubs and all the tree-ferns only grew up there, and were not to be found elsewhere in the island. It was like a different country.

The grandeur of the island worked on one's spirit and sometimes at night the beauty would swell one's heart till it threatened suffocation.

The still air, pure and strangely clear. The stars, with their brilliant hard sparkle, that mere diamonds could but poorly imitate. The rare sigh of a leaf or two in the tree tops. Sometimes, after a dance

---

1   Unpainted duralumin crumbles away if exposed to the action of sea-water. Where keel and float-shell had come unriveted (see note, page 82) the water, pressing between, had eaten away the duralumin and left a soft residue which was unknowingly taken to be putty.

at the Boomer's, I'd jump on the back of the horse-driven sleigh taking home Kirby and his young bride and off we'd slide over the sandy pathway, seeming to move at the fastest pace so close to the ground, as the horse thudded along at a gallop. Away at the end of the island towered the twin peaks with their tops buried, as usual, in the only cloud in the heavens—or were they the giant arms of Atlas holding the roof of the world off his shoulders? Then, with a swaying swing as the horses' gait took effect on first one side of the narrow sleigh and then on the other, and a slurring scrunching glide over the coral sand, we'd shoot under the wood. Now the stars were only visible in patches edged with palm-leaf spikes or foliage of interwoven tree tops. And as we slipped by ghostly boles and palm-sterns, I felt charged to the fingertips with such vitality and such power of living to the uttermost, that I marvelled at my crass stupidity in ever trying any other life but this of the island.

Next morning, it would be hard to work—at building my own coffin, for all I knew—when the fascinating doings of the islanders whispered their spell of enchantment to my blood.

Besides, if the islanders helped me, naturally I must help the islanders. For example, to keep down the population of Martin's famous rats, which once threatened to destroy the islanders' livelihood—their palms.

One afternoon I was out shooting with young Dignam. Though always very pleasant, young Dignam kept himself a dark horse as far as I was concerned. He had been to the mainland and worked on Sydney Harbour Bridge; was now a member of the island Executive Committee which decided such matters as who should work cargo or collect palm seed—done by shinning up so many hundred palms with feet linked together with a twisted wisp of palm leaf. He realized the importance of his office, I think, but was not quite sure that it sufficiently exercised his capabilities.

We set forth, joined by Mickey Nichols at the corner. Dogs, which seemed to get wind of the expedition by magic, came tearing up from every direction and yapped with mad excitement. We retained the services of the first half-dozen to arrive and drove off the rest. Arriving at a big cotton-wood tree, Dignam thrust some dry thatch-palm leaves into a hole at the foot and set them alight. He fanned the smouldering leaves with his hat to drive the smoke under the tree. He fanned and fanned till, presently, it was pouring out of every hole at the roots. It was a most comical sight: six holes belched six columns of smoke. Into each column of smoke was thrust a terrier's head, eagerly concentrating on the hole before it, motionless and solemn, without so much movement as the twitch of an ear while big tears rolled down its doggy cheeks and dropped on to the leaf-covered ashes. I noticed Dignam repeatedly glancing upwards, so imitated him and found to my amazement that smoke was issuing from the end of a branch quite twenty feet above the ground. Soon it poured or puffed from holes in nearly every branch till the tree was a spotted fairy-tale affair, with a tuft of smoke at every spot.

"Look up!" shouted Dignam, and I looked up to see a huge rat turning out with the smoke from a hole halfway along a branch. It scurried out with long tail sweeping behind. Along the branch away from the trunk. Before I had the gun up it had disappeared in thick foliage and jumped to the next tree. Out of the same hole tumbled five more, helter skelter, scrambling and jostling each other. Although they appeared to move slowly, they had all disappeared in an amazingly short time. I fired at the last one. "Did you get him?" asked Dignam. "I think I shot his tail off," said I. But we could not find it, and Dignam was not nearly as pleased at my success as I expected; in the first place, he explained, the Committee paid threepence for each tail, and we had lost that; in the second place, if he caught the same rat later, he would not get threepence for its tail if it had already been shot off. However, I made amends by donating my empty tobacco-tin for the tails of those later caught by the dogs; they curled in nicely. And when he took the gun, he was much more successful than I—in fact he nearly bagged Mickey at a range of two feet. Mickey clapped his hand to his back and whirled round to show a white, startled face. For an instant, then, I stood motionless as did young Dignam, though I was sure the flame of the explosion had flared past Mickey's head at least nine inches to one side. They began hunting for a wound, but could find none, so decided it must have been a piece of flying bark.

When we finished our scrambling hunt through the tangled undergrowth and over sprawling roots, my tobacco-tin held seventeen tails (fortunately, all of Martin's tree-dwelling rats).

As for Martin's underground birds, I forgot all about them till one day I went fishing in my rubber boat which the *Makambo* had brought from Norfolk Island. I blew it up on the lawn—to "Auntie's" amusement which bubbled inside her like a geyser about to burst into play. I carried it under my arm to the lagoon, rowed over to Goat Island half a mile away, anchored by means of a stone on a shark-line, and began to fish with dried shark for bait. My ambition was to hook a six-foot kingfish, up anchor, and go for a tow behind. It was very pleasant in the sun, dancing about on the waves in the buoyant rubber boat. I was kept at a high pitch of excitement by the dark shapes gliding over the white sand or brown coral in the pale green water below. I had not been fishing for more than three hours when the agitated movement of my line indicated success. With supreme skill I played, and with cunning care landed a goggle-eyed fish with a startling bright coat of diamond pattern, the odd diamonds being yellow, and the evens pink. It was not hooked by the mouth, but behind one ear—a fact which caused me, profound satisfaction, to think how few fishermen have the piscatory ability to catch a fish the same way. Nor was that all, for scarcely; had my line touched bottom, when I felt another bite. I struck, and the line cut through the water in circles and curves. Now I would pay the line out, and now, I would pull it in. With extraordinary skill, I finally landed a brute with wild-looking fins like the wings of a dragon and a back with a crenulated comb like a cock pterodactyl. Its broad head was covered in wicked-looking knobs and spikes, its fearsome wild mouth snarled at me. It must be the rock fish with poisonous fins arid back that I had been especially warned against! I jammed it in a corner of the petrol-tin with an oar, and tried to get the hook out of the mouth without the mouth getting my fingers in. Every time it jumped an inch I jumped a yard, till fortunately it spat the hook out and stood on its head in the tin, occasionally flapping its tail above the top. Immediately my line was out again, I hooked another fish: this had the strongest pull of all. In the excitement of playing it, I upset the tin, and the poisonous creature jumped out on to the canvas boat bottom among my bare feet. Sitting hastily on one end of the boat, with a leg along either side of it, I now found myself between the devil and the deep sea. I played the new fish with one eye on the line and the other on the creature wallowing in the water on the boat bottom. In the course of its struggles, it worked its way between the canvas bottom and the inflated side. Hastily, I jammed it there with the tin. It struggled violently while I returned my attention to the fish on the line. I played this to the side, only to find it was another poisonous brute twice as big as the first. At this moment, with a hiss of escaping air, Number One unmistakably punctured the boat's air-bag. I dropped Number Two into the boat and in my hurry dropped the line as well. Pulling away the tin, I poked Number One out from the punctured side into the middle of the boat. Here it met Number Two and proceeded to take strong exception to its presence. My only hope was for them to poison each other to death. Unfortunately, each protected itself by wrapping my line round an incredible number of times till it was a sort of cocoon. Meanwhile the air continued to hiss from the punctured air-bag. A wavelet broke over the edge of the boat. With a dramatic gesture, I severed the anchor-line and began paddling for Goat Island, perched on the round end of the boat with a leg laid along either side. Each time I dipped in an oar one side, the boat spun round the other, but as the punctured half collapsed and the boat filled with water, it held a steadier if slower course. Halfway to the island, the tin floated out of the boat. Five yards from the rocks a wave washed out fish, line, lead and hooks. On being tipped out myself and wading ashore—safe, if damp—I thought I deserved relaxation, so climbed up the island and went to sleep on the long grass near the top. I was awakened by a loud squeak under my ear. I sat up in amazement to find the ground squeaking in every direction. This savoured more of the supernatural than of the matter-of-fact. I was mighty puzzled. I felt tentatively under the long matted grass. There I found a hole like a rabbit burrow. I reached in slowly, with my hand, until at arm's length it received a stinging nip on a finger; I withdrew-it at great speed. After I had finished dancing round I again advanced, with one hand now padded, and extracted a young mutton-bird the size of a parrot, and evidently one of Martin's underground birds.

One morning, when there was a cricket match on and I naturally could not work in consequence, I was helping "Auntie". She wanted some of her wild hens for the oven, so young Dignam and I were stalking them with a rifle.

"Now," said "Auntie", "be sure you shoot them through the neck *and nowhere else.*"

Along came a big-cheeked, big-chested Australian named Campbell, visiting the island from the mainland. He worked in a bank; he was breezy and boisterous, seeming never to stop talking with a loud talk—perhaps more noticeable in contrast to the soft-speaking islanders. It was a pleasant surprise to discover, when you got behind the noise, what a good-natured, good-hearted chap he was. "Here!" he shouted, "I bet you I get one first shot."

"All right," said young Dignam, "but don't forget to hit it in the neck, and nowhere else."

Campbell took cover behind a palm tree, aimed carefully, and did get the hen first shot, and what's more, did hit it through the neck; which at twenty-five yards' range was not a bad shot. The hen was consigned to "Auntie" in the kitchen, and all seemed well. But suddenly out she popped, the red of righteous indignation in her face.

"I should just like to know who shot this hen!" she demanded.

"I did," said Campbell.

"And didn't I tell you to shoot it through the neck *and nowhere else*!"

"Why! So I did," exclaimed Campbell, surprised.

"Heavens! Heavens! Heavens above, man!" she exclaimed. "Hadn't you got the sense to see that its backside was behind its neck when you fired!"

When we had pacified "Auntie", I challenged Campbell to a

shooting match, and the target suggested was a fat, pestilential spider in a web across the pathway. It was ferocious, green and fat, with hairy legs. However, I thought it safe enough at the distance.

To my surprise, Campbell obliterated it first shot. Another was picked for me, at the same distance. With my skill as a marksman at stake, I took the most careful aim, determined that it should be a deadly shot. I fired.

A crashing explosion was followed by a continued clatter as of shrapnel striking a roof. I stood tensely still! We all stood tensely still! "The bullet", I thought, "must have struck a launch on the lagoon and blown it up. This is terrible!"

Suddenly from among the trees burst "Auntie"

"Goodness gracious me!" she exclaimed. "Why! Captin, now you are trying to murder me I do believe!"

"Auntie", it seems, was fetching a pailful of sweet potatoes from beside the shed under the trees. She was bending down fully when a five-pound cluster of palm seed, cut by the bullet from the tree above, fell twenty feet on to the corrugated-iron roof beside her. Here it exploded and hundreds of flying palm seed, hard, shiny, and each as big as a pigeon's egg, burst abroad with infernal clatter. Poor "Auntie", suddenly struck in every part of her anatomy, must have thought the end of the world upon her.

As she stalked away, emptying seed from her pocket, extracting it from her hair and shaking it from her clothes, the spider leisurely moved across its web and disappeared.

Chapter XIII

PALM ISLAND PLANE FACTORY

The *Makambo* returned from Sydney; she brought materials for me, and I began rebuilding the wings. Often, lying awake at night, I feared I had undertaken more than I could perform. And the first thing I read on studying the blue-print sent was that each bay of the wing must be trammelled to 15/100 inch. "Wing" I knew, and "bay" I knew, but:

"Roly, what is a trammel?" I asked.

"Trammel!" said he. "Isn't that what a bishop carries when preaching in a cathedral?"

"It seems to me that fooling round with this blueprint will get us into an unholy mess. I think we had better throw it away, remember how the broken wing comes to pieces, and rebuild if just the same. When in doubt, ask mother-wit."

"That's just what I think, too," said Roly.

But it occurred to me that it might be easier said than done.

"Roly," said I, "there appear to be thirty riblets in this wing, and ten ribs, of which seven have one shape, and the others each a different shape."

"That's what it looks like to me," said Roly.

"So that, if we first strip off the ten old ribs, then build on ten new ribs—provided, of course, that they are of correct shape, in correct place, and fastened to the spars exactly as the old ribs were fastened—that's all there is to it. Apart, that is to say, from riblets, fillets, slots, leading-edges, trailing-edges and that sort of thing."

"Exactly what I think," said Roly.

Each rib was made of twenty-one pieces of spruce no thicker than thick cardboard; yet every piece must be in place, glued there and tacked, and the rib fit tightly on to the spars. However, we plugged away, and slowly the job seemed to yield us its secrets. Until, at the end of a week's work, we knew something about aeroplane construction. We could fit trailing-edges; plug and glue old screw-holes; cut, glue and tack pieces of rib together; and clean, screw, measure, saw, shave, and shape like a pair of factory robots. A curious thing was to find every inter-spar metal strut inside the wing to be full of sea-water, though five weeks had already elapsed since the plane was wrecked. I said to Roly: "We must drill holes in the metal struts to let out that water."

Roly Wilson (left) and Frank Payten with the best wing, which had every rib broken, but was otherwise sound.

"That's just what I think," said he.

Next morning, I said to him: "You know, I think we ought to drill through the woodwork to let that water out."

"Do you know," said Roly, "after you left yesterday I was thinking just the same thing."

Next morning I said: "Roly, I think after all that we should drill the metal struts themselves to let that water out."

"Well, now," said he, "how curious! Because that's just what occurred to me after you had gone yesterday."

We finished the woodwork of the first wing. It looked pretty good to me. We prepared it for its cover by painting it, in the first place, with waterproof lionoil. Every corner, stick, and cranny had to be well done. Secondly, it needed a coat of dope-resisting paint to prevent the cover from sticking to each rib. The trouble was to find this paint. We had forty gallons altogether and went round and round in solemn procession, Roly and I, inspecting every label. But however hard we looked, none of them would read "Dope-resisting Paint". Yet it was on the invoice, so must be there. The only tin not otherwise accounted for was one labelled "Thinners".

"I suppose that must be it," said I.

"I suppose so, too," said Roly; so we slapped on a coat of "thinners" before laying a piece of the light-brown linen fabric, fourteen feet by ten feet, on the frame for a cover. The question was, should the cover be sewn on tight or loose? Roly and I disagreed. I said the dope would shrink it tight, so that, if sewn on tight at the start, it would split in half when doped. "Sew it on loose," said I. "No, sew it on tight," said Roly. By nightfall, we still had not agreed, so left it draped over the wing skeleton. Next morning, I said: "You know, Roly, I believe you are right and it ought to be sewn on tight."

"That's a funny thing," he said, "because I was just thinking you were right and that it ought to be sewn on loose."

We split the difference and when young Mrs. Kirby offered to do a day's sewing, she stitched it on tightly loose, or loosely tight, with most dainty, trim, and good-looking stitches, as one might expect from that young lady, while all day Roly and I, whenever we trod on a tack with our bare feet, tried not to say anything more forcible than "Bother!" or "Drat it!" Next day, Minnie, sister of Stan, the young wireless operator and Postmaster, volunteered. Minnie was a generous, warm-hearted creature who used to turn up one day a week and help "Auntie" Dignam over the housework, singing away from morning till night. She was like a tall radiant sunflower that looks happily and generously at all comers until, on a slight touch contrary to its fancy, it curls up its petals, angry or hurt. Yet, with next day's sun, joyfully uncurling them again, forgetful of all that has passed.

Minnie sewed away in great style till she arrived at a corner where I said the fabric should be turned in and sewn with just so many lock-stitches to the inch. Now Minnie was an expert at sewing. She was the island wizard at converting chiffon, ninon, voile, georgette, or what have you, into correct feminine attire. The fabric, she said, must be turned in at the corner and sewn with so and so many stitches to the inch.

"But, Minnie," I argued, while Roly, as I could see in the corner of an eye, barely suppressed his ill-timed mirth, "naturally there would not be the need to put so many lock-stitches if it were a petticoat."

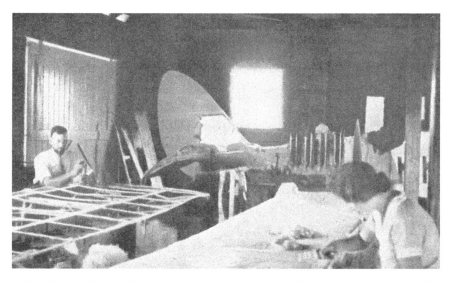

Palm Island Plane Factory; Minnie sews the fabric on one wing while the author fits new ribs on another. The engine and propeller are just visible behind Minnie's head.

No, my way was wrong, the stitch was wrong, the, number of stitches quite wrong. At last I said: "Well, I'll have to fly the jolly thing, so why not let me have it the way I want, even if it is the wrong way?"

"Now you've done it," said Roly, as she stalked off. However, with next day's sun she was as cheery as ever and had apparently quite forgotten our yesterday's tiff, as well, I might add, as the existence of any sewing to tiff about.

The curved surgical needles remained stuck in the fabric. I began to think I must have been posted as an impossibly exacting taskmaster and that we should be forced to do all the sewing ourselves, when Gower Wilson's eldest daughter, Eileen, heard with surprise that we had no sempstress, and enrolled herself on the spot. What a jewel we had then! If her father were 100 per cent loud and masculine, she was 100 per cent quiet and feminine, yet inherited his good nature, patience and capability. A paragon! And, unlike Gower, she did not insist on her job being all devised and schemed by herself—yet always thought about it, and usually suggested an improvement in method. Nor did I ever hear her suggest anything for an improvement that failed to be one. There was a lot of sewing. Twenty-three feet of it around the edge of the wing alone, and then tape had to be sewn over the top and bottom of each four-and-a-half-foot rib, with a lock-stitch every three inches right through the wing. The night after the sewing of the first wing had been finished, I woke up suddenly to be told by the subconscious part of my brain that I had forgotten to lock the bracing-wires across the inside wing-bays.

Poor Eileen had to take the fabric half off again.

"You know," said Roly, "I thought you would do something like that."

One morning he drew me aside. "Look here, Chickey," he said, "I know another girl who would help with the sewing."

"Who's that?" I asked.

"Ah, ha!" said he.

"Oh, ho!" thought I. "So that's how the wind lies, is it?"

Now there were four of us in our factory, and it was a revelation to me, the pleasure to be derived from plying a craft, using hand and eye: hard, interesting work that lent a keenness to one's appetite for everything. How craftsmen and artisans were to be envied for the pleasure in their work!

We were ready to begin doping, and life became more arduous. Not because of the work during the daytime, but because of the hours I must spend in thought. Having no previous experience, I must plan every operation in my brain before doing it. In doping, for instance, to spoil a fabric cover would be serious. There was a right way to dope, a right time for doping, and a right consistency of dope to use. It might seem childishly easy after a few days' practice or with directions from somebody who knew how to do it. But I must do it right at once without either. The first three coats had to be of red dope, P.D.N.12. The temperature I knew must be 70° Fahrenheit during application, but must it remain at 70° all the time the dope was drying? It was not often it reached 70° now, even at mid-day and with all the doors closed. In the morning we could be seen hanging round the thermometers like dogs eyeing a juicy mutton chop. Fortunately we had two, one of which read four degrees higher than the other. This fact we took to be an act of God and promptly discarded the one with the lower reading. And if the other reached 70°, then immediately men, coats, brushes and dope began to fly in all directions. That dope's motto ought to be "stick and stink". As for "stick", my fingers remained all the time coated with a skin of dark-brown lacquer except when it became thick enough to peel off with a knife, though Frank, after doping, seemed to get it off his hands all right—I think he scrubbed them with the wire saucepan brush.

The first wing was not a complete success. One panel, especially, bagged so much that I tried to take a tuck in the slack of it, doping another piece of fabric over the scar. It then appeared more efficient but scarcely more beautiful. It had a gaunt look like that of a half-starved mongrel with its ribs showing. A mistake somewhere—I wished I knew where it was.

The puzzle was solved by a wireless from Sydney which stated that the dope-resisting paint had been omitted. The fabric had stuck to every rib instead of drawing tight over the whole, like a drum-skin. At any rate, it was a relief to know the mistake was not more serious, and as the fabric could not be taken off when once doped, we proceeded to finish it, making the best job we could. Altogether it received three coats of red dope, P.D.N.12, and then five coats of aluminium dope. V.84. And what arguments we had as to the manner of applying it! Frank's idea was to slap it on good and hearty with the biggest brush he could find; Charlie Retmock, who reminded me of Girt Jan Ridd in *Lorna Doone*, painted steadily and ponderously as if the wing were a barn door; young Stan, the Postmaster, dashed it on fast with furious abandon and energy; young Tom, the island buck, made rather small strokes with a flourish, and did not exceed the speed limit even when the doorway framed no island damsel (and it was queer how often they happened to pop in just when Tom was on the job).

They might differ on the question of how to dope, but there was one point on which they all conspired to agree—that they should not admit my own superior skill at it. After the first coat it was necessary to dope another strip of tape over each rib. This tape had a serrated edge like a cock's comb, so that its grip on the fabric would be spread and not along the line of one thread only. My method was to lay a trail of dope along the line of rib, lay the tape on top, and rub it home with three fingers, one on top of the rib and one on each side. Next morning I came up to find a deputation awaiting me.

"Here!" cried Frank, pointing to a rib I had thus taped the day before, "you can't do that sort of work here, you know!"

"No, I say, Chickey," Roly added, "you can't go to Sydney and have them think that is the sort of work we do at Lord Howe Island."

"We wouldn't mind," said Frank, "if they knew it was your own work; but of course, after one look at you, they are bound to realize we have done all the important work on the plane."

"No, really, Chickey," Roly said, "you'll have to do that again."

"And take good care", added Frank, ripping off the tape, "that you don't do any more such slovenly work in future!" I explained how it was always advisable for that rib to protrude a little, a mere trifle, as it enabled the wing to secure a better grip of the air, to prevent its skidding on the sharp corners. Unfortunately, they could not appreciate my proficiency in the profundities of aerodynamics.

Frank had offered to do all the doping for me. He didn't want any pay in return, he said, but would appreciate the gift of my old altimeter. I told him it had never worked when I needed it, even before it bathe in the sea; but that only appeared to make him the keener—I think he considered it would be a suitable alarm-clock to wake him up in the morning.

The doping turned out to be totally unlike the short task we had expected it to be. For one thing, it was seldom we had two hours in the morning or two hours in the afternoon warm enough for it. And as we had to allow each coat several hours to dry, we considered it lucky if two of us could do a coat to a wing in the day. So that, if Frank had tackled it alone, at his rate of progress it might have taken him till eternity, since, before he reached the last wing, the first would have needed re-doping.

One morning, Mr. Giles was among the visitors who dropped in to inspect our factory. He was a retired Australian architect now living on the island—about seventy, tall and with a short white beard. "Huh!" he snorted, "I should like to know why *you* want to grow a beard—young man like you!"

"Well, you see," I replied, "it's like this: growing a beard is so similar to undertaking a flight that I thought it might be good practice. First comes the idea which you dare not tell a soul, knowing how the cold water of ridicule will be emptied on the hot stuff of the idea. You retire from your fellows to hatch the foundation of your plan. You are stretched on the tenterhooks of anxiety. Why? Because you fear there will be patches of unoccupied territory or wide open spaces you cannot cover. Will the course be an all-red one, or since you are starting from New Zealand, an all-black one? Or will there be the terrible bleached sandiness of desert to make the project hopeless from the start? Should you set your jaw to a Great Circle course, or make an attempt direct to the point? In the event of failure, have you the courage to face the pitying condescension people reserve for those who fail? In the event of success, have you the endurance to be pleasant to everyone who demands to know why you did it, how you did it, and what you did in doing it? Or, alternatively, are you prepared to make another lifelong enemy of every questioner ignored? And are you prepared to stand up to the damaging criticism that will be poured out in any case? Now that, after a fortnight's seclusion, your scheme begins to hatch and darken the shell it creeps from, dare you face your friends with such a poor insignificant indication of the splendid project you know it will be—only you know how splendid? With curling coat-collar and muffling scarf, you furtively steal abroad in the midsummer heat. With shrinking limbs, you slink past your club, fearful of probing questions and scathing comments on the hopeless, hare-brained nature of your projection. Should you by misfortune come face to face with an acquaintance, you, licking your lips, advance some feeble excuse for it before any has been demanded. Yes, if you can grow a beard, a flight should seem dead easy."

"Well, anyway," grunted Mr. Giles, "I don't agree with half the funny things people say about it. I think it nearly suits you. Perhaps," he added dubiously, "if you were to trim it like mine, it would be quite all right."

"But seriously, Chickey," Roly said, when Mr. Giles had stamped off, "tell me why you do grow a beard!"

"Well, you see, Roly," I replied, "it's like this: you know how, when you go out to a tea party, you often find yourself running your finger up and down the seam of your coat, feeling like a gowk for lack of something to say; well, I thought a beard would provide a ready-made, ever-present topic to poke into any gap in the conversation."

"You know," said Roly, "that's just what I thought all along."

The *Makambo* was due to call again a few days later on her way back to Sydney, so I thought I had better reassemble the motor before she arrived, and went down to Kirby's to enquire about the cylinder-heads.

"Oh," said he, "the valves must first be thoroughly ground and the cylinders thoroughly cleaned. When I do a thing, I like to do it properly."

"But don't you think I ought to reassemble the motor before the boat returns?" said I. "It's not much use keeping the cylinder-heads till they shine fit to shave by, only to discover after the *Makambo* has left that a new one is required. How about just a little grinding of the valves? After all, they were perfect when I left Norfolk Island."

Well, he washed his hands of a job unless it were done properly, so I set to work grinding them myself at his bench. It was a job I disliked intensely, but I believe I should have ground them twice as much as I actually did, had not Kirby scoffed such a lot at my grinding them such a little.

Reassembling the motor was simple enough in its way. All the tinfuls of nuts, bolts, washers, screws and parts must be used up. If anything were left over, I nosed round the motor till a place was found for it. In the end the motor seemed quite all right except that it would not go. There was no spark in either magneto, so I packed them off to Australia on the boat.

I always disliked boat day; having to clear half the shed for cargo. And then, it was a disquieting day of unrestful holiday. One walked about, here, there and everywhere quickly, as if afraid of missing something about to occur somewhere else. One's neighbour, whom yesterday one felt one knew so well, seemed to-day a stranger, inaccessible withdrawn and immersed in his own affairs; and if tolerant of one's presence, scarcely making more than a brief, superficial contact with one.

We could cover no more wings until the *Makambo* returned again with the dope-resisting paint. However, Roly and I carried on with the rebuilding of wing and aileron frames. The second wing we finished in, three days, the third and fourth only took two days each. The boat was soon back, and life became more arduous still. Now repairing, covering and doping went on all at the same time. And there was always a scramble and jostle for room, though the islanders had lent me the only other shed large enough to hold a spread wing—the seed-packing shed. Even so, there was only room there to work on one wing, and room in the cargo shed for the wing being covered.

Roly and a visitor with the newly enamelled floats which were attached to the fuselage by 36 bolts and 12 bracing wires.

I gave up going barefooted; the soles of my feet had worn thin and the sand had grown cold to the feel. It was the edge of winter, the days were shortening, rain squalls were more frequent, and as the warmth went out of the sunlight the glow of my island life abated for me; and I had to think day and night. It was not a question of making as few mistakes as possible—when the plane was finished there must be no mistake at all. And all the time I felt the urgency of hurry; the stormy, strong westerlies were setting in. It was not so much that they provided an obstacle to the last span of ocean, as that they diminished the chance of obtaining the run of fine days necessary for the last stages of assembly and launching. Once the fuselage and the floats were assembled, or the wings and the fuselage, they must remain out at the mercy of the weather—there was no room to take them back under cover. And once the plane was on the lagoon, there it must stay until it left the island.

The engine, with oil can for petrol tank, on a portable test bench which was not strong enough; Ted Austic, the island cricketer (on the right), built one which, looked the same but was bolted together instead of tied with rope.

With the dope-resisting paint had arrived the magnetos, and one morning I set out to fix and time them. This was another job which scared me beforehand. But after I had locked all the doors and, sitting on a petrol-case, had mastered the principles of the operation, it turned out dead easy. In the first place, when the piston was in a certain position in the cylinder, a spark was needed to fire the petrol mixture. Very well, (1) swing the propeller till the piston was in that certain position, (2) a spark being then needed, turn the magneto till on the point of sparking, (3) push home the magneto till its cogwheel married the cogwheel on the motor opposite it, and the job was done.

Now we set about testing the motor. And that caused us as much excitement as heating up a toy steam engine at school—when it grows hotter and hotter until you know that either (1) it must soon start, or (2) it must soon blow up. I went off to find Ted Austic; he was one of the island's star cricketers, who used to saunter along with a peaked cap on the back of his head and a vast curl in front like a shrub overhanging a cliff. I had no trouble in coaxing him away from his task of building himself a house. Hammering long spikes into lengths of wood, he made a horse for the motor to ride on like that used for wood sawing. I climbed up with a gallon tin of petrol and balanced it on a rafter in the cargo-shed roof to represent the petrol-tank in the top wing of a plane. My old length of rubber tube led the petrol from the base of the tin to the carburetter. The motor we stood inside the cargo-shed on the edge of the pit so that the revolving propeller should not strike the floor. I led an earth-wire from each magneto, attaching the loose end of it to the metal of a screwdriver. I told Roly to grasp a screwdriver in each hand and earth the current if the pace grew too hot. "Now listen, Chickey," said he, "are you sure this is all right? I'd sell my job for a brass tack any time, but I notice everyone seems to have urgent business elsewhere all of a sudden."

"Sure, it's as safe as a wheelbarrow," I replied, hoping he would not notice the resemblance of my own hand to an aspen leaf.

"Now," I warned him, "if I yell 'Earth' bang those screwdrivers down as if your life depended on it."

I pulled over the propeller with distinct respect, like a kitten reaching for a toy that squeaks every time it is touched. At each fresh swing of it without the motor's showing the least sign of life, the less I liked the job myself. It might catch on fire, it might explode, it might fly to pieces, it might—"Brrrrrrr!" With a crackling roar it suddenly started at full throttle. "EARTH!" I bellowed, and jumped for the back of the stand. Whatever Roly did, it had no effect. It roared like a mad lion caught in a trap—it was pulling enough to send a plane through the air at ninety miles an hour. The wooden stand jumped and danced frantically on the edge of the pit. "Hang on, Roly!" I shouted, "hang on!" and one on either side of the motor, feet jammed against a niche in the concrete at the edge of the pit, leaning right back, we began a tug-of-war with it. The stand teetered, gibbered, and stammered on the edge of the pit; the roar reverberated from the roof, the blast tore at the roots of our hair and the shed was full of whirling eddying papers. If ever there were a pandemonium, here it was. Till, at last, snatching the pipe off the carburetter, the petrol ran out of it and the motor died.

"Gosh!" exclaimed Roly, "hell holds no horrors for me any more!"

After the motor had run for a while, the compression became good, greatly to my relief. As there had been none beforehand, I was much afraid that Kirby had been right and that I had not ground the valves thoroughly enough. I hurried off at once and imparted the glad tidings to him, knowing how delighted he would be. Whether in consequence or no, I cannot say, but he turned up next morning and offered to help me again. I gratefully accepted. All the forenoon he worked away in the cargo shed while Roly and I were in the other. On our return we found he had discovered the one thing on the fuselage left undismantled by me. True, it had no mechanical value, being only a down pipe to lead away waste oil and prevent that from dirtying the fuselage. But Kirby had spotted a dent in this length of piping and, with his usual thoroughness, had decided to take it off for me to eliminate the dent and replace the pipe. He pointed out that a job should be done properly, and that the pipe should have been attended to when the fuselage was renovated. I pressed out the dent and then tried to replace the pipe. First I tried to do this with the fuselage in its present position; but failed because the end of the straightened pipe now wished to project exactly where the fuselage happened to be supported on the trestle. Later, the engine was lifted by block and tackle fastened to a rafter, and dropped back into position in the fuselage. This rendered my efforts to replace the pipe even more ineffective. When at last the fuselage came out of the shed and was fixed on to the float chassis, both motor and float-struts were in the way of that pipe. I lost more knuckle skin over it than over the whole of the rest of the plane. And I never did get it back securely; it was only by replacing the dent as before that I got it back at all.

Kirby also spotted the old lock-washers still on the propeller-shaft collar-bolts. "Look here, Chi," he said, "you ought not to use those old washers! Surely you ordered new ones!" Now I had particularly settled in my mind to secure those bolts myself, on the principle that if the job were wrongly done and thereby were forced to pass to another world in haphazard watery fashion, I should have the consolation of thinking that alone was responsible for my lack of a ceremonious funeral. Not wanting to hurt Kirby's feelings, I replied that I had no other washers. But I reckoned without his new determination to help me. Sacrificing the pet lamb of his thoroughness on the altar of his goodwill, he proceeded to screw home every nut on to an old washer and I was compelled to watch the whole operation from beginning to end, acutely conscious of Roly with his back turned, full of hardly contained snigger and of the new washers weighing down my pocket like lumps of lead.

Roly and I came to the conclusion that it was not fair to make him associate with us in our slipshod work, and after much consultation, asked him whether he would undertake the sign-writing; the registration marks ZK—AKK to be painted in three-foot letters on top and bottom of the wings. If so, he could do the whole job entirely in his own way (and be as efficient as he wished). Certainly he would, said he, and immediately collared our dope, trestles and the packing-shed to begin setting out the letters on the first wing. Roly and I were forced to abandon all idea of doping and moped off to look for a job in the cargo shed until Kirby had finished. But, by Jove! he did make a thorough job. I have never seen sign-writing better done, and with frequent applications of dope, Roly and I very nearly succeeded in taking out the dents made by his elbow in the wing surface.

Chapter XIV

ELIJAH SPREADS HER WINGS AGAIN

Often it seemed that we should never finish those wings, but the time came when we did. And what a job it had been (or so I, not being a craftsman, thought). Rebuilding the four wings and two ailerons, painting them with oil, then with dope-resisting paint; covering, sewing and taping them; applying three coats of P.D.N.12, doping on serrated tape, then four coats of V.84; fitting the automatic slots, replacing the fixtures and fittings for struts, rigging-wires, and aileron controls. But at last the overhauled motor was back in place, the fuselage beautifully enamelled inside and out, the floats as carefully painted, with ninety-six new screw-threads scoured out through their manhole rims; the wings loosely assembled in pairs ready to fix to the fuselage, the bent float-boom repaired with a steel sleeve, and the bruised longerons strengthened with steel fishplates (drilled for me by "Auntie's" brother, Mr. Thompson, Chairman of the Island Executive Committee). *Elijah* was all ready to rig, and so I yielded to the temptation of a day glints from the fish as it darted about on its zigzag path trying to escape. Then up to its tail glided a long, powerful fish with a greenish-yellow tinge to its back, like the first tint of autumn, and perfectly streamlined as though built for long-distance records. It chased my blue every inch of the way, flashing its long three foot of body in swirling turns after it. But it was only amusing itself with careless, royal indifference to its prey, merely deigning to associate with such an ordinary fellow as a bream for the purpose of trying out its own paces. "King-fish I see!" exclaimed Gower. "Ah! you held too tightly to that bream! Pull in and fix another hook."

I fixed a hook just as Gower had done, I baited it exactly as he had, I threw it out precisely as he threw it out. Nothing happened. Gower pulled in the line, and repeated all the operations as I had done them—in thirty seconds I was fast to another fish. Just as it broke my line, three kingfish glided' past in formation, like military aircraft. "By Jupiter!" I thought, "well named KING FISH."

"School of Kingies," said Gower, laconically, "now you'll get all the fishing you want, Skipper."

Hardly was my line back in the water, when it flew through my hands, the gut making a sibilant noise like a violin string drawn between finger and thumb. There was no case of biting; the fish had evidently picked up the bait while travelling at speed, and judging by the way the line cut through the water, it expected to go on travelling at speed.

"Put as much brake on the line as you can," said Gower, "or he'll run it right out at once. Dip your hands in the water if the line's burning them. Give him line as slowly as possible. There's not much chance of your catching him on a number-ten gut, he can swim away till the crack of doom for all the holding a number ten is good for; but I suppose you want to try. Keep a drag on, it may make him turn. He's slowing now—he *is* turning. He's turned! Let him swing half round the boat in an arc. Hold him steady. If he turns away, try to stop him, but not too hard. Now he's finished his half-circle, try to head him towards you. You've got to play him right out, don't forget! Ah! he's turned towards you, Skipper. Haul in fast. Keep the same tension on the line all along. Let your line coil easy and round on the bottom of the boat, if there's a kink as it runs out, that's the end of the lot. Look out, he'll pass the boat like lightning and your line'll snap like cotton if you check it. There he goes! Let it run, let it run! Now brake! Steady! Brake! You've got to turn him again before he runs the line right out. Dip in your hands and all if they begin to smoke. What are you three swearing at up in the stern there? All fast to kingies, eh! Well, no need to swear, because you'll lose your lines. Now, Skipper, every man jack in the boat is fast to a fish except Frank in the bows here, who seems to have a shark-line down for some reason unknown to me unless it's because he wants to avoid catching anything. Your only chance is to keep your fish to this end of the boat. Ah, I saw his back then; and it's a big 'un all right, four or five footer. You men keep your herrings away from the bows here, the skipper's fast to a four-foot kingie, and I should think it's his first ever. He may blow in here out of the blue as cool as a cucumber in his plane, but he's certainly excited right now. Keep the brake on him, Skipper! He's tiring. If you can keep him away from those other lines for a few more minutes you might get him. Now he's running off at our end, let him have it easy awhile till he's well away from the other lines. Now hold him again! He makes shorter jog-jog rushes now—he's tiring. Feel your fish all the time. Here he comes, right for the boat! Coil your line easy, and steady, and round. He's certainly a beauty. Steer him up close; don't try to lift him—that line wouldn't lift a tenth of his weight out of the water. In closer! Head 'im in. I'll try and grab his tail. Ouch! give him line, give him slack! He cracked his tail at me like a whiplash. Half a gallon of water down my neck to your account, Skipper. Steer him up again. Hey, you men, keep your minnows away from this end of the boat—this is a KING-fish here!"

At this moment the impossible happened. For probably the first time in his life our worthy friend in the bows hooked a shark. Round the boat in a circle it sailed. There were cries of "Blast you and your shark!" "Hell take it!" "Pull that rotten creature in!" "Aren't I trying to?" said Frank, now fully awake. Round went the shark and the thick cord neatly gathered in all four lines. As they were drawn together there was a brief wild tangle—lines twitching, tails swishing, backs swirling like autumn leaves on the drop. Next instant all four lines had lost their life in our hands and came up in dead confusion and a hundred knots, while Frank, with a sardonic grin, hauled in a miserable little shark not even worth the skinning.

The ground outside the cargo shed had now become an island meeting-place, and some volunteers carried the float undercarriage

During the morning tea-break the author waves the capricious bubble-level over the fuselage.

Ready to attach the first wing.

over to some bags of sand laid on the uneven turf. Others carried out the fuselage with motor in place, the floats were lifted and tediously secured to the fuselage by thirty-six bolts and twelve bracing-wires. The next task was to level the fuselage accurately for rigging the plane. I thought this would be an easy one, but I was wrong. With great difficulty we wedged the floats up on the sandbag foundation. Millimetre by millimetre, with here a wedge and there wedge till the spirit-level proved the fuselage to be level laterally. Then we worked to get head and tail level, but by that time one side was higher than the other. By the time the sides were level, the ends were out of true. And when the ends were level, the sides were out again. But at last, after exasperating failure for an hour and a half the plane seemed level all round. I heaved a sigh of relief and thought it a fine job until I happened to turn the spirit-level end for end. The bubble immediately rushed up it like a balloon trailing up Mount Everest. The instrument itself was not level! Nor could I find an accurately level level on the island. This was a difficulty I was mighty puzzled to overcome until I thought that by using the same level the same way on both plane and rigging it would make no difference if it were out of true because as far as the aeroplane was concerned it really would not know the difference.

Next we attached the wings and I was face to face with the job of rigging them. Whenever I had seen a rigger at work trueing up the wings of a plane, I had always watched the mystic ritual in the same awed silence in which I should watch a Druid preparing a victim for sacrifice. I studied the book. The wings, it said, must be dihedrally rigged $3\frac{1}{2}°$ upwards, correct to $10'$ of angle and measured with a variable inclinometer. In other words, must be cocked up at the tips; but when I asked several men to lend me their variable inclinometer, they looked positively shocked as if it were an improper demand.

"Well, Roly," I said, "you'll have to make an inclinometer."

"All right," he said, "I'll make, one if you can draw one."

So I marked an angle of $3\frac{1}{2}°$ on a piece of wood with my little celluloid protractor, and drew it out to three feet long. Roly took it home and planed it down till it was a long thin wedge, making a solid angle of 3½° at the point. His work was so accurate that I could not find the slightest deviation from the true anywhere. A fixed inclinometer was made. This we laid along the wing spar with the level on top again. Then cocked up the wing by adjustment of the rigging-wires until the bubble was in the centre of the level. Whereupon the wing must be cocked at an angle of 3½° with the horizontal as though about to be raised above the plane's back like the wings of a hawk about to settle. We also used our inclinometer laid across the wing to cant the leading-edge above the trailing-edge until the wing made an angle of 3½° with the horizontal this way also. "Stagger" was another thing we rigged for. This word was probably introduced to aerodynamics by some gentleman in the habit of finding his way home by dead-reckoning after a late night with the boys. For a stagger of 3½ inches would imply that his upper wings were coming along 3½ inches ahead of his lower wings.

At the finish the rigging appeared to have been so simple that I found myself looking all round the plane for something else to do which must have been forgotten. But apart from adjusting the control-cables to make the ailerons droop a quarter of an inch each side, there seemed to be only tedious little odd jobs left. And by lunch time next day the plane was finished. By Jove! She looked grand to me—superb—and handsome too, with her white enamelled body and floats, her bright aluminium wings with Kirby's jet-black lettering—till my pride went flat like a slumped omelette on finding that a large pivot-bolt had been left out.

"Roly," I said, "look at this! It must have come from somewhere."

"That's what I think too," said Roly.

"We never bought a new bolt like it, therefore there must be some important joint without one."

"Exactly, what I was thinking," said Roly.

We snuffed round the plane like ferrets after a rabbit but could find no place lacking such a bolt. I refused to do another thing; I'd go fishing in my rubber boat until I could think where it belonged.

"A fine excuse!" scoffed Frank, who passed at that moment with a bagful of tackle for himself. "I bet you a bob I catch more than you do, anyway."

"Done!" I cried, and was so intent on winning the bet that I forgot all about the bolt; but not so the lower part of my brain, the poor drudge of man which never seems to rest—I was woken up in the middle of the night and given the solution of the problem. There had been a duplicate rudder-bar so that the plane could be flown from the front cockpit if required; when painting the interior I had dismantled it, thinking it would never again be needed. That was where the bolt had come from. *Elijah* was in perfect order, I decided. She was ready for launching.

Chapter XV

WILL SHE FLY

The difficulty in launching the plane was the six-foot drop from the edge of the bank to the sand. There was a steep, wooden boat-launching slip, but this, however, was guarded by the sheds facing it at the top and the plane would be unable to pass between bank and sheds without one wing folded. It was all very awkward.

I came to the conclusion that the only possible conveyance that could be used to launch it was the little cargo trolley; but that was no longer or wider in the wheel-base than a perambulator, and in crossing the uneven ground the plane would appear like an eagle being taken for a ride on the back of a beetle.

I did not like it at all, and was scratching my head when Gower passed. "How much does it weigh?" he asked.

"Half a ton."

"Why not carry it, then?"

"Gower," I said, a little breathless with my sudden idea, "will you launch her for me?"

"My way might not be your way."

"You can do it entirely your own way. I'll not interfere at all."

"The boys might think . . ."

"I'll ask you in front of everybody to do the job for me."

He produced four beams which were placed under the floats and maimed by four men to each beam. With a baton, he might have been conducting an orchestra as he walked backwards, in front of them. Between the sheds and the barbed-wire fence on the edge of the bank there was not nearly enough room to pass.

"Come Up close to the fence till the port wing projects over the bank," urged Gower. "Now drop that side as low as you can and lift the starb'd wing as high as possible into the air." With one wing-tip nearly touching the beach and the other high over the shed roof, the bearers shuffled along. It was a great strain, especially for those on the beach side, and a single slip was likely to mean a crumpled wing. I followed behind biting my thumb land frowning till my head ached. Afterwards, Quintal told me that the barbs pressed into his side at the Corner. But all the bearers held on and finally dumped the plane into the water. Everyone cheered—it was a mighty fine piece of work.

I went aboard and began to prepare for a trial at once, thinking that if I waited I should get "nerves" imagining all the things that could be wrong with the plane and the different, kinds of accident that could result.

I taxied well out, faced into wind and opened the throttle.

Elijah gathered speed, was hydroplaning, and left the water as easily as a fairy dancing off—there was a splutter, the motor choked, picked up again, spluttered for a few seconds, suddenly choked once more, coughed out a few backfires and then stopped dead. I wrenched back the throttle-lever to prevent the motor from bursting into life again unexpectedly and then concentrated on alighting. Fortunately, I was still over the lagoon and it was easy enough.

I anchored off the jetty and, standing on a float, worked away to remove the carburetter without dropping more tools into the lagoon than I could help. The jet was blocked by a small piece of skin. I had cleaned the salt water from the carburetter and wiped it with a rag soaked in linseed oil to prevent further corrosion. This oil had dried in a thin, transparent skin which the petrol must have loosened and peeled off. There were enough pieces in the carburetter to choke the jet fifty times. "Awkward for you if you had delayed the discovery till halfway to Australia,' remarked Gower. And after we had cleaned every part as thoroughly as possible (yet there were bends and passages into which the eye could not possibly see), he sagaciously remarked: "I wonder if you have left one piece behind."

Again *Elijah* danced off the surface with thrilling ease. I flew low over the lagoon, waggling the wings a little; then more and more until the plane was rocking from one wing-tip on to the other. Now I hopped over imaginary hurdles above the water—first gently, and then with more and more severity until I was putting strain on the machine. The plane was all right so far; I drew in a deep breath. Now I increased the number, speed and severity of the evolutions. *Elijah* had never been more fit in her life, I thought. I jumped her up two hundred feet and trimmed the elevators for hands-off flying. I left the stick alone—she flew with wings dead level. Ha! so the Lord Howe Island rigging was perfect first shot! By Jove! By *Jove!* Then the thrill of flight ran riot in me. Was it the sense of power? Controlling with scarcely an effort that hurtling, dangerous projectile. Or the thrill of the artist expressing his mood, with the air a perfect canvas, smooth, still, with no unevenness, yet with firm texture for the seaplane to grip—no floppy, thin, tropical air, this. With a slight movement of wrist—stick between thumb and finger as though it were a brush—the seaplane swept a broad stroke across the lagoon. I drew back the stick—smoothly and unhurried it seemed, yet the plane had curled upwards like a flicker of flame painted in the air; a swirl—she was round on a wing-tip and headed back over her course quicker than the artist could flourish his brush. Another twist—no more than needed to paint a curved line, and the plane had swept, and boldly drawn, the length of the lagoon beach, a man's height above it, and—sss! had rounded the rocks where the pink crab must be bubbling with rage at this strange intruder. Stick firmly pressed to one side, she had rocked on to the other wing-tip and curved round the promontory; zoom! had shot vertically upwards to jump the cargo shed; plop! had dropped back to flatten out just above the lagoon surface; roar! had darted straight at the hill behind the scene of her wreck; phut! had flattened out against the precipitous hill face, at the last moment twisting sideways, float-bottoms nearly brushing tree tops; had turned about, floats within a few inches of the surface, motor roaring at full throttle, to shoot straight at Goat Island, and—zip! at the last moment hurdled the island with a

181

laugh from me at young Dignam on the top ducking behind a rock. Ha! ha! what sport in the world could touch this? *Elijah* rioted in her new life; now she was a bird and threw her weight about the sky like a wild, mad plover. Sweeping up till she stood on her tail, and as she lost way, toppling over sideways as though shot, to drop dead for 500 feet till the wires screamed in the wind, and I reached, through fierce exhilaration, an ecstatic consciousness of vital power; while blood and flesh strove and fought against the startling acceleration of being hurled earthwards. Beautiful plane! Amazing *Elijah!* Returned to such life as she never had before . . .

I hated "joy-riding", but the least I could do was to offer a flight to my helpers. Roly, after consistently swearing he would not go up in this plane for fifty pounds, now accepted my offer (minus the fifty pounds) with such alacrity that he quite forgot to don the look of a martyr going to the stake which he had practised at every suggestion of a flight. And when he climbed out of the plane afterwards, anyone would have put him down as a proud young father of twins.

I sent the boat for "Auntie"; she returned word: "oh, she didn't think she would come." I sent a second time; she replied: "oh, I had enough work without taking her up." I sent a third time; she arrived back Herself, groaning and sighing: "Oh, Captin, do you think it's all right? . . . Oh, Captin, will I be ill? . . . Oh, Captin, are you sure I won't die?" She had some trouble getting into the cockpit—over the slippery float, up the high step on to the wing and into the narrow entrance. During the flight she sat very still, scarcely moving her head an inch. When we were back on the water she turned and said in a quiet voice: "Oh, Captin, that was a wonderful thing! And to think I should have missed it if you hadn't made me go up!"

Minnie arrived full of chatter and giggles. Eileen was intent and quiet as if unwilling to waste the enjoyment of one second. Gower described exactly what type of windscreen he thought would improve the excessive blast in the front cockpit (I had discarded the original in New Zealand to obtain better streamlining). And had I seen the big school of bluies at the mouth of North Passage? he wanted to know.

But Frank was the passenger who surprised me. Poor slow old Frank, I thought, will realize we have left the water just about when settling on it again. But to my surprise, we were barely in the air, when he coolly started directing me where to fly and grasped the layout of the land as quickly as if he had spent a month in planes. He pointed to his house, half hidden by trees, and signalled for me to do a whirl about it while he joyfully waved his hands to his missus. I thought: "Well may you wave your hands now, my boy, for when your missus finds you have been up contrary to orders, I bet you'll be wringing them!"

Suddenly he gripped the cockpit edge and stared beneath as still as though frozen. Curious to know why, I banked the plane steeply, and found him looking down at his small enclosed garden. A horse, two calves, a number of hens and a sprinkling of I ducks were, apparently, running their annual steeplechase through it. As I looked, the tail-on-end calf in the lead, instead of jumping the row of peas (or beans) in classical style, charged (very unfairly, I thought) right into the middle of it and took the whole lot along with him between his horns; while the horse in the rear was making great strides among the potatoes. Unfortunately they vanished from sight under the trees, taking the fence in the corner with them (though I could not see how far they took it). A pretty foul race, I thought, considering how the hens were riding on the horse's back, or the horse on the ducks', if not both.

I tapped Frank on the shoulder. "Ha! ha!" I shouted, "I put my money on the calf!"

But he must have misheard me in the uproar, for his only answer was to shake his fist at me.

Next morning, with a stiff sou'-east breeze and a lopping sea, I was still taking up passengers, becoming more uneasy and peevish at each trip. "I must be flying jolly badly," I thought as the plane swerved to the right on alighting and nearly capsized; also I seemed to take longer to leave the water each time. I stopped operating to pump the bilges dry with my new, specially constructed bilge-pump. Yet there was scarcely any water in them and when Roly said to me: "You know, Chickey, you must have water in that starboard float; I can see it trickling off the bottom as you fly low over the cargo shed," I pooh-poohed the idea. For one thing, how could he see water trickling off a plane moving at that speed? Besides which, had I not just pumped all the bilges dry?[1]

The time came for Kirby's flight. He had decided to take aerial photographs of the island. Good! Now one would learn how it should be done.

I followed his efforts with the greatest interest. First he leaned out to work into a good position—the rim of his hat blew over his eyes. He withdrew to the shelter of the cockpit and tucked hat brim under crown. He leaned out—the hundred-mile-an-hour slipstream caught the side of his goggles and blew them across his eyes until the edge of a goggle centred each pupil. He withdrew into the cockpit and adjusted the goggles. He leaned out—the hat brim escaped and blew over his eyes. He withdrew into the cockpit and adjusted the hat brim. He leaned out—his goggles caught the wind, blew askew and blocked one eye completely. But they were mistaken if they thought they could deter Mr. Gerald K. He left them there and contented himself with the sight of one eye. His face grew redder each moment; he looked hot and his freckles threatened to become purple spots. The expression on his face intensified at each little delay; he had come up resolved to secure photographs, and by George, said his expression, he was jolly well going to secure 'em! He introduced the camera into the slipstream—the wind caught the bellows and puffed them away to leeward like a bellying concertina. He withdrew into the cockpit and adjusted the camera. He leaned out holding it side up, with the bottom protecting the bellows. All was at last ready for a photograph;

1   There was a fixed metal bilge-pipe to the bottom of each compartment of the float, and the pump was screwed to the top of the-pipe to pump the bilge dry. Unfortunately, in the compartment with the big leak (see note to page 82), the bilge-pipe itself had an air-leak at the top, so that the pump sucked dry and the compartment seemed empty when still full of water. The air-leak was caused by the pipe buckling when the float, as part of the N.Z.A.F. Moth, was dropped on the deck of the cruiser at Samoa.

unfortunately, fumble as he might, he could not, find the trigger. He leaned out; everything was ready; he looked up to make sure some land was in sight of the camera when the cockpit trap-door caught the wind, flew up and rapped him sharply on the knuckles. Oh, how my heart ached with compassion for him! He adjusted everything afresh and all was positively ready, when by maladministration of the controls, I had the misfortune to tilt the plane on to the other wing-tip. He sat patiently, in the same position, camera in one hand, trigger in the other, looking at the clouds with his one available eye and neither to right nor left till the plane returned to an even keel, when I came to his rescue, reached forward, held the trap-door open and tilted the plane the other way until he had some of the island to photograph instead of only the wing as his previous intention had seemed to be. From one end of the flight to the other, I don't believe he saw enough of the island with a seeing eye, to tell if it were red all over, or merely puce with pink spots.

Chapter XVI

BALL'S PYRAMID

It came to the last flight before leaving the island—the flight round the summit of the Pyramid which had filled so many hours of day-dreaming for me.

We flew across the waist of the island; I could see the swell advancing line after line on Middle Beach, and a field of coral at either end of it with white sand between, as plain to view as though the sea bottom were under glass. It was strange to watch the rollers as they slid to the island before beginning to comb, suck up sand and leave a cloud of it behind in the water, just as if a long line of horsemen had galloped over a dusty plain. Further down the coast, just before Mt. Lidgbird was a tiny bay let into the dense jungle at the water's edge. Like a finger of sea pushed into the thick tangle of tree and palm, with a perfect miniature beach at the end for fingernail and rollers breaking white on it for the quick of the nail. We flew within a wing-span of the trees and shrubs on the side of Lidgbird. They gave the impression of gasping for life in their struggle to maintain foothold on the precipitous mountain face. Twelve miles of ocean separated Pyramid from Island. It came to my mind that the prospect of a twenty-four-mile flight over water would have set me thinking pretty seriously not so many months ago. In fact, it was not twenty-two months since I had first flown solo on August 13th, 1929. Twenty-two months! It seemed more like twenty-two years. Oh well . . .

I stared at the Pyramid the whole way. At nine miles' distance I was disappointed. I had expected its grandeur to intoxicate me at once, whereas this broad side of it merely resembled a Canine tooth of rock biting through the surface. It was difficult to imagine it 1,800 feet high. Even at five miles it only looked less small. But when the plane shot up to it, round at the back I found a wall of rock towering sheer above me for two or three hundred feet, and below, dropping clean to the sea. This link between eye and sea deluded the optic nerve into the belief that I was clinging to a rock wall with a 1,500-foot drop if my hold gave, and I clutched the control-stick and instrument-board, suddenly gripped by fear of height. The Pyramid was the remaining half of a rock cone, cleft by some mighty axe from point to base. I drew off, expecting a terrific bump from down-blast of air to leeward of it. But it must have been too pointed to disturb the air-flow. From the side, it resembled a colossal rock dagger upthrust through the ocean bed, hilt in Neptune's mighty grip below. I flew back and began circling it 1,500 feet up, tightening the circle each time round the pinnacle, the plane banking more and more steeply till it seemed to be pivoting on one wing-tip while I half expected it to meet its own slipstream round the rock, and felt that I had only to reach my hand above my head to touch the crags. In several places about 200 feet below the summit, I could see clean through—it was cracked right off! It looked as if very little were needed to topple it over—what sport, the plane dodging a boulder of that size, if the motor vibration brought it hurtling and spinning down! I had to keep awake to study the rock above me, to fly the plane in a nearly vertical bank, and keep an eye skinned to avoid hitting crags under the tip of the down-tilted wing.

Though the other side was not sheer, it was too precipitous for anything to grow on its face except at one little green spot halfway up—by Jove! that must be the spring a thousand feet up the side, of which Roly had told me—what a strange and unaccountable phenomenon!

What an awe-inspiring work of nature! I returned thinking myself lucky to have had such an experience and a view of so unique a sight.

But apparently, Phil Dignam did not agree with me. He found

open planes infernally uncomfortable, he said; for one thing, he was infernally cold; for another, he was infernally blasted in the face by the slipstream; for a third, he was infernally inclined to think we were going to be dashed to bits on top of the Pyramid; for a fourth, spinning round the rock on one ear made him infernally giddy; and for a fifth, he thought he was in for an infernal crash when I shut off the motor suddenly and glided the last three miles before alighting. But in my humble opinion, the real trouble was one he kept infernally quiet about—that he was infernally near being airsick, in fact.

Ball's Pyramid, 1,800 feet high, an awe-inspiring sight.

I spent the afternoon in feverish rush, stowing my gear, loading with petrol, wirelessing for weather reports, preparing mail, and making myself a chart for a course to Sydney—in an ill moment of braggadocio I had determined to make direct for Sydney, 483 miles across water, instead of flying to the nearest point of the mainland, 360 miles away, and then working down the coast.

Just before midnight I went for my last run along the beach. I had grown to enjoy my two-mile sprint before turning in every night, running barefoot and without halt. When the moon was in the full it laid a quaking white pathway across the lagoon and a-straddle the reef; and when near its zenith and the tide was right up, I must weave my way along high-water mark as the waves burst on the sand and rushed at my feet with sibilant rustle. Often, when the moon made the stars look pale in a clear sky, I was attacked by yearning to be among them, flying again; the yearning that preys on an airman when he cannot satisfy it, fastening to him like a terrible vampire, draining his reason and injecting subtle poison into the vitality of his being, goading him till ready to pay any price whatever—health, life, or fortune—to satisfy the insatiable creature—the thwarted craving to fly.

But to-night I felt sad. My stay on the island had drawn to its close; the happiest nine weeks of my life, I thought. And here I was leaving it, not even through compulsion, but voluntarily; and on a crazy enterprise, which I knew only too well in my heart of hearts was the most foolhardy I had ever embarked upon, to fly across 483 miles of ocean with a motor that had not only flown some 35,000 miles already, but which had just been to the bottom of the sea as well. And why was I leaving? "God alone knows," I thought. And leaving this island paradise for what? If I did succeed in reaching Australia, what reward was there? Only detestable city life, unnatural, miserable, noisy. And this foreboding . . .? What was in for? Well, perhaps without the premonition of something in wait for me, life on the island would not have held the same wonderful value—any more than if I had come to it from flabby living.

Chapter XVII

OF THAT DAY

On waking, I was surprised to find that I had slept all night without a stir—a heavy, dreamless sleep. Queer that I had no worry about, or turning over in mind of, the coming flight. I felt that I was going to take part in an event in which nothing I might do would have the slightest effect on the issue. In fact, I felt like the victim and not the executioner. But that was absurd. Actually, success depended on my own efforts alone. Either on my piloting, navigating, reasoning, or on my recent work in rebuilding the plane.

I went out to look at the dawn coming over the palm tops which made a frieze to its pale, flawless sky. What beauty! Calm, peaceful, satisfying. And what a crime that I had never before realized the strange grand wonder of the island!

Later, it occurred to me that there were other quite different things I had failed to appreciate. The value of "Auntie's" placid outlook on life, for one; the charm of the simple daily life, for another. How that grilled bluie positively melted in one's mouth, after parting a little piece of the flesh so easily, dipping it in melted butter, a dash of salt, a suspicion of pepper—ah! What a dish! What a life to lead—that of a gourmet, calm, uneventful—only using sufficient self-denial to insure that everything eaten should taste as delectable as this.

Between the road and the house when I left it, long slender leaves of young palm brushed their edges across my face. Padding along with my soft shoes on the sand of the island highway, here and there the crest of a palm hung above the path like a bundle of sword blades silhouetted against the pale blue sky. The early morning light that penetrated to the ground under the trees seemed so fresh and clean with the faintest green tint in it. The dewy still air in the wood was amazingly young, tender, virginal. By heaven! What a paradise! Could anything be conceived more desirable than to live out one's life in it to a peaceful end?

I overtook Charlie Innes going to see the 'fun'. He pushed a fixed-wheel bicycle. I borrowed it and rode up to Gower's house, coming to a group of closely-set palm trees before it. I rode through them, twisting and turning, and evolving tight figures of eight round a couple of trees set close together. I had not touched one—good! Eye, nerve and hand were in co-ordination. There was a hitching-rail nailed across between two. At first, I thought it lower than the handles of my bicycle. Then wondered if I could possibly ride under it? And finally thought, "If I can, then I shall go through to-day."

Doubled up, with chest between the handle-bars, I went at it. I shot under. Ugh! The rail scraped my back. Well, I was through—that was the main thing.

Cocking my feet on the handle-bars, I rode downhill, bumping and jumping over the paddock of coarse cattle grass, to reach the bottom at full pelt. Having no brakes, I banked steeply uphill to take way off the machine, turned a complete circle and finished up in front of the boat-sheds. The people there looked strangely at me on seeing my antics, but I could not fag to interpret the thought behind the looks. Anyway, what did I care? I had squeezed a little more enjoyment out of life . . . or had I?

Gower drew the dinghy under the propeller and I broke the brandy on the propeller-boss—I had ordered it from Australia with the materials. The mooring-bridle was cast off, motor started, and I was in the cockpit.

No dashboard clock—I should miss that. And the mathematical tables all soaked off the cockpit interior by the sea—I should miss them too. No wireless either, but I had a pair of carrier pigeons in a cage. Frank's uncle had given them to me.

A breeze was blowing from island to reef, so I tried to taxi down wind to the reef. To my great surprise, I could not turn the plane. There was a stiff south-easterly blowing, but surely not strong enough to prevent a turn down wind. She would make the half-turn till broadside on easily enough, but stubbornly refused to complete the other half down wind. When the motor burst into power, the off wing promptly dipped into the sea and threatened to capsize the plane. As each engine-burst meant the new propeller's cutting into heavy spray, I gave up trying and set the plane off across wind, down the lagoon, until eventually she caught up with the reef nearly at Goat Island. I swung into wind and opened up. As she gathered speed, I felt her slue hard to starb'd and begin to trip over the floats. Instantly I cut off the power. Would she regain an even keel without overturning? Ahh! She settled back. Near go, that! I must have started when not facing dead into wind. But I had judged the wind by the lie of the waves and by their look. Well, I could soon see if I had been wrong; centralizing the rudder, I let the controls otherwise alone—the plane would now weathercock into wind and indicate its true direction. Great Scott! She was riding broadside on to the wind as I had judged it, but a seaplane riding free infallibly weathercocked truly and pointed dead *into* wind. I must have been mistaken, of course; if so, that would account for her violent slueing. But how could I have made such a large error as all that! Climbing up, I stood on the cockpit edge and streamed my handkerchief overhead. No, my original estimate had been right—south-easterly—the plane was not weathercocking truly.[1] Very strange; unprecedented! Well, I could not begin puzzling over abstruse questions of aerodynamics now; my job was to get the plane into the air. I must take good care by firm use of the rudder that she did not slue off course again. I restarted the motor headed into wind and tried once more. The seaplane ploughed through the water, throwing up a deluge of spray, but soddenly, heavily, refused to leave the surface.

I throttled the motor and tried to turn the plane down wind to

---

1 Later experience suggests that the starboard float was so full of water that a few more gallons would have sunk it. It is amazing that the seaplane did not capsize while turning, and it was only by a miracle that it could take off.

make back quickly to the reef for another shot. It was hopeless. Every time I let loose the full blast of slipstream on the rudder to swing the tail round, the off wing tipped into the surface and the plane began to capsize. Very strange! It must be the steadily freshening breeze which pushed one side of the tail strongly enough to counteract the force of the slipstream on the other. I switched off. To let the plane drift back was the only alternative.

I was mildly surprised that she drifted so slowly with that wind driving her back. But I didn't care. What did it matter? How crude was this struggling, this mechanical materialism! Weigh it in the scales with the superb beauty of a natural life and where did it come then? My spirit seemed to have gone stagnant.

I stole forward, sat on the leading-edge of a wing-root, one arm over a bracing-wire, and abstractedly gazed at the sparkle and dazzle of the wavelets, tossing away their crests in little showers of spray; or watched a piece of coral appear at my feet, slowly lifting my fascinated eyes to follow the intricate clump of dark brown and dully-plashed purple while it receded, growing less and less distinct, then disappearing for good, as I thought, only next moment to refract its distorted form to eye again—or was it to imagination only? Gradually I fell into a trance, my spirit becoming, as it were, crystal clear all consideration of material things in the present and in the future was swept clean away and I sat absorbed only in the astounding wonder, the exquisite beauty of nature all around.

The pounding roar of surf broke into my reverie and I dragged my gaze from the lagoon deep. The plane was nearly on the reef where the combers thundered on the coral, charging it in lines of seething, dazzling white.

I slipped off my seat and swung the propeller, then clambered back into the cockpit. I moved parallel to the reef until the motor was warm enough, then turned into wind and opened the throttle. The plane threshed its way across the lagoon till I feared for the motor—it must be white hot, it had raged so long at full throttle in slow air. The beach before Dignam's loomed ahead and I switched off. It seemed as if *Elijah* were heavily reluctant to leave the island.

Nor had I ever seen that fairer. The palm tops streamed before the wind like mermaids' wild hair. And among the other dull-green foliage with the sun right in face, there was a continuing ravelling glint of light on upturned leaf. The beach was spotlessly clean, washed yellow to high-water mark by the lagoon, with a rim of sand above bleached white by the sun. It led away to the mountains' haughty majesty. If only I could be rid of the intolerable burden of having to make myself struggle to leave. All I wanted was to feel resigned and to have no care. Leave! I was going to leave all right. And here was a sure omen—the island itself was farewelling me. The mountains had doffed their heads of cloud. Lidgbird and Gower that I had seldom before seen clear—that always brooded in some cloud or other. Cloud like a long airship moored on the summit; or a great ball of fluffy white; like the thick, flat round of a dirty mushroom top; or sometimes, the tall, pure white cone of a dunce's cap; sometimes a grey whirlpool of cloud dropping from heaven with the base of its funnel buried in the mountain; and occasionally, a dull cloud above the whole length of the island like a flat tombstone slab. But to-day, the mountains stood bareheaded. Oh! I was going to leave all right. The strange feeling was that I had no say in the matter, was being swept along, powerless, at the dictate of some supernatural force. Bah! I must not let that get hold of me . . . Time I pushed on with my job . . .

I reached up to open the top tank petrol-cock and let the liquid spill and fitfully patter on the taut wing surface as the wind blew its stream. I also inserted a length of rubber tubing in the back tank and began syphoning petrol out of that. Load! I must lessen the load. I caught sight of a luscious great island orange half under the cockpit seat; I fished it up and let it drop into the sea from finger and thumb. Another—no, no, not food yet! But I jettisoned thirty-five pounds' weight of petrol. That left me nine hours' supply. I sat on the cockpit edge, legs dangling above the water, and watched the breakers appear larger every minute as the plane drifted backwards to the reef. At last she was in position for another attempt. As soon as she gathered some speed, I tried rocking on to her own bow-waves, at each rock mounting them a little higher as I could tell by the lessened drag on the floats; I snatched at the stick—nearly jumped her off; levelled her on the water again. Now—another jump! She was out of the water. No good! Back she sank again. Now the palms were so close ahead, there would not be space in which to rise above them or turn. A few yards further! Nearly off! No good! I closed the throttle. Oh well, what did it matter? I was bound to get off some time. It was only a case of bearing this intolerable heaviness of spirit at the wearisome grind. I'd get off all right—I'd go on dumping gear and petrol till the damned plane did leave. I opened the petrol-cock. Gower and Roly Wilson, who had been abortively charging after me in a dinghy from one side of the lagoon to the other, at last caught me up. Gower stepped aboard and suggested I leave behind my kit of spare parts. I thought for a moment and then agreed reluctantly— perhaps it was only a pigheaded idea that they offered any slight chance in the event of accident. After disturbing the tightly-packed cockpit, there was some trouble in stowing the pigeon-hutch. I let Gower do it; he was there, and after all, I felt so indolent. It was this pounding rush across the lagoon followed by the lazy drift back; and the exquisite beauty of the island, the inordinate sparkle, dazzle and flash of the lagoon—brighter, livelier than ever before, as though deliberately out to show what intensity of joy in living life on the island could hold. Even the mottled wave reflections on the under-wing surface tried to seduce me from effort with their fantastic dancing. I jettisoned another five gallons—that left eight hours' fuel. If adverse wind should be met, it was not enough, as the flight would take close on seven hours in still air.

Well, I must try again. I changed my tactics, deliberately keeping the plane down on the surface till long after she had run the distance ordinarily sufficient. Now! She left the water. Off? Yes! No—touched again! I held her down for another cable's length. Now, back—with the stick right against my stomach. Would she hold off? Yes—no—yes. She was off. Horrible take-off! Heavily stalled, nose pointing to heaven, she had no right to be in the air at all. For all I knew, the tail might still be brushing the waves. By heavens! But I'd stay off now, though. The plane lurched like a mortally wounded bear. I wrenched the stick hard over to the other side. The plane seemed not to have flying-speed at all. I had no control over it. It made no response. Then slowly it righted and lurched heavily to the other side. I pushed the stick hard over. The plane righted to an even keel. Suddenly the port wing was struck down to the sea by an air-bump. The plane seemed to collapse on its side as though the wing supporting it had been shot away. I struck the control-stick right across, hard over. It felt lifeless; the ailerons flopped like the arms of a dead body. The plane had not responded. It continued its slither to the sea. "That's the finish of it!" I thought. My anxiety ceased and gave place to resignation. The wing, within a few inches of the water, seemed to cushion on a surface layer of air. The plane slowly righted. Only the slots, hanging out like twin tongues of dead-beat dogs, gave me the least control. A wall of palms right in face blocked the path. Impossible to turn right or left. The only chance was to keep the plane down in the thicker surface air and try to gather speed sufficient to jump the palms. They rushed at me. I must keep the plane down. Every nerve rebelled, urging me to try and rise now. No! That was certain destruction. I must keep down till the last. Now! I jumped the plane as high as possible. I knew the jump must take away what flying-speed it had gained. I knew it must drop after the jump. Would it regain flying-speed before striking the trees? Down . . . down . . . I felt as though settling in a parachute jump. The foliage came up at me. The plane couldn't do it! I saw the leaves turned over by the wind look up at me like a sea of pale faces. No good! It couldn't do it. Oh well, I didn't care. "Go on, you cow," I thought, "crash then, if you want to—I don't give a damn." On the instant, a strong gust of wind reached the plane; I could see its blast spread on the tree tops; it gave the controls grip, and the wings lift. It saved her there.

Now I had the saddle to mount. Now, as I was, I dared not turn. Slots still out, the plane laboured heavily up the slope. The motor must be defective! I snatched a glance at the revolution-indicator. No, it read 1,800. Strange how unstable and uncontrollable the plane had been. Due perhaps to a downwash of air off the saddle, for it gained height better, once over. The slots quavered, then shut. I felt prickly with heat all over.

I began a wide turn; the plane scudded, away before the wind. I could not go back to salute the people on the jetty. Let me take it easy for a minute or two! I tried each magneto separately and steadied on a course of West 20° South, where lay Sydney, 483 miles away. 9.30 local mean time. The sky was a clear, hard blue, the stiff breeze chasing the plane along combed over the rollers travelling in the same direction. The sea glittered in the staring light from the sun behind my right shoulder. But surely at such an early hour of the day it could not be as far north as it appeared? Unless my compass were wrong! I uncased the slide-rule and computed its true bearing. Of course, I had forgotten that—now near mid-winter—it was at its farthest north; the compass was all right. As the tail wind was driving the plane slightly off course to the north, I changed direction 10° to the south to counteract it. Every now and then I twisted round in my seat, as I wanted to see from what distance the island was visible on such a clear day. I found the task irksome; I only wanted to sit and idly muse, to fly on and on doing nothing. To observe for drift was a labour scarcely to be borne. And as Australia presented a face nearly—2,000 miles long, what on earth did I care if I made a bull's-eye of Sydney or not? However, though the face might present a 2,000-mile target, it had such a receding chin that for every degree I flew south of the course, the distance would materially increase until it would soon become greater than the plane's range. Conversely, with every degree I flew north of the course the distance would shorten. Unfortunately my wits seemed strangely dull and I did not take in the fact. Though obviously, I need not worry about anything like that in such perfect weather. In fact, I should heed but one sextant shot at 12.30 in order to make a perfect landfall of Sydney. I ought to prepare for it now. No, I could not be bothered. I'd wait till the time came.

Fifty-five minutes out, the mountains were still visible above the horizon like two tiny warts on the face of the ocean. In sight over a hundred miles away! What an easy mark! One would not need much navigation to find them to-day. Yet, now that I came to think of it, Norfolk Island had been invisible at 15 miles distance on just such a clear day. Evidently, one never could tell . . .

I found we had made 113 miles at the end of the first hour with a tail wind of 40 m.p.h. Perfect weather and nearly a quarter of the way in one hour, by Jupiter! Thank God! I only wanted a dead-easy crossing, I had nothing left in me to handle a single difficulty. I found the wind had swung round from being south of the tail to north of it. A pity I had allowed for its coming from the south. The plane was now 10 miles off course to the south as a consequence. Not that a trifle like that mattered on such a day. Would there be any of my friends in Sydney to meet me, I wondered?

I leaned back in the cockpit idly eating an orange. It was a good job I had practically no work to do. I never in my life felt less like doing any.

An hour and a half out: puffy white bursts of cloud ahead—like high explosive. I couldn't object to a few clouds.

Suddenly I stiffened, every muscle tense. The motor had back-fired with a report loud above the roar—a thing it had never done before in full flight. I think my heart missed a beat. The carburetter! Another piece of skin in it! I sat stock still, hot for tenseness of muscles, waiting for the final splutter and choke. It continued firing. What was wrong with it? I reached up and tried the starb'd magneto. That was all right. I tried the port, and the motor running on that alone dropped fifty revolutions, fired roughly, harshly. So that was it! A defective magneto. The only parts I had not repaired myself! The motor ran harshly for two minutes while I listened intently, eardrums taut. Then suddenly, it broke again into an even, smooth roar.

Thank God it was not the carburetter! After all, I had two magnetos, even if one failed.

By the end of the second hour out the wind had backed from E. 13° N. to E. 30° N. but still it was driving the plane onwards. 217 miles in two hours. Nearly halfway! Keep blowing, wind! I could not bear anything but a dead-easy passage.

Again through the wind having changed, I had not corrected

sufficiently for drift, and the plane was now 25 miles off course to the south. Every mile to the south added length to the flight; but I did not seem to take in the fact. However, it could not make much odds under such perfect conditions. I altered course 10° to the northward.

The plane flew under the first clouds. They became larger, began to tower, and the spaces between grew less. I could see a possibility of being unable to obtain the sextant shot. Not that I really cared. Halfway across already and a 2,000-mile target ahead. Not much worry about navigation!

Soon, there was an almost unbroken ceiling of cloud hanging above. It sagged like a sheet tacked up at regular intervals. The wind was increasing in force and backing persistently. At two and a half hours out the sky was completely shut off by the dull-grey, threatening cloud. Dropping too, by thunder! I must definitely give up the idea of obtaining a sextant shot when three hours out. In fact the grey of the ceiling was rapidly becoming darker and lowering. I spurred myself into making some hurried drift observations. The wind was 50 miles an hour from the north-east, by Jove! The plane would be 43 miles off course to the south and, with the drift, was heading obliquely for the receding part of Australia. 43 miles! Unfortunate that I had allowed it to become so much. I at once changed course another 10° to the north. Looking up I found the clouds ahead, dark, heavy grey, infused with black. And the wind was backing rapidly—a storm, by heavens! How intolerably foul! Staring ahead, I could see an apparently solid curtain right across the path of flight. I scanned it to the north, but could see no sign of a break anywhere; I searched to the south—there was not a single gap from horizon to horizon. And it hung heavily from cloud ceiling to water surface, barring my passage. I fastened the safety-belt.

I felt chilled, and made tight the scarf around my neck. At three hours less two minutes, the aeroplane struck heavy rain; it stung my face. The rate the drift was carrying the plane south was almost alarming. The wind had backed till now it was right in the north. Again I changed course another 10° which put the wind dead abeam. More than that I dared not correct—so I felt—I could not reason. My reason was quite numb or dead. But I sensed that once I began making a head wind of that gale, I destroyed my chance of reaching the mainland. Drift—40° to the south, I judged. The plane was being driven half sideways like a crab. At three hours to the instant, the plane flew into a downpour twice as heavy as the first. I had forgotten that it could rain so heavily. I kept my head down as much as possible, but the water caught the top of my helmet, streamed down my face and poured down my neck. My spirits were in the deepest depression. How I craved to escape just this sort of thing!

On the instant the plane left this downpour, which I had thought as heavy as I could possibly bear, if seemed to strike a solid wall of water with a crash. God! I ducked my head. I could see in the corner of my eye water leaving the wing's trailing-edge in a sheet; to be shattered almost on the instant by the air blast. On either side of my head water poured into the cockpit in two streams, which were scattered like wind-blown waterfalls and blew into my face. Immediately, I was flying as "blind" as if in a dense cloud of smoke. I throttled back till the motor was making no effort and began a slanting dive for the water. God! What a fool to let myself be caught in this, so high above the water, and yet so low. Panic clutched me. The water would be invisible in this deluge except for a few square yards vertically below, and as for that, once the plane began a turn and locked the compass needle with centrifugal force, "vertical" was no more to be recognized than "horizontal". But I must not panic—it meant dying, like a paralysed rabbit. I began repeating to myself, "Keep cool! Keep cool! K-e-e-p c-o-o-l! K-e-e-p c-o-o-l!" forming the words with my lips. The plane passed through small sudden bumps, which shook it as a terrier shakes a rat. I looked over at the strut speed-indicator for the speed of the dive but could see neither pointer nor figures in the smother of water. I must use the revolution-indicator. If the revs increased, the dive was becoming steeper. I must find the water surface. I dared not try to climb "blind". One heavier bump to throw the seaplane into a steep bank, dive, climb or turn, and I'd never be able to find out where the sea lay without deliberately putting the plane into a spin. But there would not be height enough to get out of a spin, once in it. I sat dead still, left shoulder against the cockpit side, and moving only my eyes—compass—bubble level—revolution-indicator—vertically downwards over the cockpit edge: travelling them from one to the other as fast as I could, only touching the control-stick with light finger and thumb to ease up the plane's nose when the motor revolutions increased. There was more chance of the plane keeping itself level than of my keeping it level, flying "blind". Thank God it was rigged true! There would only be time to flatten out if I picked up the water exactly where I was looking for it—vertically below—and to do that I must keep the plane dead true. "Keep cool, k-e-e-p c-o-o-l." I saw the compass needle-begin travelling to the left; I pressed the left rudder the slightest amount: the needle still travelled; I moved the rudder the least bit more. If the plane once began swinging fast enough to lock the needle . . . Yet if not very gentle I should set it swinging the other way . . . The needle still travelled. My foot tapped the rudder a fraction of an inch more. The needle checked. It began swinging back. A slight tap on the other rudder. Suppose that I could not see the water at all in this? It must be a cloudburst. I felt the strain. I might as well be coming down to the sea in the dark of night. There was more likelihood of a glint from the water in the dark. I left off saying "Keep cool"; I had no further need. My nerves had come up to scratch. I was conscious that I had never flown so well in my life. A flash of exultation.

Ahhh! A dull patch of water behind the lower wing rushed up at me. I pushed the throttle. The engine only misfired; it failed to pick up. I thrust the lever wide open as I flattened the plane out in a dense cloud of smoke. I throttled back till the motor was making no effort and began a slanting dive for the water. God! What a fool to let myself be caught in this, so high above the water, and yet so low. Panic clutched me. The water would be invisible in this deluge except for a few square yards vertically below, and as for that, once the plane began a turn and locked the compass needle with centrifugal force, "vertical" was no more to be recognized than "horizontal". But I must not panic—it meant dying, like a paralysed rabbit. I began repeating to myself, "Keep cool! Keep cool! K-e-e-p c-o-o-l! K-e-e-p c-o-o-l!" forming the words with my lips. The plane passed through small sudden bumps, which shook it as a terrier shakes a rat. I looked over at the strut speed-indicator for the speed of the dive but could see neither pointer nor figures in the smother of water. I must use the revolution-indicator. If the revs, increased, the dive was becoming steeper. I must find the water surface. I dared not try to climb "blind". One heavier bump to throw the seaplane into a steep bank, dive, climb or turn, and I'd never be able to find out where the sea lay without deliberately putting the plane into a spin. But there would not be height enough to get out of a spin, once in it. I sat dead still, left shoulder against the cockpit side, and moving only my eyes— compass—bubble level—revolution-indicator—vertically downwards over the cockpit edge: travelling them from one to the other as fast as I could, only touching the control-stick with light finger and thumb to ease up the plane's nose when the motor revolutions increased. There was more chance of the plane keeping itself level than of my keeping it level, flying "blind". Thank God it was rigged true! There would only be time to flatten out if I picked up the water exactly where I was looking for it—vertically below—and to do that I must keep the plane dead true. "Keep cool, k-e-e-p c-o-o-l." I saw the compass needle begin travelling to the left; I pressed the left rudder the slightest amount: the needle still travelled; I moved the rudder the least bit more. If the plane once began swinging fast enough to lock the needle . . . Yet if not very gentle I should set it swinging the other way . . . The needle still travelled. My foot tapped the rudder a fraction of an inch more. The needle checked. It began swinging back. A slight tap on the other rudder. Suppose that I could not see the water at all in this? It must be a cloudburst. I felt the strain. I might as well be coming down to the sea in the dark of night. There was more likelihood of a glint from the water in the dark. I left off saying "Keep cool"; I had no further need. My nerves had come up to scratch. I was conscious that I had never flown so well in my life. A flash of exultation.

Ahhh! A dull patch of water behind the lower wing rushed up at me. I pushed the throttle. The engine only misfired; it failed to pick up. I thrust the lever wide open as I flattened the plane out above the water. The motor spluttered; it broke into an uneven rattle, and back-fired intermittently; the plane shook from its roughness. The motor had failed! I waited, tense, for the final choke and the crash. It still fired with harsh clatter. "Now, Minerva . . . if ever . . ." The plane kept up and lumbered on. I was terribly concentrated solely on keeping the plane flying. The motor continued with an uneven, tearing noise but it could only be a matter of seconds—even if it did not fail completely—I was bound to strike the sea. The water was only visible to a plane's length ahead where it merged into the grey wall of rain-water. The plane was flying in the centre of a hollow grey globe with nothing by which to keep level except the small patch where globe rested on sea. I had to fly level without any mark ahead to fly by. Yet I must not rise above a few feet from the surface or the small hole of sea in the bottom of the grey globe of visibility would vanish. I must hug every wave whether rising or falling. The plane irritably jerked its way along as I joggled the controls unceasingly. The water pouring over my goggles distorted the look of the sea; then ran on down my face and neck. Streams of it trickled down my chest, stomach and back. I could not dart a single look at compass or any instrument: it was obvious suicide to take my eyes off the water for so long as an instant. Only one circumstance was in my favour—the very violence of the gale. Although the plane pointed in one direction, it was blown half-left so that the next wave to be surmounted was visible to me instead of being hidden by the front of the fuselage, and I could steer by the "feel" of the drift— otherwise must have wandered about aimlessly. The furious cross-sea was one vast tumultuous upheaval. Here shooting upward like a leaping flame to lick at the machine, there heaving to a great hummock. Sometimes the crests combed boiling down the slopes, sometimes they were slashed away bodily and hurled southwards till they dashed like flying-fish into the side of another watery hillock. But these tails of spume streaking south across the wave valleys enabled me to steer a straight course. I knew I was flying as I had never flown before. The vitality of every nerve seemed to have doubled. But I could not last long at the pace. Every moment I expected some muscle to lag, the plane to strike a summit and somersault into the next. Suddenly, I found myself flying straight into the water and snatched back the stick to jump the plane's nose up, thinking eye and hand had at last failed me under the strain. But at once I realized that visibility had increased while the plane was in the trough between two rollers, and the rainfall easing had unshrouded the crest of the swell ahead and above me. Next instant the plane shot into the open air. I rose thirty feet and snatched the goggles up to my forehead. It seemed like three thousand feet.

I had flown into a strange unnatural stillness as if into the dead core of a typhoon. There was not a breath of wind, nor a drop of rain. Flitting from roller to roller, I could scarcely believe I was not in a dream. Although the waves still piled up high in pyramids or pinnacles till their summits tumbled down in ruins, they might have been of solid ice for the amazing clarity with which every line and curve, fold and shade, of every wave was limned in my brain. It gave me an impression of dead, still life. I rose to a hundred feet and tore off my scarf; the wind playing down my neck soothed and somewhat cooled the slow fire burning under my skin. The aneroid altimeter caught my eye; it read 900 instead of 100 feet: so the barometric pressure had dropped an inch in the last few miles. The motor! I tried the bad magneto. This time there was no drop in the revs. Good! It had recovered. Yet, strange, with the motor still running so foully. I tried the good magneto, switching off the bad.

A ghastly silence followed. The propeller still beat the air with a dead whirr, whirr, whirr; but, had I woken up to find myself buried alive, the grave could not have seemed more terribly silent to me. For an instant, the blood stopped flowing in my veins, then suddenly released, it rushed through in hot flood. I switched on the remaining magneto again.[1] But if the water had killed one, I could expect the other, already half-dead, to follow suit at any moment. Someone had told me that I should die in my bed at eighty. The thought produced the beginning of a smile. There was a violent bump in the air; the motor fired like a chain rattling through a hawse-pipe. Next instant the plane hit another wall of grey water and immediately plunged me into blind flying. But at least I had a clear impression of the exact lie of the sea below. I at once dived the plane down steeply to the surface and the fury of the gale and deluge had again swallowed up the plane. I felt deathly cold to the bone; it had struck into my spirit also. I was being driven till I gave up my number, cruelly, inexorably. And God! I couldn't stand this any longer. Never to stop skimming the teeth of the waves in endless jerks. I was tired to death of it. And in any case, I was bound to make the few inches' mistake sooner or later. Why not chuck it up now?

No, why should I be driven in this way? And my reason was being deliberately numbed at the same time so that I should have no readiness when the crash came. Must get out of this torpor. Must think, *would* think. First, I must remember to turn into wind immediately the motor failed—alighting across the gale meant turning over at once and going straight to the bottom, with no chance of saving the boat.

At the same moment, the back-firing broke out afresh. I kicked the rudder hard, and as quick as a stone shot from a sling, had the plane swung into wind in a flattish, skidding turn. The motor's death-rattle! No, it stopped back-firing—the rough splutter continuing. I swung back across wind and drove on.

The downpour eased. Then the plane emerged; it rose as though a heavy weight were lifted from its back. I looked at the compass. It read 225° instead of 270°. 55° off course and headed to miss even Tasmania! Strange, I thought I could fly by drift to within 10° of accuracy. I looked over the side and at once the line of

---

1   The sea-water had eaten through the small spring in the contact switch of one magneto and vibration or a bump had earthed the current. The other magneto was faulty because the distributor was cracked across.

whipped-off spray showed me the reason. The wind had backed another forty or fifty degrees and was now north-west. I looked at the clock. Great heavens! Had that age of happening lasted only twenty-seven minutes of time? My hands still trembled. This depression of spirit was terrible. My brain was numb. Already remembrance of the dead magneto was slurred. Unthinking, I reached up my hand and switched off the port one again. The abrupt cessation of noise shocked my brain back to thought. But the shock passed. Well, I was still alive; and really, what did it matter? A man had to die some time in any case. I felt for the package of cake where I had put it; it was not there, but after some fumbling, my fingertips located it where it had fetched up— under the seat. Half of it was sodden with water, but I ate it with zest. Then an orange. Shades of Jupiter! I never tasted a more succulent. And there was something real about it. I slipped my goggles off and dried them; then unstrapped the helmet, wrung it out and mopped my head. Shivering with cold, I twisted the scarf around my neck, and fastened up the padded Reid jacket.

Now I must think. I MUST think. Must overcome this strange feeling that I was a puppet playing a part set for me—it was only an illusion to make me indifferent and lull me into taking no steps towards safety. I must rouse my brain. When the motor failed, turn into wind, yes. But when the plane hit, what must I do? Release the cockpit cover, out with the pigeon-cage and then boat, boat-pump, and water, if possible. Cockpit cover, pigeons, boat, pump, water. Pigeons, boat, pump, water. Pigeons, boat, pump, water. And now, what was the plane's position? I pulled out the soaked chart. Well, that was useless. Even before the storm the plane was so far south as to be right on the edge of the chart. After being blown further south at the rate of a mile a minute during the storm, it must be hopelessly off by now.

I had a small map of Australia torn from a school atlas at the island. Unfortunately, the land came nearly to the edge of it, and the small space that should have represented sea was occupied by a plan of Sydney. Even without the plan of Sydney it would not have contained enough sea to show Lord Howe Island's position.

But it was the only thing to use. Where was I before the storm? Latitude 33 . . . 32 . . . no, 34—longitude 154. Where was that latitude on the small map? Lat. 32 was there, and 36. None shown between. I must guess where 34 came. Right in the middle of the city plan. What was the longitude? 153 . . . no, 152. What was the use of these tedious calculations, anyway? I gave up the struggle to make my brains work, and resignation not unlike contentment stole over me.

The plane was flying up to a line squall ahead, parallel to the previous storm and stretching, too, from horizon to horizon. But the water on the other side was dimly visible as through a gauzy curtain. Yet, could I get through it—rain had finished off the other magneto and bumps seemed to throw the remaining one into confusion. The drops were heavy enough, striking my face like pellets of hail, but the motor still carried on.

The plane passed through the curtain of rain and entered an immense cavern of infinite space bounded only above by the illimitable vault of dull sky, and below by the immeasurable floor of dull water. To right, to left and in front, were no bounds—only space. I was intensely aware of solitude. Dotting the vast expanse were slanting pillars of rain squall, leaning against the wind. They trailed across the dull floor of water like spirits of the dead drifting from the infernal regions. The vastness lent it a nightmare air. One of those ghostly grey masses would sweep upon me, towering higher and higher in its bulk till it crushed me and I fell and fell, turning and twisting to the destruction below. And then ahead . . . surely . . . the vaulted ceiling bulged with two black-cored squall clouds, like twin fungoid growths linked each to the sea by a gross column. Framed in the space between the two columns was one of these spirits at that very moment being conjured from hell below. A slender and straight pillar of grey-white reared on end from the sea surface, rose to a height, and burst roundly at the top, with convolutions and curves like smoke expanding after the blast of a big gun. Nearly in a trance, I gazed at this phenomenon, flying straight at it as though fascinated, like a moth by a candle-flame. Till suddenly, the motor burst into rough clatter and I returned to the present with a start. I must rouse myself; heavens! I must not fly near that thing; the air disturbance capable of twisting it from the sea must be terrific.

And I must drive my reason to action again. The wind was abating and had veered back to the north. "Let me see, what was I doing before that line squall? Ah, yes, position! Where was I before the storm? Lat. 34, long. 154; right in the middle of the city plan! Now to transfer the course from chart to map! But position, course, track and drift of an hour ago seemed hopelessly entangled in my brain with position, track and drift of the present. I had to put questions to myself as to a child. My brain seemed numb, torpid. But the strange thing was this feeling of guilt when I forced myself to work. As though I had been ordered by some master *not* to think for myself.

Then, to plot the course and track in the middle of the town plan after drawing lines of latitude and longitude through it and while trying to disregard the existence of town streets, seemed peculiarly difficult. And what was the use of working out my position? Beating up to Sydney . . . what did I care about Sydney? Just let me reach any land! That cursed motor again! If only it would make the same noise continuously whether good or bad. Each time it broke out coughing I sat rigid, expectant for the complete failure; then gradually growing accustomed to the harsh rattle, slowly relaxed my eardrums, finally becoming callous to the noise, till without warning, it broke into smooth running and I went through for that again all the same gradually dulled torment of nerves. Calculations! What did I care about calculations, expecting to be dashed into the sea at any moment? Land! Wasn't that land away to the north-west? How my heart bounded! Low purple foothills and a mountain range behind. That made a short crossing, did it not? 9.30, 10.30, 11.30, 12.30, 1.30, 13.30, 9 from 13. My God! What an awful noise. No motor could stand that for long. I looked overboard, but one glance was sufficient. The cross-seas, evenly matched with huge billows, were angrily breaking each other to fragments. "Pigeons, boat, pump, water . . ." What was I doing? Oh! That land. Fancy being, so close to it and then failing. Land! Where was it? Was it possible that that long black cloud had appeared to be land? What a terrible labour it all was! Ought to sight land now! 9.30 from 13.30, 9 from 13; four hours out at 65 miles an hour—75, 85; say 85 on the average. 4 by 85, 4 by 80 made 320. 320 from 480 left 160. I couldn't be closer than 160 miles. No, that was all wrong, I must be as far from land as an hour ago, before the storm. How could I have imagined it land?

A great black cloud bulged from sky to sea. It looked heavy with storm, to the south and ahead. What was that at the foot of it? Smoke . . . By Jupiter! A ship. I turned south-west automatically. It offered me a sudden new lease of life, breeding a friendliness, that glowed in my breast. If only I could reach it before the motor gave out, all my troubles would be over! Perhaps it looked close only in comparison with the vast space of air around, for it seemed an age while the plane was reaching for it. It lay at the edge of the storm like a small waterfowl riding at the foot of a black cliff, and it stirred a warm fellow-feeling in me. A migratory bird, spent with the storm, would feel drawn to its generous fellow creatures in the same way on sighting a ship. I swooped down, and wheeled about the bows, then tightly turned around the stern. S.S. K-U-R-O-W. What an awesome sight from above! The bows, sliding off one roller, crashed into the next to churn up a wide spreading patch of frothing water. Then, as the cross-swell struck her, she lurched heavily, appeared to slide into a hollow and sink into the trough, decks awash as if waterlogged; but she wallowed out and rolled first on to one beam and then on to the other, discharging water from her decks as though over a weir. Not a sign of life was visible and nothing could be imagined more derelict-looking or less likely to be capable of giving help. I felt as if a door had been slammed in my face. I turned and beat north-west to round the storm cloud, feeling grateful that I could avoid that by going out of my way, and thinking that I would rather go fifty miles off course than face another storm. The death of the first magneto was associated in my mind with heavy rain—yet every bump also set the remaining magneto spluttering afresh. 2.05 hours. Only 4 hours 35 minutes out! It was part of a lifetime. How terrible that sea had looked! Yet there was something grand about it; and what a wild sight, the ship wallowing, decks awash under the huge seas, with that thundercloud towering above! It was strangely satisfying to muse on the grandeur of space and distance, the wildness of the sea and the power of the storm. To think such thoughts and to give up worrying about difficulties or troubles, the present or the future, filled me with a strange apathy. That was wrong. It was only the relief of yielding to a vice, which would later result in feeling degraded for the weakness of yielding. I must throw off this torpor which went with making no effort for safety.

The motor, what was wrong with it? Magneto dead! Why so suddenly? Heavy rain—yet monsoon rain never damaged it. It must be something else. The current interrupted somewhere? The insulation of the earthing-wire torn perhaps, resulting in a short-circuit. That must be the trouble. Could I do anything? If I fumbled with the leads to the switch, I might short-circuit the other magneto's earth-wire. What was the best I could do?

I felt behind the dashboard where the three electric cables curved round to the back of the switch. I gathered them together gently. Well, I would climb high, fly on with the remaining magneto till it failed and then, as the plane began its glide, wrench at the switch-wires with all my strength. I might hope to tear them from the magneto terminals. "Something would get torn when I started," I thought, humour gently stirring. Meanwhile, touch nothing.

The plane laboured to 2,000 feet but there stuck, the motor too weak for any further height. However, that would give me two minutes of glide before it reached the water. After this effort, I fell again into the depths of depression. I felt guilty as if I had done something wrong; but when my brain returned to its coma of lethargy, which it immediately did, I felt easy in mind again.

Once round the black storm cloud, the plane flew into calm air and fine weather. Away in front at great distance in space, as it seemed, sunrays poured down through an opening in the cloud vault, as though it were an entrance to a tomb in which I had been flying. It was a shock—the thought of any more sunlight existing in the world had passed from my mind. The wind dropped away to the merest breeze from the north and every minute the sea grew noticeably calmer, until after a few miles it appeared dead smooth with only a light swell resembling, from above, ripples creeping along under the surface. The change accentuated a feeling that I was in some unreal, other world, never again to make contact with a living existence where living things grew, where sleeping, and eating, and moving, took place.

The plane flew into the open under a weak, hazy sun. The air was deathly still and the sea appeared from that height to be immobile. I was suspended, a particle, in space. I was flying through eternity. It was all one to me. Let anything happen, I should not care. I was content.

Suddenly I saw the truth: every time I made an effort for self-preservation or tried to force circumstances to suit me, I felt depressed or disaster came nearer and nearer to me till I gave up to resignation. It was fate driving me into a corner like a dog and belabouring me until I jumped through the hoop, until I admitted I was weak and unable to carry out anything on my own account or against fate's ruling. Bah! I took out the sextant and made two observations, at five hours out. As I began to reduce the sight, the engine started misfiring. My attention wandered from the maths, and I listened intently, head slightly forward. The revolution-indicator dropped from 1,675 to 1,600 revolutions; when, after a few minutes, the roughness smoothed out, my jaw muscles and eardrums relaxed, I raised my head, sat back and became absent-mindedly receptive to the beauty of sky, air and sea around. With a sigh, I drove myself to work again. But not till five and a half hours out was it finished. Nor had it much material value; the sun was too far west. But I derived a satisfaction from having done the work, even if sour. Always, I flew on west; I had always been flying west, and I always should be. I sighted land ahead and somewhat to the right. Purple-coloured lowland on two sides of a great estuary. The water of the estuary gleamed in the sunlight. Ahead in a roll of white weak clouds a bright light flashed. What was that? Nothing could glitter and flash in a cloud but an aeroplane.

I watched the spot intently for a time. More flashes occurred, but I could see no plane. Turning to the land, I found that had disappeared: in its place, a long purple-hued cloud lay on the sea at a great distance. Another illusion! It thrust me down into the deepest depths of depression. When I looked back at the flashing light, that too had disappeared. There was not a sign of it. Yes, suddenly it caught my eye 30° to the left front. Then vivid flashes in several places like the dazzle of a heliograph. That, it could not be; it must be a flight of planes. They could hardly be connected with me? Then I saw advancing—great heavens!—the dull grey-white shape of an airship. Airship! Impossible! However, there was no doubt about it, and indeed how should I be mistaken in an airship? It nosed towards me like an oblong pearl. Nothing but a cloud or two was visible in the sky for miles. I looked left, sometimes catching a flash or a glint there. Turning again to the airship, I found it had completely vanished. I screwed up my eyes, unable to believe them, and twisted the plane this way and that thinking the airship must be hidden by a blind spot. There was scarcely a wisp of a cloud anywhere near. "Heavens!" I thought, "am I seeing things?" Or was I just being tantalized? Dazzling flashes continued in four or five different places to the left, but still I could pick out no planes.

Then out of some clouds to my right front I saw another, or the same, airship advancing. I fixed my gaze on it, determined not to look away for the fraction of a second. I'd see what happened to this one if I had to chase it.

It drew steadily closer until perhaps a mile away when, right under my gaze as it were, it suddenly vanished. I was astonished.

But it reappeared close to where it had vanished. I watched it angrily with fixed intentness. It drew closer. I could see the dull gleam of light on nose and back. It came on, but instead of increasing in size, it diminished as it approached! When quite near, it suddenly became its own ghost. For one second I could see clear through it and the next, so quickly as a flame can vanish, it had vanished. A diminutive cloud formed perfectly to the shape of an airship and then dissolving. I turned to the flashes: those too had now vanished. I felt stranded in solitude; it was intolerable.

The plane flew on in perfect stillness of air over dull water, of dead metallic surface—a stealthy approach into space. The bank of whitish cloud maintained its distance, seeming to draw in its skirts on my reaching for it as though I were tainted or branded for eternal solitude. Was I doomed to fly on for ever? Thrown out of the earth's atmosphere, it could not have been more deathly still or given deeper impression of space. And the sense of solitude was intensified at every fresh sight of land which turned out to be only another illusion. Could I be tottering on the edge of my mind to be taken in afresh every few minutes? Each new delusion was a blow; in the end I felt I had been driven to the utter limit of disappointment. If all the land in the world should unroll before my eyes, I'd care nothing . . . nothing . . . nothing . . . As for the motor breaking up, let it! I was weary to death waiting for it to. How wonderful to have the cool salt water put out the fire in my nerves!

6 hours 5 minutes out; there was land ahead now, but what did I care? 6 hours 15 minutes; the land still there. The longest delusion yet. But I was no more to be caught that way. "Try a new trick," I thought.

But at 6 hours 18 minutes, I was almost on top of a river winding and twisting towards me through dark, forbidding country. A solitary mountain cone rose from the lowland ahead, a high, black and inhospitable mountain range formed the background. A heavy bank of clouds lying on top, obscured the sun, which was now preparing to set right in face.

Oh, this must be Australia. If it were England it would be all the same to me. But where was the populous coast of New South Wales I had expected? This was derelict, dead. To the south lay a great bay or inlet. At the far side I spotted three, four, five ships at anchor. They were all the same colour—dull grey. War grey. Battleships! Was there not a naval base in a bay on the north side of Sydney Harbour? I must be out in the reckoning I made, and must have struck Sydney after all. I could not fag to reason about that sort of thing. I turned south and crossed the bay with its wild scrub pushing to the water's edge. Reaching the ships, I flew low between the two lines. H.M.A.S. *Australia*, H.M.A.S. *Canberra*, I read on my right-hand side. How small they seemed! And how dead, all dead! What was that strange craft the other side? An aircraft-carrier! My heart fluttered at the thought of obtaining sanctuary in it. But it, too, had a cold, lifeless air about it; I supposed I must continue to Sydney. I flew on over an artificial breakwater at the side of the bay. Alongside of it was a suburb of red-bricked, red-tiled bungalows, houses and larger buildings. Expensive-looking houses. But the strange thing was, I could see no road leading away from the suburb; it was set in a dull-brown desert, relieved solely by sparsely-standing trees of drab green. And not a sign of life nor a wisp of smoke from a chimney could I see. Had the world been raided by another planet and all life exterminated during the years of my absence? However, the great city would be lying the other side of this land. Peculiar that I should see no tall chimneys or buildings. I flew over a pool of stagnant-looking water and over the crest of the headland. Instead of Sydney, there was nothing but the same desolate wilderness without a sign of habitation for as far as I could see. Yet surely I was in my right senses? The world could not have died during my absence. Well, I'd try the warships. If a single human being were to be found, surely there would be a watchman on one of five warships. I returned and alighted beside the *Australia*; its huge bulk towered above me. The plane drifted past, away from it, and back to the *Canberra*. It bobbed about on the cockling water. The dead silence except for the soft chop, chop, chop against the floats oppressed me like a catastrophe after the roar of the motor. My nerves, all over, felt as if the slightest touch would set them twanging. Hell! What a fool to drop among a nest of disdainful battleships, to be despised and ignored for an interloping, upstart civilian, a crawler outside the impenetrably regulated life of their hive. If I tried to enter, I should meet the stinging community contempt for a pusher who did not belong. It seemed to me that I had not been so solitary as I imagined out there waiting to plop into the sea.

God! I must get out of this. I'd fly up the coast till I came to a creek, and there tie up. It would have vegetation, green things growing, friendly, peaceful. But I must know my whereabouts. How helpless I was! I could not draw alongside in a seaplane and board one of the ships. However much I wanted help, I could not force them to give it to me. Damn them! I'd make them interrupt their self-contained, supercilious, convention-ridden existence. I'd signal them; they'd be bound to notice a signal. I stood on the cockpit edge and began calling the *Canberra* in Morse code with my handkerchief.

An Aldis lamp at once flashed its baleful eye at me from the interior of the bridge. I felt that countless other eyes had been fixed on me the whole time. Yet still there was no sign of a living person.

"Where is Sydney? . . . I began. At that moment a motor pinnace shot round the bows from behind the warship.[1] I cancelled my signal and stood waiting. A petty-officer was, I think, in charge.

"How far is Sydney?" I asked.

"Eighty miles."

"North or south?"

"North."

Eighty miles! How I dreaded the thought of Sydney, of teeming crowds starving one's soul with excess of sociability and utter lack of sympathy. But my job was to try for Sydney. And here, I must leave here at all costs—immediately. The motor launch was crowded with sailors. Their nervous robustness oppressed me with sense of inferiority in myself. At twenty yards' distance it struck me like a blow—their insensibility to nerves worn thin and laid bare to every wave in the ether, like finger-tips worn off by picking innumerable stones from the ground. Close up, they affected me till I seemed like a victim flayed and lying on a slab for a number of butchers. I must go, I must escape. I must escape. If only I could be alone with nature, free from all noise except a quiet whisper of night breeze among the tree tops. Just left alone to watch the grass or anything that grew. But I could not take off out there with that

---

1   Actually only a few seconds had elapsed from the time the plane alighted to the time the motor launch reached it.

swell running. I asked the men in the motor launch if they would tow me back to the shelter of the breakwater. They slipped me a towrope without ramming the plane and I stood forward, dipped in the sea to above the ankles every time the float was towed into a wave and submerged. As I made to start the engine, I noticed mare's-tails of streaky black soot painted, on the cowling. Of course! The motor was dud. That had completely passed from my mind . . . But perhaps it had enough kick to carry me away from here . . .

However, immediately the plane moved forward, attempted to gather speed, and then began pounding the swells, the obvious futility of trying to rise was driven home to me.

That settled it, I had to stay, must petition for help, and put up with whatever befell me. The motor boat approached again. There was now an officer on board—or was it a different boat?

"We'll tow you to *Albatross*," he said. I had no idea what *Albatross* was. It did not matter, I made fast the tow-line.

Elijah was led up to the stern of the aircraft-carrier, where a long boom projected with a. rope dangling from the end. This I made fast to. A sailor let down a rope ladder from the boom. I released the pigeons—I felt sorry for them—and they took off with a flutter and a flapping, presumably for their home loft near Sydney. Then I grappled my way up clumsily, with feet often swinging out higher than head.

"Captain's waiting for you," murmured a sailor on, the boom-end.

"What's the Captain's name?" I asked in an undertone.

"Captain Feakes."

I made my way along the boom towards a commanding figure much ringed about with gold braid waiting on the deck for me.

Captain Feakes looked hard at me.

"Dr. Livingstone, I assume!" he remarked. Then added, after a pause: "At any rate, you have managed to 'discover' the only aircraft-carrier in the southern hemisphere. Come along to my cabin!"

To me it was more like a richly furnished drawing-room. I had confused impressions of fine, thick-piled carpets, of paintings, an open grand piano with music set over the keys, of miniatures, a large covered sofa, comfortable arm-chairs. And yet I could not have sworn that any of these things were there. It was like a well-dressed man, leaving the impression of being well dressed without the remembrance to name any particular garment worn. The cabin had a tone; it struck a note. Evidently Captain Feakes tossed the silvery mane of a social lion.

I looked down to make sure my sodden feet and wringing-wet trouser-ends were not oozing on to the carpet. What a strange, uncouth object I must look! With dirty canvas shoes, baggy, wet grey slacks, unwieldy padded jacket, tangled hair, matted beard and face blasted by the wind.

"Would you like some tea?"

No, I thanked him.

"Will you have a whiskey-and-soda, then?"

"Thank you, sir."

I was feeling like a little boy in front of an awe-inspiring headmaster. I must pull myself together. After all, I was the captain of one craft—even though a small one—visiting the captain of another. But my personality seemed to have left me or to have been stolen from me. I could only feel an insignificant outsider. I must act a part. What was one role more or less a day? I had already played the islander—or was it a dream that I had been joking with Auntie Dignam about her cooking only a few hours ago; that Roly and Gower Wilson had chased me across and across the lagoon, rowing furiously and accusing me of deliberately keeping them from their uneaten breakfast; that, feeling sorry for the hungry fellow, I had allowed Gower to suck at the rubber tube to start the petrol syphoning till he had a mouthful of petrol; delighted at his distorted face, spitting and spluttering? I had also acted the part of pilot—a strange set piece it had seemed—and that of boatman, that of engineer, that of navigator. So, surely by pulling another string, I could have the puppet perform a social role now.

Captain Feakes had been ashore in the unoccupied naval settlement when I flew over; and on hearing the noise the motor was making, had stood stock still while I flew over and back, expecting me to crash at any moment.

I told him that I, personally, had been waiting to do that for three and a half hours.

While I was drinking, he remarked, giving his head a slight toss as though to settle his brushed-backed silvery hair and giving his cuff exact adjustment by sweeping his hand to his tie with outward crook of elbow: "Did I say, when you came aboard, 'Dr. Livingstone, I *as*sume?'? Of course, I meant, 'Dr. Livingstone, I *pre*sume?' "

Evidently Captain Feakes must strike exactly the right note in everything. I could imagine him saying to himself before a battle, "Now, Henry Feakes, ha! A battle impends. It must, of course, be won; but it must be fought just so. No wrong, note from the guns, no discord among the gunners, and above all, the enemy must be blown up in the right clef."

He was behaving as if I were a long-expected favourite guest. And I, on my part, felt a scarcely tolerable craving to make contact with my fellow humans, to bridge a bottomless gulf of loneliness seeming to cut me off from them. Yet his sympathy and kindness only made me conscious of how unutterably isolated I was from what I craved. My spirit was terribly alone, weak . . . Yet not even my best friend could have reached across to help. I thought, "If 'man' ever flies alone out of the earth's atmosphere into space—to the moon—though he return safely, he will not live. The awful emptiness of space will change his soul and isolate it. Never again will he be able to make contact with man, beast, plant, or any thing. And across the gulf of unutterable loneliness cutting him off from the world he once knew, he will only see distantly through a film of strange, hard air. Perhaps the soul, belonging to space, will have recognized its home, and languish in utter loneliness for it until, loosening its hold on the body, it floats back again."

Squadron-Leader Hewitt of the Australian Air Force attached to the *Albatross* arrived, and he also was determined to help me in any way possible.

They offered either to have my plane drawn up on a concrete slipway inside the breakwater or to have it lifted on board the

218

Albatross. The ship was a sea-plane-carrier, and used to lifting them in and out of her giant maw by means of cranes, to deposit them in the sea. I chose to have the plane taken aboard. They asked me if, since the responsibility must be mine, there was any particular way I wished it to be done or any particular part I wished to play in the doing of it. I asked to be permitted to undertake the job of engaging crane-hook and sling-wires. I said I had grown used to that job at Norfolk Island, and felt more competent to do it than anyone not accustomed to Moth seaplanes.

When I went on deck, dark had fallen.

Two slings were prepared and two wooden spreaders to keep the wires from crushing the petrol-tank. The plane was towed up slowly under a lowered crane-hook. An arc-lamp shed a brilliance high up, but only a dim light reached the plane and the black water surface absorbed most of the rest. Standing on the motor of the bobbing machine, I tried to catch the ponderous hook each time it swung a wicked blow at me. It was a giant compared to that at Norfolk Island, and a great iron hoop encircled the hook, probably for ease in hooking big flying-boats, but as far as I was concerned, only adding to my difficulties. I had to dodge the hoop and catch the hook with one hand, and reach under with the other to hold sling-wires taut and keep their four ends fast to the plane, keep the spreaders in place, have the wires ready for the hook—all at the same time. The hook itself was so heavy that I could not lift it with an outstretched arm. In addition to the roll of the seaplane, there was the slight movement of the warship. And a slight movement of the ship would tear the hook from my grasp, cling I never so tightly to the plane, gripping the motor jockey-wise with my knees. When the hook swung back I had to both dodge it and catch it. Nor was it easy to see under the light above. Except for a few slow gleams reflected from the changing surface, the water appeared to absorb it all. But at last I had the wires taut, the spreader in place, the slings coming through the proper wing-guides and held at arm's length to take the hook. The hook was in hand under the wires and I was about to shove it hard against them ready for the lift when either the three-quarter-ton seaplane dropped away or the several-thousand-ton ship rose. The hook snatched at the bite of wire and took the strain. The fingers of both my hands were still between hook and wires. There was a moment of excruciating pain as the wires bit through my fingers. Christ! My fingers all off. A picture of fingerless stumps flashed on to my mind's eye.[1] I shrieked. If the shriek were forced from me at the start by the pain, I knew immediately I began it that no quicker signal to the winchman was possible, and put everything I knew of fiendish noise into it.

At once I felt a terrible shame. If only I had had the strength to stand the pain without a sound! Fate driving me again. By squealing I had given in instantly and admitted my hopeless weakness to accomplish anything unless it be set out in my destiny.

The hook fell away and disengaged. As I sat on the motor, knees doubled up, leaning against the petrol-tank, with hands that I refused to look at lying on top, my spirit as well seemed to have been crushed. How fate must be laughing at me now that I felt this overwhelming sense of failure.

Dead silence had followed my outcry. Only that there was a slight lick and lap of water. The hook swung like a great pendulum above me. Well, I had bragged of my wonderful skill at this job. Now I could get on with it. Get on with it! Finish it!

I cuddled the round of the iron hook in the palm of my right hand and rested the wires in the thumb-crook of the other. Everything went easily. Fate was helping me now—I had jumped through the hoop, licked to order like a dog. What a damned joke! And another—the care I now took to avoid having the rest of my hands caught. "Lift!" I said, uncertain of the strength of my voice. But it was strangely quiet now—the winchman would hear anything. The water fell away. I hooked my arms round the petrol-tank struts and leaned forward with my shoulders against the tank. The plane rose smoothly, quickly, in the dead silence. The sea's surface looked far below as the plane swung fifty or sixty feet above at the end of the gallow's arm. The water reflected the light with dull changing gleam. It might have been a sea of oil gently disturbed by subtle

---

1   Actually only the top of one finger had been crushed right off.

forces beneath. In the boat that had led the plane under its wire halter were two upturned faces, ghostly white. The arm pivoted, the plane followed it inboard and continued to swing as if strung up high in a puffy breeze. I half expected to hear the crank and creak of a gibbet chain break the silence above; it seemed deathlike; to me. White faces peered up from the deck which itself stared, in the brilliant white light of the arc-lamp. I must keep control of my senses yet—I must not drop on to the deck from this height. Round blackness rushed into my eyesight and back again and the spot of deck visible to me swelled and contracted like a light rapidly focused on a black screen. The plane stopped swinging and was at once dropped smoothly through the air to butt softly on to padded mats. I said to a man standing by, "Help me down, will you? I'm going to faint." Fool! Why had I said that? How ridiculous if I did not!

The sailor had my shoulders but had forgotten one of my legs which I could still see lying across the engine-cowling above me.

In the black void of space, solid slanting white columns of water came rushing on to me, growing to terrible size as they towered above to crush, to crush, to crush . . . I was a piece of weed in a river, waving and swaying in the flow . . . I was drowsily lazing beside a bubbling brook on a warm summer's day—how strangely glad I was of the rest . . . I fell into a sleep, I think, for I dreamed the nightmare I knew so well through dreaming it night after night at Tripoli, at Sydney, at Wellington—that I was in the air, flying, when my sight was completely blotted out in an instant, that I was flying on in black darkness waiting for the crash that must as inevitably follow, as death follows life. How I was clawing the wall when I awoke the first night I dreamed it at Tripoli! But this was the last time of rehearsing it in a dream, had I but known, next time I was to act it. But here was the end of that day . . .

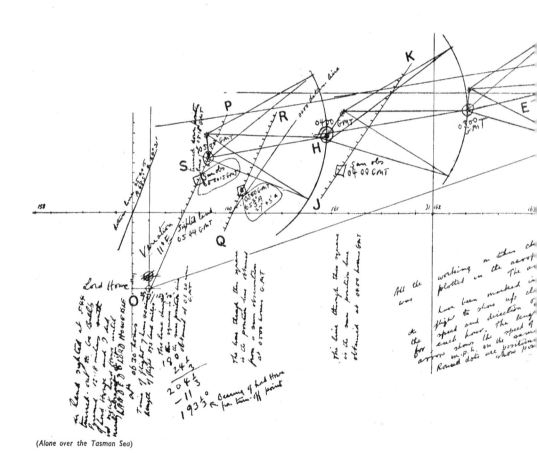

(Alone over the Tasman Sea)

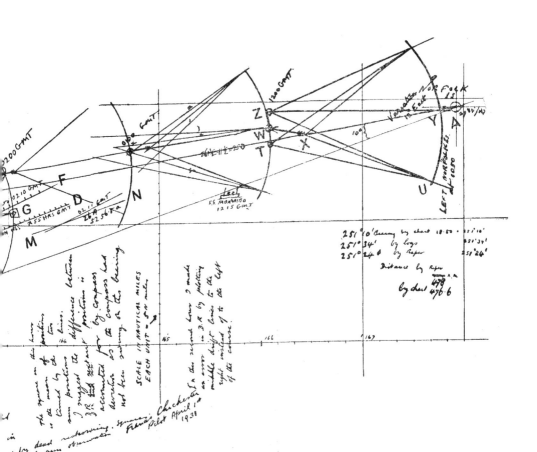

Description of the navigation methods used.
Reprinted from the R.A.F. Training Magazine " Tee Emm " (August, 1944),
by courtesy of the editor.

AN ACCOUNT OF THE NAVIGATION ON THE FLIGHT FROM NORFOLK ISLAND TO LORD HOWE ISLAND, REPRINTED FROM THE "R.A.F. TRAINING MAGAZINE" BY COURTESY OF THE EDITOR.

Here is the story of what might be called an epic of navigation. It occurred over thirteen years ago. We publish it because we feel it will be of considerable interest to navigators to-day. It also provides what is quite probably the first air-plot ever made, which incidentally we reproduce. (Not too well, we are afraid, but then the air-plot was made in the air and for practical reasons, not with the idea of ultimately being reproduced in TEE EMM.)

The flight (by a pilot known to many in the Air Force) was quite definitely an achievement. It was made in a wooden Moth, fitted with floats and possessing a Gipsy I engine. It started from Norfolk Island, N.W. of New Zealand, whence the pilot had previously flown. It covered five hundred and seventy-five miles of lonely Tasman Sea, which was not such a trivial distance then as nowadays, and on this particular occasion an unbalanced propeller, damaged by choppy waves while taking off in the open Pacific, had reduced the aircraft's speed. The journey thus took seven hours, forty minutes, yet only nine and a half hours' petrol could be carried, while the objective was another island, Lord Howe Island, of barely five square miles, with the nearest land more than four hundred miles further on. Moreover, the navigation had to be done by the pilot in an open cockpit, and, owing to vibration from the damaged propeller, he found it impossible to write while touching any part of the aircraft.

Yet it was successful. Certainly an epic of navigation. Here are the navigational details.

The navigation comprised an air-plot started afresh from the D.R. position at the end of each hour. The D.R. position was amended when possible by sun position-lines, of which five were obtained using a marine-type box-sextant and the sea horizon. The sun observations were relied on completely, and post-flight checking showed this was justified in that none could have been more than 31 miles in error.

The method of making a sun observation was to pre-compute the sun's altitude and azimuth—in one case, six hours in advance—and plot a datum position-line through the assumed position. Of course, the altitude could not be observed at the exact instant of the pre-computation but allowance for this was made according to the known rate of change of altitude of the sun at the time and in the area. The difference between the altitude observed and the pre-computed altitude gave an actual position-line a corresponding distance away from the datum one and parallel with it. The pre-computing was done by means of the cylindrical Bygrave position-line slide-rule of which one cylinder has a scale of 36 feet long.

One to three sun-shots were taken at each observation. Judging the drift by eye, treble drift observations were made every half-hour and the mean of the two W/V's found was used to decide the hourly D.R. position. The drifts were plotted on the chart itself and this is almost the only respect in which the navigation differed from to-day's Coastal Command navigation drill. As a result of this method a succession of hourly W/V vectors were shown on the chart which enabled the pilot to forecast the next hour's W/V by eye. Marking the W/V vectors with 3-stroke arrows shows an interesting conformance with the latest R.A.F. practice.

The method of plotting the wind was as under; the reference letters are marked on the chart which is on the next page:—

Plot the course-line YX from the last D.R. position Y and mark off the next hour's air distance = YX along it. From the air position X at the end of this course-line draw an arc UY of an air-speed-circle of radius equal to the hour's air distance. Plot course-lines UX, etc., from the circumference of the airspeed circle to its centre, X; these lines represent the courses on which the drift was measured, namely, 30° to port, and 30° to starboard. Plot drift-lines (YZ, UZ, etc.) one side or other of each course-line according to the drift observed; the drift-lines meet in a point, or form a cocked hat.

Now here are some points about the actual navigation.

Immediately after taking off from A, the sun's bearing at the objective O at a time five hours later, *i.e.*, 1¼ hours before the E.T.A. at O, was computed and a datum position-line OP plotted on the chart. P was now an earlier objective and selected so that the required track to it was 10° to one side of the direct track to the island.

The 0000 G.M.T. air-position, X was plotted (note that it was labelled 1200 G.M.T. by mistake). Course-lines 30° to starboard (UX) and the other 30° to port were plotted and the drift lines on each course (JT, etc.) were plotted. These gave a D.R. position at 0000 G.M.T. at Z, using the first half-hour's W/V found; or at T, using the second half-hour's W/V found. W was accepted as the mean D.R. position and a fresh air-plot started from it.

During the second hour a mistake was made of plotting the drift-lines for the centre course to starboard instead of port. It looks as if the pilot, though he did not rub out the wrong lines, realised the mistake at the time, because the D.R. position he chose is at the intersection of two accurate drift-lines; and the numbering of the various drift lines suggests he smelt a rat. From then on he gave up plotting six drift-lines per hour and only plotted the mean of each pair; though, in fact, next hour he did not plot any drift lines, but estimated the D.R. position at B; easy enough in this case, with the drift nil on the flight course and only 3° on the courses to port and starboard.

The sun was now nearly on the beam and two observations gave position-lines EF and CD. These were important because the pilot relied on them for checking deviation, there having been no opportunity to swing the aircraft on this heading. The pilot accepted G as the 0200 D.R. position instead of B, 21 miles to the north, and assumed this was due to a 5° compass deviation. From then on he subtracted 5° from each magnetic course to obtain the correct compass course.

MN was the pre-computed datum position-line for the 0210 G.M.T. sun observation. Five hours after the start, sun observations were again made, the first of these, JK, at 0400 G.M.T. showing that the corresponding D.R. position at H, was 22½ miles in error.

An 0500 sun observation put the aircraft on QR, 26 miles short of the line OP through the island. This was accepted as correct, disregarding the D.R. position, S, of the same time and the pilot continued the same course as before until he reckoned to have reached OP, when he altered course 55° to port to fly along OP.

At 052015 G.M.T. another sun observation confirmed that the aircraft was on OP all right.

The weather was now getting bad, the last two sun observations being taken through lucky gaps, one actually while turning to keep the sun in view.

A large rock 12 miles south of the objective island was sighted ahead at 0544 and mistaken for the island itself, which was not seen till abeam, 5 miles to starboard, at 0625 G.M.T.; it had been completely hidden in a heavy squall.

The aircraft was on the island lagoon at 0630 after a flight, as stated, of 7 hours, 40 minutes.

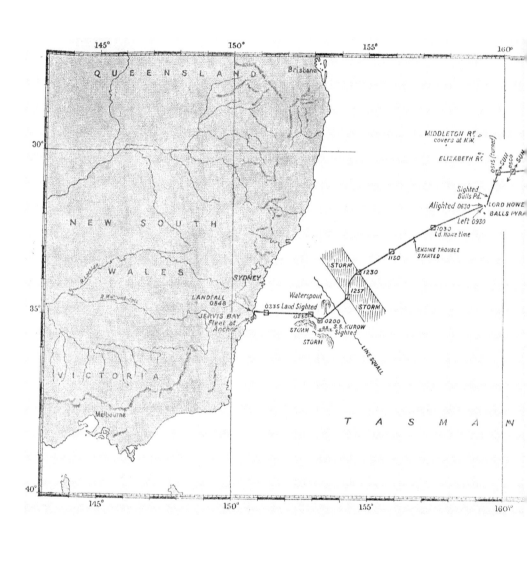

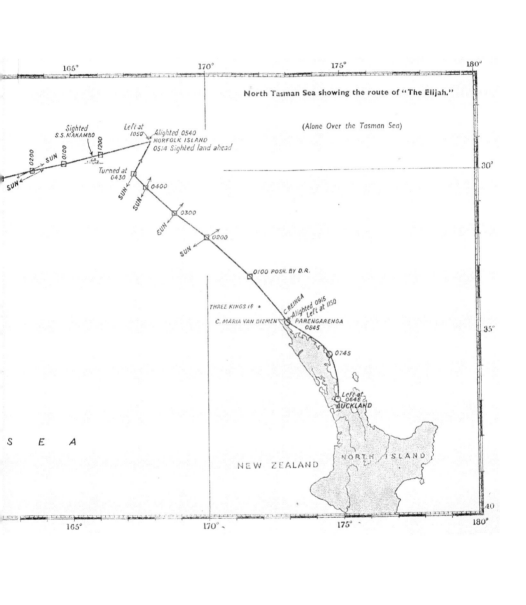

North Tasman Sea showing the route of "The Elijah."

(Alone Over the Tasman Sea)

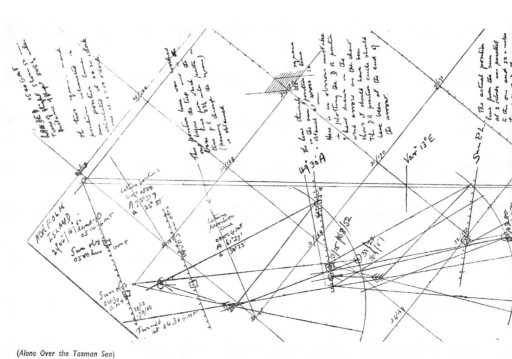

(Alone Over the Tasman Sea)

Photograph of the actual plotting done d

All the working on this chart was plotted in the aeroplane during flight. The arrows were worked in after the flight to show clearly at a glance the direction and speed of the wind for each hour's flight. The length of the arrow gives the speed of the wind in m.p.h. on the same scale. The dots in circles denotes position by Dead Reckoning. The squares denote positions arrived at from observations of the sun by sextant. Francis Chichester. Pilot.

March 28th 1931

flight from **New Zealand** to **Norfolk** Island.

www.ingramcontent.com/pod-product-compliance
Ingram Content Group UK Ltd.
Pitfield, Milton Keynes, MK11 3LW, UK
UKHW030703020325
455687UK00006B/55